Lc
Motorcycles
of the 1920s

Jack Bacon

Edited by Roger Fogg

Panther Publishing

Published by Panther Publishing Ltd in 2008
Panther Publishing Ltd
10 Lime Avenue
High Wycombe
Buckinghamshire HP11 1DP, UK
http://www.panther-publishing.com

Acknowledgements
Without the help and advice of Annice Collett, the archivist of the Vintage Motor Cycle Club, this book would have been infinitely more difficult to put together, and we are very grateful to her for the use of the Club's extensive library and resources. We have also been assisted by Jane Skayman at Mortons Media Group, and Andy Foulkes at M E Publishing with images from contemporary magazines. Bill Snelling at Amulree and FoTTofinders helped with photographs of the TT. Christine Stephens and Sue Mitchell did most of the word processing. Bill Boddy and Ian Young both gave Jack great encouragement and inspiration in the early years of his writings. Photographs were loaned from Lloyd Watson, Jonathan Vickers and Sam Edyvean. Dion, Jamie and Julia Henderson, together with Melissa A Holloway helped in the background. All photos and illustrations not credited elsewhere are the property of the Bacon family or the editor, Roger Fogg. Phillip and Robert, Jack's sons were very much involved with kick starting the process after a period when the book seemed to have become permanently dormant. Roger Fogg dealt with much of the editing process, and also used many images from his own collection. Above all Monica Bacon, Jacks widow, held the whole thing together and to her this book is dedicated.

Cover photo is of Jack Bacon on his Humber at the 1966 Banbury run, taken by Len Thorpe. Whilst every effort has been made to trace and obtain permission from the copyright owner, the passage of time has defeated all efforts.

ISBN 978-0-9556595-8-4

Printed and Bound by Digital Book Print Ltd

Contents

Preface iv
Foreword viii
Introduction: The Golden 20s 1
The British Motorcycle Industry in the 1920s 5
Roads and Garages 39
Tools 42
Clothing 43
Belts 62
Forks and Steering Dampers 118
Lighting 140
Bonniksen Speedometers 142
Cockpit Trouble 143
Tyres 248
Literature 270
Bibliography 272

Lost Motorcycles of the 1920s 7
- *Abbotsford* 8
- *ACME* 9
- *AEL* 11
- *AJR* 13
- *AJS* 15
- *AJW* 16
- *Alecto* 24
- *Alldays* 27
- *Alwin* 29
- *Ascot Pullin* 30
- *Ariel* 34
- *Atlas* 35
- *Autoglider* 37
- *Baker* 46
- *Berwick* 53
- *Blackburne* 56
- *Brough Superior* 64
- *BSA* 65
- *Castle Three* 66
- *Clement* 69
- *Coventry Mascot* 71
- *Coventry Premier* 73
- *Dalton* 75
- *Dandy* 78
- *Douglas* 80
- *Dunelt* 81
- *Economic* 97
- *Royal Enfield* 99
- *Francis Barnet* 100
- *GRI* 115
- *Hack* 117
- *Harper Three Wheeler* 121
- *Hoskison* 124
- *HP* 127
- *HRD* 129
- *Humber* 130
- *LAD* 139
- *Levis* 144
- *LGC* 159
- *Macklum* 162
- *Matchless* 164
- *Meredith* 165
- *Merrall Brown* 166
- *Norton* 168
- *OEC* 169
- *Orbit* 176
- *P&M* 179
- *P&S* 180
- *Paragon* 182
- *Peters* 183
- *Priory* 185
- *Quadrant* 187
- *Radco* 195
- *Raleigh* 205
- *Ray* 226
- *Reynolds* 228
- *Rover* 230
- *RW Scout* 236
- *Rudge* 238
- *Scott* 239
- *Scott Sociable* 240
- *Sirrah (see Wiseman Group)* 257
- *Sunbeam* 243
- *Triumph* 244
- *Turner* 245
- *Velocette* 250
- *Verus (see Wiseman Group)* 259
- *W and G* 251
- *WAG* 253
- *Weaver (see Wiseman Group)* 262
- *Wiseman Group* 255
  - *Sirrah* 257
  - *Verus* 259
  - *Weaver* 262
- *Xtra Car* 269

Preface

Known and loved by everyone as *Jack*, only his wife Monica knew him as John. His interest in motoring and in particular, motorcycling, blossomed in the late twenties, and at the age of fifteen, he acquired his first machine. This was a 1921 two stroke OK Supreme with a belt drive, and soon after buying it, Jack set a record... he was the first boy to ride a motorcycle to the local grammar school.

Jack was a scholar, earning his place on merit and becoming fluent in Latin amongst many other accomplishments. On completion of his studies, he entered the prestigious, newly formed RAF as an apprentice, again on merit, and at a time when such positions were still purchased by the gentry, he arrived the same day his hero, T E Lawrence, left that base. Jack's service record was curtailed by rheumatic fever, which cost him six months in hospital and almost his life. Given a greatly reduced life expectation, his passion for motorcycling in particular, never diminished, and he would later surprise everyone by becoming an octogenarian.

Invalided out of the RAF, he returned to his native Cornwall, where he began to rebuild his shattered life. Where there is a will, there is a way and Jack would find it! Denied the opportunity to fulfill his early promise, he sought to make a career as an electrical engineer and apply his indomitable spirit to the exiting new world of motoring. He would later say that there is not one technique used in modern motorcycle design that had not been tried in the heyday of the 20's, so inevitably motorcycles from this era became his focus.

He purchased a 1927 350 OHV Zenith very similar to the one Adrian Kessell, a famous Cornish competition rider, used until recently on grass tracks. I say similar because Jack proudly pointed out that his Zenith was a year newer than the Kessell machine,

Jack Bacon, pre-war, on a 500 ohv Raleigh

Jack on the Zenith with a friend on a Royal Enfield near Cape Cornwall

which was raced in those days by Adrian's father, Tommy. It was on the Zenith that he entered his first trial, the 1931 St Austell Club's annual Good Friday Trial. There were two sections (one was Blue Hills) and a stop and re-start test. The route was from St Austell to Land's End and back, some 120 miles. The faithful Zenith was also used at early grass track meetings at Rocky Park, St Austell, but with little success.

In 1932, a 500 Dunelt single cylinder two-stroke replaced the Zenith; this bike was very pleasant to ride but rather slow and very thirsty. Eventually its double diameter piston disintegrated and the machine was written off. Then came a 350 OHV Levis which Jack found more to his liking. On the grass he was often in the money and on one memorable occasion at Launceston, Jack and the Levis had a field day, winning every race he entered.

The next year, Jack became the unfortunate owner of one of the worst machines ever created (to use his own words). This was the 350 OHV Calthorpe which was so unreliable that any sporting activities were out of the question. The following year, he obtained a 500 cc OHV Raleigh, identical to the one he rode competitively in an End to End Trial in the latter years of his life. On this machine, he won a bronze medal in a West Cornwall club trial.

In 1936, he bought a 1928 500 OHV AJS, and this was replaced by a three-wheel Morgan. Powered by a JAP racing engine, the Morgan was fast and extremely tractable. Flirting briefly with cars, two more Morgan three-wheelers followed. His biggest complaint was the lack of accuracy when machining the clevis, which caused *many* drive failures. He maintained that if the tolerances were correct, then a *wooden* cotter pin would suffice. A great believer in the value of wood, he also proposed *wooden pistons*, a notion given credence by Frank Costin in recent times.

Four wheels never captured his attention like three, or better still two, unless the vehicle could be pressed into service for sporting endeavours. When he borrowed a BSA three-wheeler from Maynard Williams (father of TT winner Phil), for the 1939 Land's End Trial, Jack recalls that they tied a concrete block, wrapped in lead sheeting, to the front of the BSA in an effort to make it grip on the sections. Until the very end, the Morgan was the only car he had any time for, that is, if we forget a brief later 'affair' with an MG.

Those were dark times, and two days after the war came, Jack applied to re-enlist. Given his health record, the RAF reluctantly made an exception for him, but was told that 'private' was the best he could hope for... he became a corporal. Never wishing to "look too good, nor talk too wise", his 'new' mount, a fast 1928 Model 18 Norton, was kept running on petrol smuggled out of hangars in water bottles hidden in a gas mask carrier. During this time, he enjoyed a renaissance and was able to call a number of illustrious people his friend. He was famous for his ability to acquire tea when no one else could. So great was his sadness for the many friends he lost that he developed an enduring abhorrence of war.

For all that, he encouraged a new pastime... motorcycling. The machines used by this 'club' were of course, all of a respectable age. Strangely enough, it was at this time that Jack owned his newest machine, a 1931 350 Rudge, but this was soon exchanged for a more mature BSA Sloper. It was here that Jack developed his

Monica Bacon and round tank BSA

Jack and Monica in their younger days

philosophy that a motorcycle should be maintained in a condition contemporary to the actual life of the motorcycle - the appearance of being about 5-10 years old. It is also fitting that in a time of such sadness mixed with so much happiness, Jack would meet and later marry the love of his life, Monica.

The post war years were very lean; while many of his friends were moving on to fame and fortune, Jack's health was already beginning to fail. In a world ravaged by war, Jack still sought to instil a pioneering spirit through motor sport in all he met. If there was the vaguest possibility it could be raced, rallied, trialed or used for a hill climb, then so be it. I personally remember as a child accompanying him on many of these outings: a better childhood, no boy could want for. As an electrical engineer, he used a succession of 'upright' Ford Populars for work (well low and behold, were they not *very* suitable for trials? How fortuitous.)

He founded the Wadebridge and District Motor Club (now Camel Vale) and later the Cornwall section of the VMCC. He actively helped run the Cornish Stadium where one could still enjoy the thrill of Speedway Racing and the smell of Castrol 'R'. A man of letters, knowledge, and great wisdom, his passion remained for the heyday of the British motorcycle industry. True to form, he began to archive any reference to the almost 200 motorcycle marques that existed on paper at that time. Here he endeavoured to differentiate between mainstream manufacturers and those with a largely untold story. Many marques were no more than a twinkle in the eye of their founder; others had no conceivable merit... let alone a good yarn. All those who knew Jack will remember how he captivated an audience with humour and a good story.

So *Lost Motorcycles of the 1920s* was born as a legacy to those who come after, from one who remembered when motorcycling was akin to space travel. His Morgan and collection of vintage motorcycles provided the 'true grit' including a 1925 2½ BSA, a 1928 3½ Raleigh, a 1929 2¾ Humber, a 1925 4 'hoss' Quadrant and a 1922 2¾ Douglas. These were shown each year; each could be ridden, and all looking as if stored in a time capsule.

Most of all we will remember Jack for his compassionate, courageous humanity, his lust for life, and his ability to breath that life into others. Rest In Peace, John Slater Bacon.

I would like to thank Dad's executors Dion, Julia and James Henderson for their undying support, also his long time friends Bill Body and Ian Young for giving us hope in sad times; Murray Walker and Bill Snelling for giving the project credence when we were struggling to bring it to fruition. Not least, I would like to thank my brother Robert.

Phillip Marcus John Bacon, February 2008

Wooden Pistons

At one period during the war I was the 'Electrical Section' of a certain snug little flight and one of the pilots told me the story of how he, with his girl-friend on the pillion, set off from Nottingham for a day by the sea. They reached their destination, Skegness I think it was, by which time the bike was pulling very badly, so they left it with a repairer who said he would see what he could do. They returned to the establishment in the evening and the engine was running well. The repairer said that it would get them home OK but that it must be 'taken down' and a permanent repair effected before it had any further serious use. He charged them a pound but would not say what he had done.

The journey back to Nottingham was completed satisfactorily and when subsequently my informant removed the cylinder, what did he find? - A wooden piston! I know that this story seems somewhat far-fetched, but so does the one about a piston with furniture casters in place of a skirt which has been attributed to Freddie Dixon! *(The piston pictured here was given to Jack as a retirement present, something he was extremely proud of all his life.)*

Foreword

John Slater Bacon, known to his friends as 'Jack' was a proud Cornishman, born into a farming family in the village of Tywardreath near Fowey. This is the village that Daphne Du Maurier made famous in her book 'House on the Strand', and indeed she used locations on the farm in this novel.

He began his motorcycling career in 1929. In those days boys could obtain licences at fourteen but Jack was unable to afford his first bike until he had reached the mature age of fifteen, and so began his love of motorcycles, and especially those from the golden age of the 1920s which Phillip Bacon has described so well in the Preface.

Jack also wrote a column for the Vintage Clubs monthly Journal, entitled *Of Shoes and Ships and Sealing Wax*, a quote from Lewis Carol's poem *The Walrus and the Carpenter.*

"The time has come," the Walrus said,
"To talk of many things:
Of shoes and ships and sealing-wax
Of cabbages and kings
And why the sea is boiling hot
And whether pigs have wings."

His column concerned itself with a host of interesting and obscure facts about vintage motor cycles, their riders and manufacturers, their designers and sellers, their performances and their shortcomings. This in turn developed into a desire to put much of his knowledge into print in the form of a book, tentatively entitled "Motor Cycles and Three Wheelers of the Twenties". He spent an enormous amount of time doing research into the subject. There are many files of correspondence, references, jottings, cross references and literature that remain to testify to this pursuit of his interest. He was equally interested in major manufacturers, as well as the two men and a boy back shed creations. They all held equal fascination, which he duly recorded in his eloquent style on foolscap paper and on the back of works memos in longhand.

Sadly, the book was not to be, and Jack died in his 81st year, with this particular ambition still not realised. Some fifteen years after his death however, his widow Monica, together with sons Phillip and Robert decided that Jacks work should not remain in filing cabinets and on book shelves, unappreciated and unread. All the work that he put in should be collated and eventually published, in at least a form that Jack would have understood, appreciated and indeed, hopefully approved of.

The family contacted Roger Fogg, who had known Jack well, and who also had a love of vintage motorcycles, to see if he could put together the nuts and bolts of a publication. This involved getting all the notes put into a computer readable format, rather than in the type written or hand written form in which they already existed. Images had to be scanned and matched with text, permissions had to be sought and all loose ends had to be tied-up.

The result of all this combined effort is what you see before you. You may ask why the book refers to the period from the end of the First War up to 1930. Many of the makes listed in the book were made before the period, some after. The answer is that this is the age that the author was interested in, and he did not write outside of this time frame. It seems a pity in many ways that full marque histories of some manufacturers were not completed and this may be addressed in some future publication. The book concentrates on the lesser known makes and tends to exclude those for which in all probability nothing more than a prototype or perhaps just a very small handful of bikes were ever produced. But it does include many of the bikes which existed for more than just a passing moment in the 1920s and gives as complete a specification of the bikes and their makers as is possible.

Since the book was first conceived there have been many very detailed histories written on the more popular motorcycles which superseded some of the work that was done by Jack Bacon. These makes are included, but the intention is to direct the reader to already published sources rather than fully describe what is already available elsewhere. As far as can be told this work is by a long chalk, the most comprehensive produced on some of the more obscure makes of the twenties and as such is both unique and valuable, written as it was by someone who knew these machines inside out, and above all who was there at the time! This publication is as near as we can get it to a modern version of Jacks vision of his 'Motorcycles and Three-wheelers of the Twenties'.

All the rest

The comprehensive yet by no means exhaustive *Fletchers Index* lists around 200 makes of motorcycle manufactured between the end of the First World War and 1924. Scanning the pages of the contemporary publications, it's not difficult to discover others that were never included. If we then go on to say that there were probably another hundred or so made in the period up to 1930, then a rough figure of around 350 different manufacturers offered their products to the public during the nineteen twenties in Great Britain. A few well known encyclopaedic books have made valiant attempts to track down these machines and to at least establish their basic details (see the Bibliography). These publications are highly recommended and can be bought in most major bookshops.

The purpose of this book is not to go over this ground again, instead it seeks to pick out some well known and also some obscure machines and their creators in order to flesh out the bones. There are so many bikes that are not included here; Jack was interested in all of them but chose to select the fifty or so machines included here because for whatever reason, they had a particular appeal for him. It would take untold hours of research, not to mention a volume to rival the size and weight of *War and Peace* if such a task were to be undertaken, at least to the extent of the effort that has gone into creating *Lost Motorcycles of the 1920s.* We acknowledge that makes that might have been included are not here. You must look elsewhere for your history of Zenith, Calthorpe, ABC, Zenith and so on. If you were to enquire after all the 'New' machines such as New Comet, Coulson, ERA, Gerrard, Hudson, Knight, Imperial or Scale you will not find them in this book (although you will find New Paragon). What you will find instead is a unique commentary on the kinds of bike that were available throughout that magical period of our history when the products of Great Britain were the best in the world.

Sources

Throughout the book the author refers to a number of publications when discussing individual manaufacturers and their motorcycles. These are listed below together with some information about them for those not familiar with them.

The Motor Cycle and *Motor Cycling* were weekly magazines that were required reading for all those interested in two- or three-wheeled transport. Started in the very early years, they contained all manner of news, comment, adverts and photographs. Each year, to coincide with the Motor Cycle Show held at Earls Court in November, there were 'Show Issues' which carried detailed analysis of the very latest that the industry had to offer the public.

The *Buyers Guide* was a supplement to these Show Issues which listed every model currently being manufactured, together with specifications and prices. These 'Show' numbers have proved a valauable source for the information given in this book.

The *Trader* was a weekly magazine designed specifically for the Trade, and carried news and information that may not necessarily have been of general interest, but in retrospect gives a real insight into the ups and downs of the people who made and sold motorcycles for a living.

Fletchers Motor Cycle Index published from 1913-1924 was originally published by Fletcher and Son Ltd of Norwich, and was subsequently re issued by Autopress Ltd in 1964. This also gave many details and specifications and has been used by many authors and motoring historians in checking facts and settling disputes of all kinds.

Roger Fogg, April 2008

Jack Bacon on his 1928 500 OHV Raleigh outside 'The Gables' in Tywardreath; same place as the photo on page iv, but 40 years later.

An advertisement for New Hudson from the Golden 20s

Introduction

The Golden '20s

Whilst this book chronicles the comings and goings of the motorcycle industry it may be useful to understand at least some of the political and social events of the twenties. To acknowledge how manufacturing was influenced by external forces is an integral part of its history. The effects of fashion, art, culture and the socio-political climate meant that people did not just experience motorcycles as an entity on their own. They were part of a whole scene, and dependant on where you fitted, influenced your need, choice, taste and ultimate purchase of a two wheeler. This, then, is a brief background against which these bikes were produced.

By the 1920's many people had been made old by the horrors of war. Young men of 18 had seen the reality of trench warfare: women who had served as nurses had seen injuries that shocked. Women had also shown that they were more than capable of doing men's jobs, and did not want to return to being maids for other people. The returning soldiers were promised a 'Land Fit For Heroes', but there was much unemployment: in 1922 The British Legion estimated that there were one million ex-servicemen who were unemployed. Resentment, coupled with the growing sense of the lack of rewards which these people felt they merited, would culminate in Britain's employers facing workers action. In 1926 the Trades Union Congress called a General Strike in defence of miner's wages and hours. For several months the miners held out against the employers, but most were eventually forced to go back to work as a result of the hardship they faced. Britain was also faced with industrial problems; nineteenth century industrial techniques had peaked and were no longer appropriate in a competitive world.

Post war Europe was in chaos and a return to the Empire days simply did not happen. Basic industries such as ship building, coal mining and textile manufacture began heading for a slump. In Germany the Weimar Republic had to face a severe economic downturn because of the war debt and the one sided Treaty of Versailles. This crisis would lead eventually to the rise of the Nazi party. Communism began attracting large numbers following the Oktober Revolution in Russia.

The Roaring Twenties. Power Petrol advertisement (opposite) and a record sleeve from the period (above)

From the Boys Book of Motorcycling, published 1928

There is scarcely a world's record that is not held by a British rider and machine and a British victory in an international race is now almost a foregone conclusion. We build so many more motorcycles than the rest of the world put together that motorcycle manufacture might almost be said to be a British monopoly. How long this desirable state of affairs will continue nobody dare say. One thing is certain, however, and that is that we cannot afford to rest on our laurels, since both Germany and Italy are taking up motorcycling very seriously, and signs are not wanting to show us that within a very few years they will be producing machines that will provide a serious challenge to our supremacy.

Towards the end of the decade came the Great Depression- this at a time when Britain had still not recovered from the effects of the first war. With the war having permanently eroded Britain's trading position in world markets, even the new industries, such as the motor and electrical industries, were not managed and developed efficiently enough to compete in world markets against foreign competitors possessing more up-to-date plants.

In 1929 the US stock market crash caused a shock around the globe. World trade contracted, prices fell and governments faced financial crisis as the supply of American credit dried up. The effects on industrial Britain were immediate and devastating as demand for British products disappeared.

There were still extremes both of wealth and poverty in the twenties. Large numbers of people continued to live in cramped housing conditions and had to exist on poor wages. They were the people who worked in the factories, the people who produced the raw materials and goods that were for home use as well as being exported all over the world. Many lived in the cities, and this population continued to rise as Britain lost more of its agricultural workers to industry. Yet there were still plenty of people who were extremely wealthy, not just those who always had had money such as the landowners and aristocracy, but also the newly wealthy entrepreneurs - rich from their businesses with a lot of disposable income.

Not for nothing was this time called The Golden Age. The Original Dixieland Jazz Band had brought a new kind of music to the country from America, and people flocked to the dance halls and clubs to hear it. The Kaiser's war was responsible for the widespread increase in smoking, the wearing of wristwatches and the paper bank note. Inventions such as the gramophone and the crystal radio began to be mass marketed and instant music began to popularise dance worldwide. The early twenties saw a great change in the drinking habits of the affluent, the imbibing of cocktails was considered degenerate, but exciting. Most people still retained their pre-war values but the behaviour of the bright young things was written about with distaste by journalists.

Flapper girls, for instance were a new breed of young women who bobbed their hair, wore short skirts and flaunted their disdain for what was seen as conventional behaviour. F Scott Fitzgerald wrote *The Great Gatsby* describing the decadence and hedonism of the post World War One period, whilst in Britain D H Lawrence wrote many novels, short stories and poems about the dehumanising effect of industrialisation and modernity from the viewpoint of the working classes. There were new attitudes as well to Church and Religion and a desire for personal freedom was born.

Some significant inventions and discoveries of the twenties include the Thompson machine gun, insulin, frozen food, television, rockets and penicillin. Art Deco was a popular international movement and affected the decorative arts, in particular industrial design. This style was seen as elegant, formal, functional and ultra modern.

Despite all the problems mentioned, this period was a time when Britain's pride in its Commonwealth, its People, its skills and its traditions was at a high point. The British Motor Cycle reflected in part the glories of the Empire; there was nothing that the rest of the world could do to match it!

"NONSENSE," SAID SOPHONISBA. I JINGLED A FEW COINS.

Sophonisba, a popular cartoon character depicted by Nickless, from Motor Cycle Review, May 1926

The British Motor Cycle Industry in the 1920s

After the First World War motor cycle production resumed with a vengeance in order to cater for the needs of the returning soldiers who had recently acquired the skills and abilities to ride and drive mechanised vehicles. They had the money and desire to own such machines, and it was a boom time for those who were prepared to produce motorcycles in order to meet this demand. Of course there were major manufacturers who were turning from war work to concentrate on civilian production, but in the early twenties there were also many 'two men and a boy' outfits, assembling bikes from a store of proprietary parts that were being made to cater for this trade. There were even cases of motorcycles being offered to the trade without a badge and to which a transfer could be added; they could then be sold under any name that appealed. Many of these were short lived. Production figures were very low, sometimes in single figures, and as a consequence many have passed into history leaving barely a trace. Perhaps a small advert in the back of the motorcycling press is all there is to prove that they ever existed at all. These are rich hunting grounds for writers such as Jack Bacon.

He was able to understand the relationships between the people employed in the industry at the time. He knew that Mr 'A' designed bike 'B', took it to manufacturer 'C', who then produced it at address 'D', under patent 'E' which, after a period of time evolved to become the slightly different model that was offered to the public after road testing in the Motor Cycle Show of 1924.

During the twenties the motor cycle underwent many changes in design and specification. There was a move away from the traditional diamond frame, as used in a bicycle, to a more elongated flat tank style used to accommodate the wide tank and lower saddle position and which eventually evolved towards the end of the twenties into the saddle tank frame where the tank straddled the tubes rather than sitting between them. Transmission improved too. Although many machines at the start of the period had gearboxes and some kind of clutch or neutral, as time went on there was a move away from belt to all chain drive which eventually became universal by the end of the twenties. There was also a shift away from hand change towards foot change gearboxes, although this didn't really become fashionable until the mid thirties.

The engines were in a constant state of development too. Pioneers such as Sir Henry Ricardo experimented with four valve heads and twin exhausts on the Triumph. Overhead valve machines, largely as a result of racing successes began to dominate in terms of performance over the traditional side valves. Two strokes became increasingly more sophisticated and reliable.

Sidecar outfits were still very much a part of family life at the start of the twenties, but by the end of the decade small saloon cars had begun to oust them from their dominant position. Weird and wonderful inventions were tried out constantly, some of which had not the slightest hope of succeeding; the patent taken out for a joint petrol /steam V-twin engine was an example. Yet this was the time that was described as the Golden Era for the British Motorcycle Industry. British designs were of the most advanced, many speed records were held by British Machines, and they were exported all over the world.

Marketing also began to change in the twenties. No longer was it the best way to refer to a motorcycle as the 'Model 5' for example. From a selling point of view it was common to invent names for the machines, perhaps reference to racing successes would be part of the package. Thus models became 'Super Sports', 'TT' or 'Export Big Twin'. Motorcycles that had proved themselves in competition were replicated and sold to the public. Fashion dictated that new machines had to have sloping engines and twin port exhausts. Many manufacturers were quite convinced that their name on successful winning machines could be used to sell even their most mundane products.

By the end of the twenties and with the Depression looming, fewer of the smaller makes remained in business. All the established firms experienced difficulties, some even went under. Budget models were introduced, built down to a price in order to survive. This really was the end of an era, and, although there would be great glories and models to come, the huge range and number of people engaged in the manufacture of motor cycles would no longer reach the dizzy heights of that period.

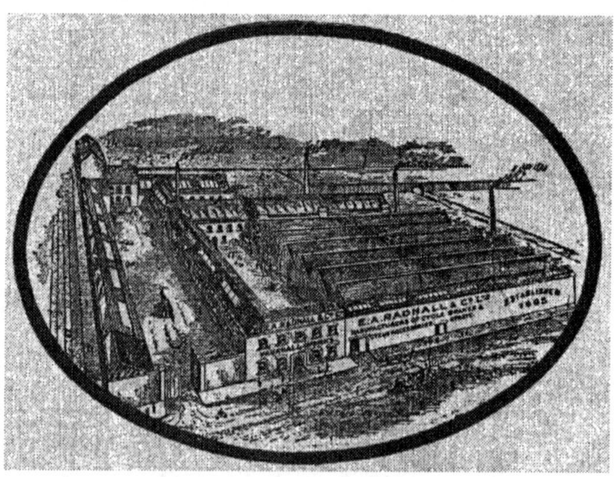

The mighty industrial empire that was the Radco factory, as reproduced in their brochure. In effect it was quite a small factory on the banks of a canal in Dartmouth Street, Birmingham.

Lost Motorcycles

of the

1920s

ABBOTTSFORD

One of the smallest-ever three wheelers was the Abbottsford which made a brief appearance circa 1920. This was not a three-wheeler in the accepted sense, but rather a scooter with two rear wheels. The idea was that it would appeal to persons in search of utility transport but who were too nervous to cope with a conventional lightweight.

Wheels with 16 x 2 inch tyres were used, the front one being mounted in a rather long conventional steering head. The rear wheels, efficiently guarded, were on an axle attached to a pair of quarter-elliptical leaf springs which were sufficiently short to prevent too much rolling on corners.

The seat was mounted on four uprights and behind and below it was a useful carrier with a capacity of 168 lbs., a useful point since it was envisaged that the machine could also be used as a light delivery vehicle.

Beneath the seat and mounted vertically was the 1½ hp engine with overhead valves and a capacity of 142.5cc. Described as a 'John' it had a bore and stroke of 55 x 60 mm, identical dimensions to those of the little Norman engine which was current at that time. Starting was by hand and a cone clutch was provided. Single speed transmission was by chain via a countershaft.

The Abbottsford Scooter and Engineering Co Ltd, of 5 Surbiton Road, Kingston-on-Thames, should have had a winner with this attractive little outfit. However, it seems highly improbable that it could have been profitably marketed for the mere £35 which was being asked. Surrey certainly had more that its share of lost causes largely because it was close to London and Brooklands which spawned many small engineering firms in the surrounding area to service the automotive and aeronautical industries. Such firms were often inspired to produce their own version of a record breaker, reality intruded and such ventures led to their ultimate demise.

A serious attempt to attract the nervous rider was the stated reason behind the three-wheeled Abbotsford miniature. (Photo: Mortons Media Group Archives)

ACME

The impression has been given in other quarters that the amalgamation between the Rex and Acme concerns took place immediately after the First World War but in fact each make was produced independently for the years 1920 and 1921.

Acme machines were made by the Coventry Acme Motor Co. Ltd., Earlsdon, Coventry. They concentrated on an 'eight horsepower' model for 1920. It had a long wheel-base, was rather heavy and at £194 must have been one of Britain's most expensive machines.

An imposing big twin, the 8hp JAP engined Acme has a long wheelbase and spring saddle pillar. both of which add to the riders comfort

This was indeed an impressive motorcycle and owed much of its good looks to a particularly pleasing design of tank, which held over two gallons of petrol and a quoted five pints of oil. The top of the tank was not parallel with the ground but sloped all the way from front to rear.

The engine was a 976cc (85.5 x 85.5 mm) twin side-valve JAP An unusual feature was that the magneto, which was positioned high up and forward of the front down tube, was chain driven direct from the crank-shaft and not from the timing gear. A neat aluminium enclosure protected the magneto chain and primary drive.

Three speeds, a clutch and kick start were provided by a Sturmey Archer gear box with the control on the seat tube, but final drive was rather conservatively through a one inch belt. Mudguarding was thorough and footboards were standard.

Much the same machine, now the model 'A', was the main plank in the platform when the 1921 programme was announced - but it was listed complete with sidecar. The tank had either been slightly altered, or else a previous error had been corrected as the oil capacity was now given as 3 ½ pints. A B&B. carburettor was specified in place of the previous year's Amac.

Crankcase 'suction' drew oil through a side feed and the system was backed up by a hand pump. Other details which help to complete the picture included a grey-panelled tank, Brampton forks and a stirrup front brake: noticeable was the absence of inverted levers.

The Model 'B' sold as a dual purpose mount, had a similar specification but incorporated a 654cc (70 x 85mm) JAP engine.

The following year the Acme became the Rex Acme, shown below.

Above, an early Rex Acme and opposite, a 1927 Rex Acme 350TT

AEL

A E Lynes & Co. Ltd., of Moor Street, Coventry, were cycle manufacturers who turned out a limited number of 'component' motor cycles during the early twenties dangling in front of agents the carrot 'Our discounts are the largest in the trade'. To attempt a detailed description of the machines would be rather pointless since there was nothing to distinguish an AEL from the products of a score of other assemblers operating at that period. Such an exercise would also be rendered difficult since the firm did not deign to publicize their wares in *The Motor Cycle Buyers' Guide.*

The models on offer in 1921 were single speed and two speed Villiers types and a two speed JAP, no engine capacity being quoted.

For 1922 an ambitious programme was announced but one cannot help feeling that this was a 'kite-flying' exercise. Theoretically there were three Villiers models and three JAP models - single-speed two-speed and three-speed in each case. There was also the 2¾ hp OHV AEL Blackburn 'Specially built for hill-climbs and speed'.

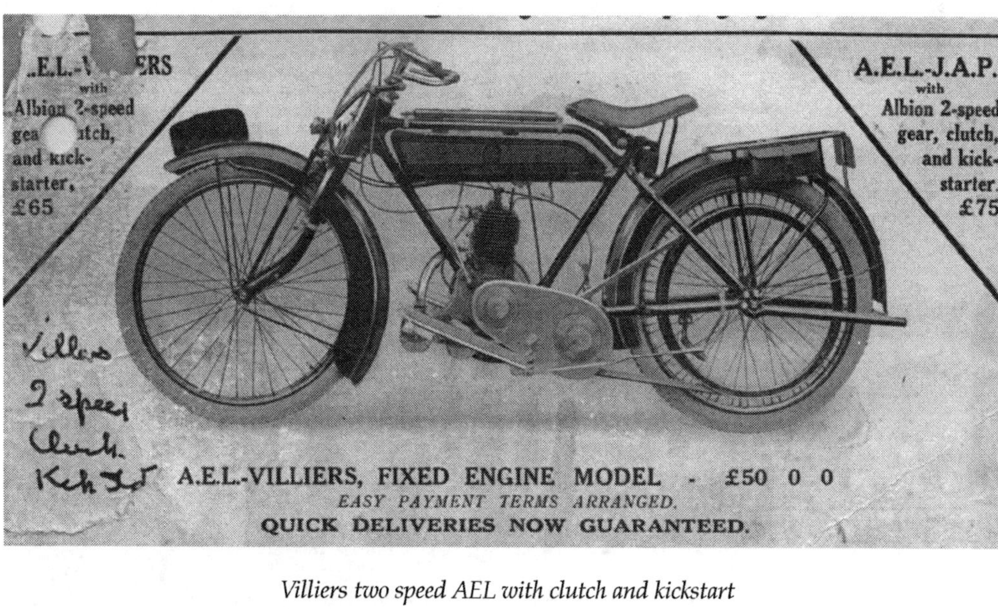

Villiers two speed AEL with clutch and kickstart

A more realistic picture of the situation is revealed in Fletcher's which shows that year's model as a 2¾ hp Villiers and a 2¾ hp JAP, each with Albion two speed clutch and kick start boxes and belt final drive. Serial numbers were given as 2900 to 3001. The range and specification was the same for 1923 and the serial numbers of 3002 to 3036 indicate how few machines were produced. It seems likely that 1924 was the last year that any machines were offered, but since no serial numbers are quoted it is possible that no machines were made.

In 1926 the company went into voluntary liquidation. Mr T Appleby of Birmingham, no newcomer to this situation as far as the motor and cycle business was concerned, was the liquidator. The trading figures show a sorry state of affairs throughout the life of the company; they are recorded as typical of the fate of the small motor cycle manufacturer of the twenties.

MOTOR CYCLE SENSATION

STUDY THESE PRICES.

A.E.L. J.A.P.

293 c.c., 2½ h.p., with 2-speed Gear Box, Clutch and Kick-Starter - - - - - - **£50**

A.E.L. VILLIERS.

2-Stroke, 2½ h.p., with 2-Speed Gear Box, Clutch and Kick-Starter - - - - - - **£48**

A.E.L. BLACKBURNE.

350 c.c., with overhead valves, 2¾ h.p., complete with 2-Speed Gear Box, Clu'ch and Kick-Starter - - - - - - - - - - - **£70**

Gent's Cycle - - - £6 : 0 : 0
Lady's Model Cycle - £6 : 10 : 0

SURPLUS STOCK.—We have a quantity of Cycle and Motor Cycle parts to clear at reasonable prices. List upon application.

The Coventry Nut & Bolt Mfg. Co., Ltd.

MOOR STREET, COVENTRY.

AJR

In the Senior, Junior and Lightweight Races at the Isle of Man in 1925, A J Robertson rode three machines of his own building, retiring in each event.

Even for a newcomer to the TT his performance was not spectacular. In the lightweight event he failed to complete the first lap, but in the Senior he managed to complete five. His riding was consistent at least - four laps each at 44 minutes, and one at 42 minutes 28 seconds. Such times might possibly have given him a place in the 1910 to 1914 era.

However, nothing daunted, early in 1926 he introduced from 65 Queen Street, Edinburgh, a range of AJR motorcycles as the result of 'experience gained from these events, coupled with his knowledge of Scottish requirements'. It is obvious, however, that he failed to take into consideration Scottish pockets, or, for that matter, the finances of motorcyclists as a whole, as his machines were hopelessly expensive.

The production AJR, apart from having a separate oil tank, looked uncommonly like an AJS, even to the side spring forks, and whilst a functional enough machine, displayed as much originality as its name suggested.

It was claimed that models could be built suitable for service in all parts of the globe, which would have necessitated a drastic alteration to the home model

AJ Robertson. (Photo: FoTTofinders)

with its 3 ¾ inch ground clearance. Common to all models were JAP OHV engines, B and B carburettors, and Sturmey Archer gearboxes, as befitted a sports model of the day. The primary chain enclosure was scanty, there was no carrier, and the mudguard stays were formed from flat strip.

Cheapest model in the range was fitted with the humble 346cc (70 x 90mm) single port standard engine. This was offered at £65, compared with similar 'component' machines of established makes for as little as £47, or the pedigree 350 OHV AJS at £53.

For £77 (£4 more than a model 18 Norton) there was a choice of a 246 cc (62.5 x 80mm), or a 344cc (74 x 80mm) model. Each employed the two port sports engine, weighed 240 pounds, and had 650 x 65 tyres. The five hundred with 70 x 80 tyres and turning the scale at 260lbs, had a 490cc two port JAP engine and carried a price tag of £92 10s 0d, which was not much saving on a comparable HRD of vastly superior appearance and with real TT breeding.

It will be obvious then, that whatever the merits of the AJR, it was priced out of the market from the start.

In the 1926 TT the manufacturer-rider retired from the Senior and finished twenty second in the Junior, an achievement scarcely calculated to stimulate sales, so it can hardly have been a surprise to anyone when an announcement appeared in September 1926 that manufacture had been discontinued.

AJ Robertson and AJR in the 1926 TT races. (Photo: FoTTofinders)

AJS

AJS had a proven track record that dated back to well before the first war. Their post war models were entirely new, not just revamped versions of older models. A huge coup for the factory came in 1921 when the Senior TT was won by Howard Davies on one of their newly introduced 'Big Port' 350cc machines. Racing successes boosted their sales throughout the period, and towards the end an OHC model R7 was introduced. The company produced well manufactured and reliable single cylinder and V-twins with a range of sidecars of their own design and manufacture. However by 1931 even this very large company could not survive. They were taken over by Matchless and production was transferred from Wolverhampton to London, although the marque name continued into the sixties.

Further reading

AJS of Wolverhampton, S J Mills, 1994

AJS Wireless

Your report that a 'five valve' AJS was recently auctioned for £400 has dashed to the ground any hopes I may have had of gradually increasing the size of my, at present tiny collection of vintage radios. Whilst £400 seems a lot of money it is still, taking inflation into consideration, appreciably less than the receiver would have cost when new! A feature of some of the early AJS sets was a neat panel meter which may or may not - I only ever saw one in a picture - have been to measure signal strength.

Other motor cycle manufacturers who produced wireless sets during the early years of broadcasting include Levis, Excelsior and BSA. The last mentioned also produced the motor sound box etc., for the Regal gramophone which was a 'cooking' version of the Columbia.

One of the reasons that vintage radios are so hard to come by was that those taken back against new sets were often destroyed by the dealer to keep them off the market. During the twenties the same fate would have befallen motor cycles over five years old if a certain well known Plymouth dealer had his pleas answered!

AJW

During the 1926 - 1927 season a new make started to appear in trials programmes - the AJW, manufactured in Exeter – and early in 1927 the occasional advertisement found its way into the motor cycle press. Among the entries in the Cardiff-Leicester-Cardiff Open Trial (28-29th January, 1927) was one WPC Stephens riding a 498 cc Model, but only the 996cc V twin figured in the 1927 Buyers Guide.

Appropriately, AJW the South West's motorcycle, was well represented in the 1927 London-Lands End Trial, for the AJW Motor Company of Friernhay Street, Exeter, entered three 996cc sidecar outfits to perform in the hands of the designer-manufacturer AJ (Jack) Wheaton, accompanied by FH Knill and ALS Denyer. At that time, West Country riders fortunate enough to contemplate the purchase of a new machine set more store by how the mount of their fancy performed on Bluehills or 'The Roost' than on what it looked like in a dealer's showroom. So it must have been a source of gratification to the little factory that AJW stole the show.

Reporting on the performances at Beggars Roost *The Motor Cycle* said *'The thrills of the day among the big side-car outfits were the ascents of A.J. Wheaton and F.H. Knill'.* Even the London papers such as the *Daily Express* and the (now defunct) *Daily News* were lavish in their praise. The official results showed Knill to have won a

AJW 1927 9.96 Model

Gold and Wheaton a Silver. Denyer retired, due, I seem to recall, to a broken sidecar spindle.

For the first two or three years of production AJW concentrated on 1000cc twins. There was initially a single model for 1927, powered by a 996cc (78 x 104 mm) British Vulpine (Anzani) V-twin engine with push-rod operated over-head valves.

The exhaust pipes were brought back along the left-hand side, one above the other. Gear ratios via a Jardine box, were 3.5, 5.45, 8.5 and 12.57 to 1. This was possibly at that time the only British big twin with four speeds; 'hit or miss' gear change was by means of a foot-operated lever. Engine and box were installed in a rugged duplex frame topped by an imposing plated saddle tank. The front guard had a sensible amount of valance and the rear was devoid of a carrier. The overall appearance was suggestive of that of the Brough Superior, but at £105 for a 1000cc OHV twin it was cheaper by far.

The demand for luxury big twins was, if only on account of price, distinctly limited and was already being met by such competitors as Brough Superior, Coventry Eagle, Zenith and McEvoy. It was not surprising then that Wheaton, anxious to gain a bigger share of the market by offering as wide a choice as practicable, put

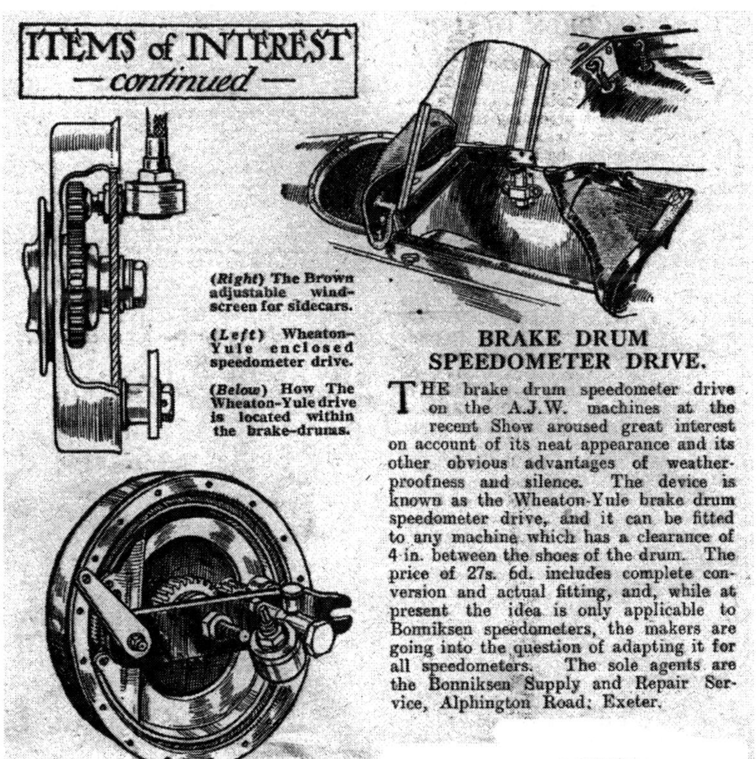

ITEMS of INTEREST — continued —

(Right) The Brown adjustable windscreen for sidecars.

(Left) Wheaton-Yule enclosed speedometer drive.

(Below) How The Wheaton-Yule drive is located within the brake-drums.

BRAKE DRUM SPEEDOMETER DRIVE.

THE brake drum speedometer drive on the A.J.W. machines at the recent Show aroused great interest on account of its neat appearance and its other obvious advantages of weatherproofness and silence. The device is known as the Wheaton-Yule brake drum speedometer drive, and it can be fitted to any machine which has a clearance of 4 in. between the shoes of the drum. The price of 27s. 6d. includes complete conversion and actual fitting, and, while at present the idea is only applicable to Bonniksen speedometers, the makers are going into the question of adapting it for all speedometers. The sole agents are the Bonniksen Supply and Repair Service, Alphington Road, Exeter.

The speedometer drive (left). (Photo: Mortons Media Group Archives)

AJW 8.30 Standard. Price £125 0s 0d, or fitted with 8hp Sports JAP engine, at £115 0s 0d (Photo: VMCC)

on a comprehensive selection of models for 1928. Indeed, no other British manufacturer offered as large a range of big twins.

Small-scale assemblers did not, as a rule, put much originality into their designs, but AJ Wheaton was, as will subsequently be seen an exception. For 1928 an interesting feature was introduced in the form of an enclosed drive for the speedometer, accomplished by accommodating a steel and fibre pinion within the front brake drum. Most other enclosed drives, and there were shortly to be several examples, came from the gear box and the accuracy of the instrument was questionable due to the rear wheel not always making 100% contact with the road. Following 1927 practice there was a hand pump which, by means of a two way tap could be used to deliver oil either to the chains or to the rocker boxes. Whilst this was a commendable idea, the effect was to render untidy the top of an otherwise elegant tank: AJW was not the sole offender! The most expensive models in the range costing £155 fully-equipped (electric lighting and horn, speedometer and clock) were the 'Two-Port Special' and the '8-45 Special'.

These both enjoyed the new duplex cradle frame designed to afford the utmost protection to the crankcase. Leckie saddles were equipped with adjustable friction dampers to check spring movement and the brakes were interconnected. Both brakes could be operated by a pedal on the left hand side, or by a lever on the right of the handlebars. A lever on the left handlebar operated the front brake independently.

The difference between the two models lay mainly in the power units. The 'Two-Port Special' was fitted with 996cc (78 x 104 mm) 'Summit' (Anzani) twin OHV engine and the '8-45' with a corresponding 980cc (85.7 x 85 mm) JAP. The Two-Port (as its title suggests) had cylinder heads each with two exhaust ports and consequently there were two exhaust pipes and silencers, disposed one above the other on either side of the machine. On the '8-45' the exhaust pipe from the front head ran parallel with the ground for some distance and then swept up into a tubular silencer at about wheel spindle height. The final tail pipe extended well past the rear number plate. From the rear head a pipe dived behind the seat tube to terminate in its own silencer which was mounted symmetrically to its opposite number.

Looking particularly compact for a side-valve twin on account of its side-mounted, bevel-driven magneto was the '8-30 Standard'. The JAP engine had the same bore and stroke as its OHV counterpart. Separate exhaust pipes were brought back at low level on opposite sides. They discharged into tubular silencers steadied by brackets which had the appearance of having been forgotten until the last moment. A fourth model the '996 Standard' used the 996cc Summit OHV engine with single exhaust ports.

The four versions so far listed all had Jardine four-speed gear boxes; the overall ratios being identical to those quoted for 1927. At the cheaper extreme of the range the 'TS 996' also employed the single exhaust port Summit engine, but the gearbox was a three-speed Sturmey Archer with ratios of 3.5, 5.2 and 10 to 1.

At the 1928 Olympia Show the AJW 'Super 4' appeared. It never went into production and in that respect, as far as 'fours' at that particular show was concerned, it was in good company. At the time the 'Super 4' was probably the most advanced four-cylinder motor cycle ever shown to the public. That nothing ever came of the project is a matter for regret: possibly there was some inherent fault in the design or an insurmountable obstacle to production.

Many a motor cycle has been described as 'A Car on Two Wheels', but no such claim was made for the 'Super 4' since one sat astride it and not within it. Despite

The AJW Super 4. The caption to this pictuire reads 'Originality is apparent in every line of the remarkable water-cooled four-cylinder AJW'

this fact the vehicle, except for the fact that it had a saddle, footrests, handlebars and, of course, two wheels, owed little to conventional motorcycle practice but was designed from first principles, applying car techniques where applicable.

Designers, both before and since, seem to have concentrated their ingenuity on evolving a suitable four cylinder engine and then (some more cunningly than others) contrived to coax it into a tubular frame. Wheaton, however, took as his starting point a ready-made and well-proven engine and proceeded to design for it a two-wheeled chassis

The engine was a 985cc (56 x 100 mm) British Anzani intended for light car use. It was of straightforward four cylinder design with side-by-side valves, detachable head and three main bearings. There was no induction manifold, the car type carburettor being mounted between the second and third cylinders on the opposite side of the block from the valves, as in the case of so-called Hotchkiss engines fitted to Morris Cowleys and Oxfords of that period. At the time that the first details were released, it was proposed to use some form of combined magneto and dynamo for ignition and lighting. The engine actually used in the prototype would have given place to a re-designed one had the machine gone into production.

Two channel steel chassis members with two tubular cross-braces formed, with the engine bolted into position, a particularly strong, rigid and probably easily-produced main assembly. Duplex steering, closely following OEC practice, avoided the use of front forks, the chassis members being splayed out to allow adequate steering lock. Attached to the front of the cylinder head was a bracket to support a head-stock which accommodated the handlebar stem. The handlebars were connected to the steering assembly by a drag-link.

Rising from the chassis were two supports for the saddle and an inverted, U-shaped bracket for the rear guard. Two plates at the extreme end of the chassis were drilled to take the knock-out rear spindle and from the under-side of the chassis were two hangers to carry the foot rests. A conventional rear stand was fitted in addition to a prop stand. To enable the front wheel to be lifted clear of the ground, the intention was to provide a pair of miniature screw-jacks which could be carried in the toolbox.

In front of the engine, and not very conspicuous was a ribbon-type radiator. Water circulation relied on the thermo-syphon principle; there was no fan. Behind the engine and below the saddle, the petrol tank had only its filler cap exposed. At least one contemporary illustration shows a level indicator tube similar to the gauge-glass on a steam boiler. All engine oil was carried in the sump. What would have been the tank-top on an ordinary machine was a panel which housed a speedometer, a clock, an ammeter and the lighting switch.

980cc AJW

The means whereby a three-speed gearbox can be sited behind a four-cylinder engine with its crank in line with the frame, in such a manner that final drive can be by chain presents a problem to any designer who contemplates such an arrangement, particularly where only limited-scale production is envisaged. How the difficulty was to be overcome, if in fact it ever was, is shrouded in uncertainty. An otherwise admirable drawing of the general layout stops short at what appears to be the flywheel. The pressman describing the prototype seems to have been skating on thin ice and speaks casually of building gear shafts 'in behind the flywheel and car-type cone clutch'.

One also gathers that a bevel-driven countershaft carried the sprocket for the final chain, which seems reasonable enough though a little more detail, particularly as to the means of enclosure, would have been appreciated. However, he goes on to state that the kick-start mechanism was on the countershaft. It would thus appear that the engine could not be kick-started without a gear being engaged and the machine being on its stand. To add further to the confusion, *The Motor Cycle* description of the model exhibited at Olympia mentions a Sturmey Archer three-speed gearbox, whereas the accompanying sketch shows what may well have been a Sturmey Archer kick-start pedal, but an illustration elsewhere shows no pedal at all!

A removable side panel enclosed all the working parts which was held in position with bonnet clips as used on cars of that era. Both front and rear wheels were most thoroughly guarded. A bulge in the left-hand side panel allowed an exhaust pipe connected directly to the end of the manifold to emerge at a little below the level of the bottom of the saddle springs. It was only exposed for a short distance and terminated in a neat, plated cylindrical silencer.

When the Super 4 was envisaged it was a 'dream bus' and it still would be at the time of writing some forty-five years later. 100mph was tentatively mentioned and the price was to have been in the region of £140 fully equipped. At anything like that price, even in those hungry days, the demand should have been there, but possibly the matter of the transmission was never properly sorted out.

As to the models actually listed for 1929, it is noticeable that more extensive use was made of Sturmey Archer three-speed gearboxes of the new horizontal-mounting type. On all machines the top gear was now lower. The overall ratios were 4, 6 and 10 to 1 (Sturmey Archer) and 4, 6.22, 9.22 and 14.35 to 1 (Jardine) A new model was introduced following existing AJW practice, but incorporating the 680cc OHV JAP V-twin engine and the Sturmey Archer box.

The range of 1000cc twins catered for all tastes if not all pockets, not that cycle-wise they differed much from each other or from their predecessors. In effect, there was a basic frame offered with various permutations of engine and gear box. Not many of any one model can have been made, but for the record the range was as follows -

Model	Capacity	Features	
680 TS	680cc	OHV JAP	Sturmey Archer 3-speed gearbox.
Standard	980cc	SV JAP	Sturmey 3- or Jardine 4-speed
8-45 TS	980cc	OHV JAP	Sturmey 3-speed. Racing engine opt. extra.
4 Port TS	996cc	Summit	Sturmey 3-speed
Racing	996cc	Summit	Jardine 4-speed
Sports	996cc	Summit	Sturmey 3-speed

Due to an extension of activities into the two-stroke and single cylinder OHV classes and because the twins were offered in so many versions, there were over a dozen different models for 1930. The new two-strokes were pleasant enough little bikes with Villiers engines and Albion gearboxes. The only feature that distinguished these machines from the products of other small assemblers was that most of them enjoyed, or possible more accurately 'employed' foot-operated gear change of the non-positive type. The cheapest two-stroke was a 196cc Sports. Rather more expensive, the 'Black Fox' came in 172 or 196cc form. For the Silver Fox there were 247 or 343cc engines, and any Fox model could be supplied in trials trim at extra cost. A straightforward, up-to-date, but quite undistinguished, 500cc OHV used the Sturmey Archer three-speed gearbox and the 'cooking' variety of JAP engine. Racing engines by Blackburne or JAP were optional bringing the prices to a prohibitive £89 and £95 respectively.

The twins must now have been on their way out but were still listed in a matter-of-fact manner which seemed to indicate that if there was a depression, news of it had not reached Devon, although at £89, fully equipped, the 680 OHV JAP should have been a good buy. Much the same range of 1000cc twins continued but a spring frame was available for the OHV JAP. Why it was not optional on the 4-Port Special is surprising - but doubtless Mr. Wheaton would have obliged!

1930 was, of course, the year which caused many small assemblers to cry 'enough' but not so AJ Wheaton. The marque was kept alive during the hungry years of the thirties, although for some time probably all that kept the wolf from the door was a 500 OHV sold at cut-throat prices through a large London dealer. By this time, any magic which the name AJW had ever attracted was wearing a trifle thin. Subsequent to the Second World War further examples emerged including a speedway model and an attractive 494cc side-valve vertical twin JAP-engined Grey Fox and whilst there was still evidence of imaginative design the appearance of the early models was sadly absent.

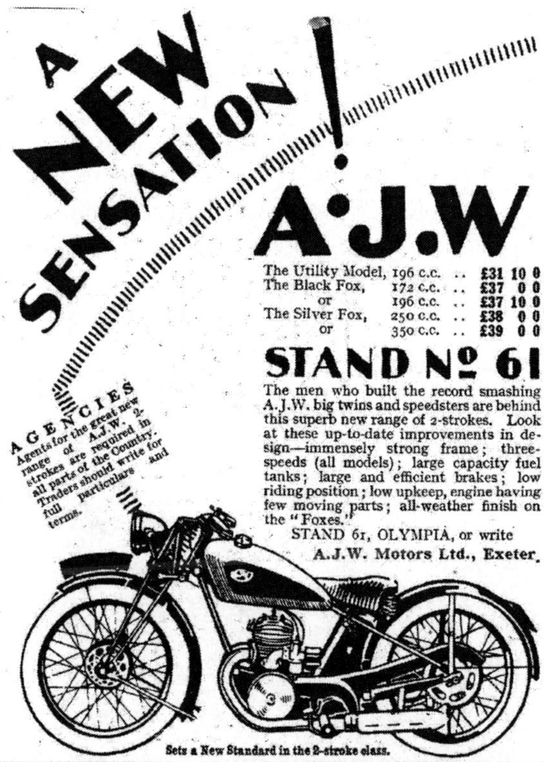

ALECTO

'The first two stroke to break records' was what the motorcycle press said about the Alecto. Whilst the question arises 'what is a record?' and official records of the time do not usually differentiate between two strokes and four strokes, the fact that a machine of this make held no less than twenty-one long distance records at Brooklands in 1920, must give the statement a certain degree of credibility. The manufacturers, Cashmore Brothers of Balham, London, used the slogan 'designed by riders, for riders'- but most small manufacturers, and some of the more important ones, were riders in the twenties.

The feature which lifted the Alecto out of the rut, at a time when most small producers were content to rely on proprietary components, was its engine, the design of which saw few changes during the time that the marque was current. It was, however, always installed in a most pedestrian cycle and the price asked for a complete machine was so high that one marvels that any sales were made at all.

By the middle of 1921, the manufacturers were in serious financial difficulties and GHW and LAV Cashmore were bankrupt, with liabilities according to a contemporary report of the proceedings of £8,833. Assets were estimated to come to £10,000 but it was not until1925 that the second and final dividend was declared.

Alecto Sports.(Photo: VMCC)

Following the bankruptcy proceedings, manufacture was undertaken by Whitmee Engineering Co Ltd, still at Grove Road, Balham, and in July 1922, it was announced in the press that manufacture was now 'in full swing' under the management of 'Mr Cashmore'. Which of the two original partners this was, if indeed either, must remain a matter for conjecture. It was also stated that an enlargement of Grove Works, (sometimes described as Alecto Works) was 'contemplated'.

It will have been gathered that the Alecto engine was a two stroke. Its design was not revolutionary but there were two or three distinctive features. The engine was 'square' i.e. the bore and the stroke were equal, the piston was made of Magnalium, and there were, for better or for worse, usually two exhaust ports. A bore and stroke of 76mm gave a capacity of 345cc which the designers preferred to rate as 3½ hp. The magneto, initially a CAV was behind the cylinder driven by an enclosed chain from the off-side. Also on the right hand side and facing outwards was an Amac two-stroke carburettor. Following car practice, the big end was split and white metalled. Lubrication was usually by drip feed, and oil reached its destinations by way of a system of internal oil-ways.

The 1920 model was just about as unimaginative as it could have been - long narrow flat tank, belt drive, stirrup front brake and small section tyres. The two speed Burman gearbox, however did have a kick starter. Both plated exhaust pipes discharged into a large cylindrical transverse expansion chamber and the tail pipe wandered aimlessly along the right hand side. Blue and red was standard finish but all-black could be specified. The price was £83 7s 6d, subsequently increased by 5%. During 1920 a 'Model B' with stronger frame and heavier forks was offered complete with sidecar.

For 1921 detail improvements were made to the engine - they included modification to the attachment of the exhaust pipes to the cylinder, hopefully to prevent the egress of oil. The two speed solo had risen in weight from 165 to 189 lbs. There was also an alleged TT model with direct belt drive but which it was pointed out, could be converted to two speed without structural alteration. The price? A mere £75! A more substantial model complete with sidecar sold for, or was offered at, £125 0s 0d.

The 1922 range did not include the single speed TT model and a virtually unaltered two speed solo had been reduced to £65. The heavier sidecar model was available in two or three speed form. *Buyers Guide* lists just a single model for 1923, and it describes it as having no clutch or kick starter. The source also lists two speed chain cum belt and two or three all-chain models, all with clutch and kick starter, which information, however, must be taken with a certain amount of reserve, bearing in mind that the work was probably compiled in retrospect.

In October 1923 'the amazing machine with the heart of a lion, the speed of a hare....the strength of a lorry' was at Olympia in its 1924 guise. All the latest improvements and exceptional value for money were claimed but alas, the range was still hopelessly outmoded and overpriced. The lowered frame described for 1923, now formed the basis of a 'sports' model with two speeds, kick starter and chain cum belt transmission. The exhaust pipe, however, led into an expansion chamber box beneath the engine and had two outlet pipes.

The remaining models which made up the 1924 programme, still employed the old high frame and long tank, although the gear lever had found its way from the side of the tank to the seat tube. Two exhaust pipes now fed into a box beneath the engine. From it a large bore exhaust pipe ran purposefully if not very beautifully along the left hand side, the final run being parallel to the ground but at high level. There are conflicting reports as to the method of lubrication but the indications are that it was by mechanical pump. Three speed Burman gearboxes were standard for this part of the range and there was the choice of belt or chain final drive, but one looked in vain for 'all the latest improvements'.

1925 is the last year for which the Alecto is listed, still with stirrup brake and 2¼ inch tyres. There were three models almost identical to their 1924 counterparts. Lubrication was now by drip feed, possibly it might never have been otherwise. The Sports still only had two speeds (3.5 and 7 to 1) and belt drive. The standard solo came with three speeds and either belt (£51) or chain (£56) drive. For a machine that made such little effort to keep up-to-date, the Alecto was lucky to survive as long as it did.

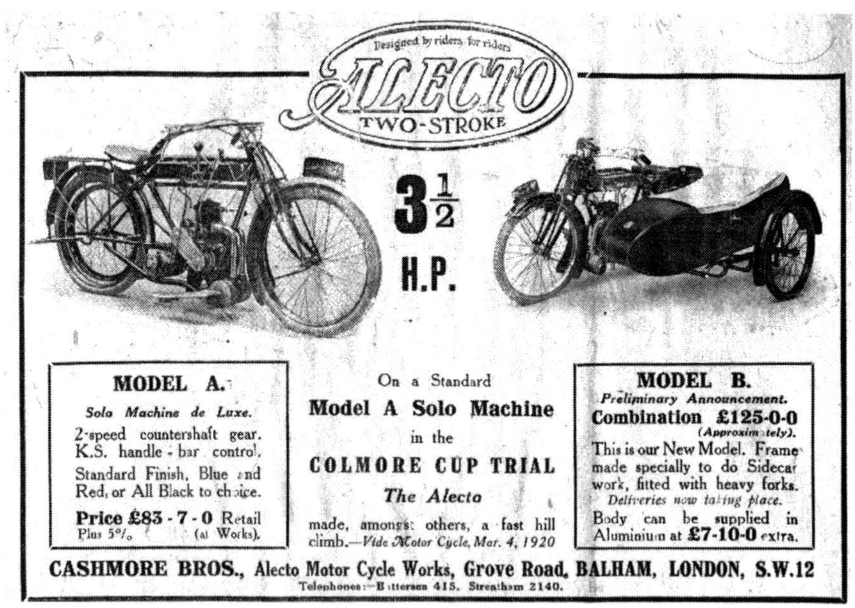

Alecto 1921 models

ALLDAYS

A rather interesting machine which seems to have been almost completely overlooked by historians is the Alldays, product of New Alldays and Onions Ltd, Great Western Works, Small Heath, Birmingham, who introduced a two-model programme for 1927.

The 2¾ hp model utilised the 349cc OHV oil-cooled Bradshaw engine, the manufacture of which was at the time in the hands of Dorman of Stafford. It had a Binks carburettor and BTH magneto. The exhaust pipe swept rather inelegantly around the front down tune and then ran along at low level on the left-hand side of the machine.

A Sturmey Archer gearbox was fitted and the standard ratios were 5, 10 and 15 to 1. The gear lever was mounted directly on the box and was of the type which readily lent itself to foot operation.

The frame was of fairly straightforward design for which great strength and excellent steering qualities were claimed. An interesting detail is that the front down tube terminated in a forked lug which secured the front of the crank case at two points without the use of engine plates.

5/6hp Alldays priced at £85. (Photo: VMCC)[6]

Although not of the 'saddle' type the tank was of particularly fine design and of welded construction throughout. The brakes were, of course, internal expanding but slightly puny - five inches for the front and six inches at the rear. The front forks had the appearance of being Druids.

Following similar lines but of somewhat heavier construction, was the 6 hp incorporating the well known 680cc side-valve JAP twin engine, but in this case using a B and B carburettor and Lucas magneto. Again the exhaust pipe was brought out to the left-hand side. This model had a separate oil tank and eight inch brakes.

Both models had sidecar lugs and they should have provided a useful choice of sporting dual-purpose machine. Unfortunately the prices were on the high side (£55 and £75). Alldays was not a name associated with high performance motorcycles and times were highly competitive. Thus the Alldays scarcely got off the ground, for before the end of 1927 manufacture was discontinued.

Alldays advertisement 1927. Right, Alldays Matchless from 1912

ALWIN

The Alwin scooter was announced for 1920 by the Alwin Manufacturing Company, Luther Road, London, SW. The initial particulars given were brief in the extreme and any further information is hard to find.

Like various other scooters (most of which disappeared after a short while, unloved and unsung) it had no seat, one stood on a platform.

The two-stroke engine was described as being of 1¾ hp. It drove the rear wheel via a shaft. If there was more than one speed the makers did not seem to think that it was worth mentioning.

Judging by a hand-out illustration, the rear number plate was like a normal front one (i.e. legible from both sides) and was mounted on top of the rear wheel enclosure.

The machine was built on a pressed steel chassis and rear springing was incorporated, which perhaps was just as well, since the 3 disc wheels were fitted with solid tyres.

Alwin scooter 1920

ASCOT PULLIN

During the last two or three years of the vintage period a vast number of revolutionary designs were announced. One of the most outstanding of these and one which did not disappear from the scene immediately after being shown at Olympia, was the Ascot Pullin. In fact it was the last of the thoroughly unconventional British motorcycles of the twenties to be produced in anything approaching serious quantities. This machine was the brain-child of CG (Cyril) Pullin who was recognised as one of the most brilliant designers of that period. It was built by Ascot Motor and Manufacturing Co Ltd, of Letchworth, Herts.

For many years the motorcycling public had been brain-washed by the technical press into the belief that what was wanted was an 'ideal' motorcycle which was literally 'a car on two wheels'. It needed to be clean to ride and easy to keep clean, be quiet and docile and to require a minimum of maintenance. Furthermore as well as being economical to run and not *too* expensive to buy, the performance had to be at least comparable with that of a conventional 'Super Sports'. Here then was a machine which offered all these attributes and more besides, but it

Ascot Pullin. (Photo: VMCC)

turned out to be a commercial failure, not only due to the Slump but also because the demand for such a machine did not in fact exist.

In some ways the Ascot Pullin can be likened to the LE Velocette of a couple of decades later which was also built to fill a demand, the size of which had been over-estimated. But whereas the latter, unconventional though it was, embodied only about a couple of patented features, the former incorporated no fewer than twenty-five. (What machine built from scratch ever boasted more?)

There was no frame, as such, and its place, as in the case of the LE Velocette was taken by a body formed from a single sheet of steel. In the case of the AP it was dished at strategic areas to prevent 'drumming'. Into this housing was built a fuel tank and a one-gallon oil tank, each with its own contents gauge. The fuel tank held no less than four and a half gallons, an unnecessarily large quantity if the quoted 150 mpg could be relied upon. Just forward of the saddle was an extra tool-box (with 'lighting-up' table inside the lid) which also served as a 'tummy rest'. Removable side panels gave access to the power unit.

A steering head was welded to the main body and the steering column was supported by taper roller bearings. The front fork blades were also of pressed steel and a single fork-spring was enclosed. Even the handlebars took the form of steel pressing into which was built an instrument panel equipped with speedometer, clock, oil pressure gauge, ammeter and lighting switch. (A Norman 'Nippy' moped of recent times used a similar but less elaborate arrangement.) There was even internal illumination for the dials - which is more than could be said of most cars of that era! Twist-grips were provided to control the throttle and the ignition, and a magneto cut-out button was fitted. Thumb-operated levers flanked the dash panel which operated the air slide of the carburettor and the steering damper. A windscreen, telescopically adjustable for height was fitted to some machines.

Typical of the luxurious specification was the size of the tyres - 26 x 3.25 inches while 27 x 4.4 inch tyres were offered as an extra. The wheels were interchangeable and ran on taper roller bearings. Both front and rear brakes had eight inch drums. The brakes were not only hydraulically operated but were self-adjusting. Initially engine oil from the tank was the brake fluid but later a special fluid was used. To comply with the law the front brake was also cable operated from a hand lever. An enclosed drive for the speedometer came from the front hub. Removal of the wheels was facilitated by the provision of a central stand with extendable plungers for extra height, and by a front stand.

As might be expected the OHV engine and the gearbox formed a single unit, and it was made the more compact by arranging the cylinder horizontally. This layout also ensured an extremely low centre of gravity despite a ground clearance of six inches. The bore and stroke of 82 x 94 mm gave a capacity of 496cc, which was sometimes quoted as 497cc. For half its depth the cylinder was recessed into the crankcase and the exposed half was vertically finned. Finning was sparse on the two-port head, possibly to prevent over-cooling. The rockers which ran on roller bearings were so built up that it was possible to alter the angle between the valve operating arm and the push-rod arm. This feature may have been intended to provide a fresh range of valve clearance adjustment after wear had taken place or it may merely have been incidental in the design.

Four long studs secured the cylinder head direct to the crankcase thus holding the cylinder barrel under compression. On a platform which formed the part of the crankcase immediately above the lower and recessed half of the barrel was a 'Mag-Generator', the BTH equivalent of a Magdyno. It was gear-driven through a Vernier Coupling similar to that already in use by AJS. A down-draught Amac carburettor with horizontal mixing chamber and vertical air intake was mounted directly to the inlet port.

Lubrication was of course mechanical but a flow regulator was interconnected with the throttle. An oil filter was readily removable for cleaning as was the whole pump mechanism. Rotary release valves, one in each half of the crankcase, provided lubrication to the timing gear and to the primary drive.

The drive from the engine to the gear-box was by double-helical gears and as was usual with this type of primary drive, the engine ran 'backwards' - ie opposite to the direction of rotation of the road wheels. A multi-plate metal to metal clutch ran in oil. The three speed gear-box used ball bearings throughout. The drive came in through a spring loaded shock absorber on the left-hand side and went out via a second similar shock absorber on the right-hand side.

The kick starter was on the left. It had an exposed quadrant which engaged with a free-wheel pinion, again closely following AJS practice. An interesting device was an interconnection mechanism between the kick starter and an exhaust valve lifter. Final drive was by normal roller chain, a fairly effective enclosure for which was part and parcel of the main body pressing.

The exhaust system was particularly neat. Two pipes ran parallel to the ground and discharged into cylindrical silencers with fish-tails. The exact shape of the fish-tail seems to vary slightly from one illustration to another.

Looking as if it did not altogether 'belong' was a useful rear carrier fitted with two conventional tool-bags. Also giving the impression of being afterthoughts were the battery (mounted directly above the rear hub where it could receive the full effect of road shock), likewise the leg shields, when fitted.

The general finish was striking - dark blue cellulose body relieved with cream panels, black mudguards, etc, and, at a time when this not completely unmixed blessing was in its infancy, chromium-plated wheel rims.

Despite mild cams and a low compression ratio the maximum speed was variously given as 70 and 75mph. Pullin, who was the first rider of a 500cc machine to attain 100mph at Brooklands should have known what he was talking about when he claimed a speed of around 100mph for the Ascot Pullin if fitted with fiercer cams and a high compression piston.

The foregoing notes describe the 1929 model when it was first introduced in October 1928. When in due course it appeared at Olympia mention was made in the press of a transmission free-wheel which could be put into or taken out of action at will - but I can trace no subsequent reference to this feature. Prices for 1929 were £73 for the Sports and £75 for the Utility, reasonable enough for what was without doubt the most completely equipped British motorcycle which had ever been produced.

Ascot Pullin 1928

There was a single model for 1930 at £78 15s 0d. and the weight was now quoted at 390lbs as compared with 340lbs previously. The cylinder head and barrel had been redesigned giving deeper finning and a new position for the plug. The method of tappet adjustment was altered and the rockers modified, otherwise there was little change. The machine illustrated in The Motor Cycle Show Guide had cylindrical silencers fitted with half fish tails, but elsewhere it is depicted with no silencers and what looked like straight-through exhaust pipes, but which presumably contained internal baffles.

The Ascot Pullin was a lot of bike for the money, but in all probability buyers lucky enough to have that sort of money and looking for a refined machine with plenty of life turned their attention to the BSA Slopers, and sacrificed some of the frills leaving the substantial difference in price in the bank.

1930 was the last year for which the make was listed and by the Spring of that year London dealers Rennos were offering brand new machines at 49 guineas and all parts at 41 per cent off list price. That they were still doing so by the Autumn gives some idea of the state of the motorcycle trade at that time.

ARIEL

The Ariel origins go well back into the Victorian period and their involvement in the cycle trade. After World War I Jack Sangster came into the business, but his main interest was the Ariel light Car. The motorcycles of the time used the old fashioned White and Poppe single cylinder side-valve engines, plus V- twins of proprietary manufacturer. Ariel were rather behind the times until Val Page joined the firm. Under his leadership a new range of 550 SV and 500 OHV models with good performance were introduced. Saddle tanks and cradle frames were brought in to update the range and a whole range of publicity stunts(Harry Perrey rode his Ariel to the top of Snowdon and another time he got one across the English Channel on floats), helped to boost sales to 1,000 machines a week in 1929.

Further reading;

The Ariel Story, Peter Hartley, Argus books, 1980, reprinted by the Ariel Owners Club

ATLAS

Produced by the Aston Motor and Engineering Co Ltd, of Whitton Lane, Aston, Birmingham, the Atlas was an ultra-lightweight of real distinction which changed but little during the period in which it was built.

Not content to employ one of the many available engines 'ready to drop into the frame', the makers designed and produced their own miniature power unit and a remarkably fine piece of work it was. The bore and stroke of 55 x 60mm gave a capacity of 142.5cc or in the parlance of that era, 1¾hp. The disc type crank was machined from a drop forging. It ran on a combination of roller and plain bearings. Phosphor bronze bushes were used for big and small ends. There was of course an outside flywheel and this was formed from a steel stamping.

At the rear of the engine was a CAV magneto, chain driven from behind the engine sprocket. The primary chain drove a plain countershaft running on ball bearings. An aluminium enclosure protected both chains and they received a modicum of lubrication via a steel pipe connected to the compression release valve. The carburettor which could be either a Senspray or an Amac was attached to the front of the cylinder and faced forwards. Only a very short pipe discharged from the transverse expansion box. Lubrication was by petroil. In its original form the Atlas had only a single speed. The final drive from the countershaft was by belt.

This was a true ultra lightweight touching the scale at a mere 75 lbs although the layout owed nothing to the push bike but followed normal motorcycle practice throughout. The front forks were of the type which afforded a 'fore and aft' movement with a horizontal spring.

Both brakes operated on the belt rim but the method by which they were activated strikes one as being unnecessarily complicated. A heel pedal applied a block to the 'V' of the rim. A second block was brought into contact with the inside of the rim by a handlebar lever but additional pressure also brought the foot brake into operation.

These are the particulars of the machine as it was introduced in December 1921 at the attractive price of £31 10s 0d. At that time an initial 25 machines were nearing completion. During 1922 the weight was quoted at 95 lbs fully equipped, and the tail pipe had been somewhat lengthened.

For 1923 the price had come down to 26 guineas. Similar models with plain two-speed or two-speed and kick start were offered at 29 guineas and 32 guineas respectively.

The single speed model was dropped for 1924 but the two two-speed models continued to be available at the same prices. This was possibly the last year during which the Atlas was marketed.

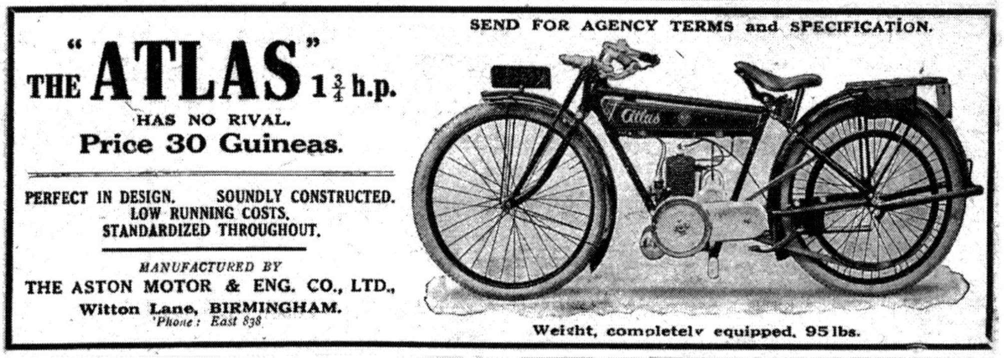

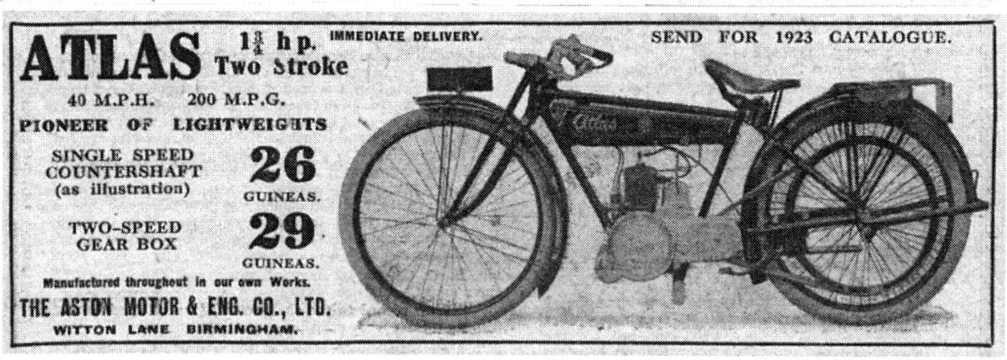

AUTOGLIDER

Of all the scooters which appeared on the market immediately after the 1914-1918 War, the Autoglilder was sounder than most. It was also probably one of the best sellers and during 1920 was being handled by nearly fifty agents in the British Isles as well as being represented in China, Japan and India. The manufacturers and 'Patentees' were the old-established Birmingham firm of Townsend & Company, Great Charles Street, but later the concern became Autoglider Ltd, of 26 Lower Tower Street.

Initially the machine was designed so that the 'rider' stood on a platform fixed to a sprung chassis which was the subject of a Patent. "It is impossible to enjoy the delights of gliding..." the makers said, "...with a seat". Soon, however, they bowed to convention and models with seats were introduced.

The construction of the 1919-1920 'stand-up' model was quite straightforward. The two stroke engine was a 70 x 76mm (292cc) Union but it had a chain driven magneto mounted forward, not the side mounted direct coupled type usually associated with this make. Unusual too for the Union, lubrication was by petrol carried in the cylindrical tank mounted vertically on the tall handlebar stem. This engine (as was the case with subsequent ones) was situated immediately over the front wheel which it drove by chain via a metal-to-metal engine shaft clutch. There was only one speed, a ratio of 7 to 1. The clutch was of the makers own design and was available for fitment to other makes of machine using similar engines.

Models with seats were available for 1920. These came in two versions, one a straightforward runabout and the other a 'Service Model' which used the rear of the machine to form a three cubic foot locker with a parcel rack on the top. The latter type was intended for the use of commercial travelers and the like. The 'seat' versions, both of which were exceedingly attractive and well thought out vehicles, still used cylindrical tanks but mounted horizontally across the handlebars. Common to all Autogliders were disc wheels fitted with 16 x $2^3/_8$ inch Autoglider Palmer tyres. In 1921 six distinct models were offered. These probably consisted of one stand-up and the two seated models with a choice of Union or Villiers (flywheel magneto) engine in each case.

Soon however *The Invincible Autoglider, The Machine without a Rival,* went the way of its counterparts leaving a small number of not necessarily more worthy scooters behind.

Above, an advertisement for the Autoglider, and below, a 1929 Autoglider 269cc de luxe

Roads and Garages

Although many fine motoring roads had been created in the years leading up to the war, the conflict had inevitably taken valuable resources away from repairs and maintenance to pay for the war effort. The process of tarmacadaming - that is the mixing of small pieces of gravel with tar then laying it on a well prepared foundation and rolling it flat, had been around for a number of years. The gang of road workers with their steamroller were a familiar sight to all highway users, however there were still many minor roads that remained in much the same state they had been in since the days of the Stage Coach.

The back roads were muddy in winter and dusty in summer. Horse drawn traffic still dominated all other vehicles until the mid twenties, with the result that the surface layer consisted of a rich mixture of animal droppings, loose stones, horse shoes and nails, deep cart tracks and even deeper potholes. There was not a lot of surface drainage and the resultant puddles were hidden by fallen leaves, whilst flocks of sheep and cattle shared the same road with heavy goods vehicles and ordinary cars to make life interesting for the ordinary motorcyclist.

However by way of compensation, the roads were well marked with sign- and mile-posts. There was usually someone around to ask for help or directions, and often there were good inns and hotels. It must not be forgotten either that at this time the whole country was covered by a vast range of rural and mainline railways, so that no matter where you were, you were never very far from a station. In the event of a terminal breakdown, the offending machine could usually be pushed or hauled to the nearest local halt and put on a train home.

Typical rural road around the time of the Great War

PG Rose's garage at Par, Cornwall, in the late twenties

Garages and repairers began to proliferate. Members of the armed forces had gained all kinds of useful experiences with mechanical locomotion whilst serving King and Country and were keen to capitalise on this knowledge. At the turn of the century, petrol had been very difficult to obtain, its main use in Victorian times being that of a dry cleaning fluid! So, with the substantially increased number of people taking to the roads who needed fuel and sometimes repairs, a great many establishments started to cater for these needs. Petrol began to be served in purpose built 'petrol stations', which used specially constructed underground tanks in order to store the fuel. It was dispensed using a hand cranked pump through a pipe directly into the vehicle. The previous system of selling petroleum in 2 or 5 gallon metal cans began to look old fashioned.

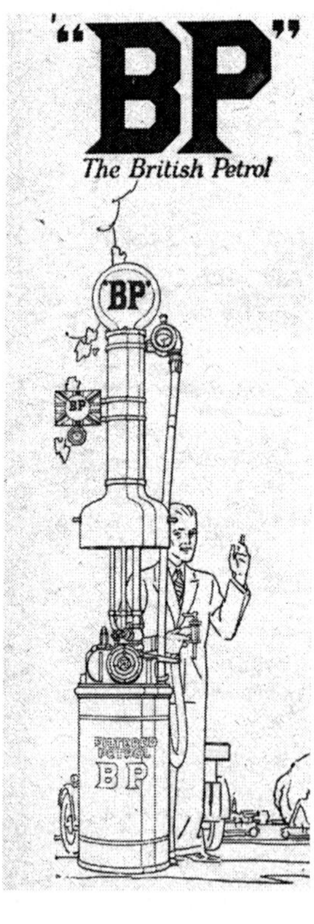

This was a very interesting cross-over time when the pioneer garage owners, mostly blacksmiths who had learned in their youth how to repair farm carts and wagons, and whose mechanical knowledge of the internal combustion engine had been gained by trial and error, began to be replaced by mechanics who had specialist knowledge of the vehicles they had to deal with. Thus for example, there had to be people who knew about electrical systems, metallurgy, or tyres.

The buying and selling of new and second-hand machines then, of course, became part of the equation. Agents for new models proclaimed their machines perfection, high efficiency, scientific design, ample power, best investment, go anywhere reliability, in fact all that could be reasonably desired by a customer willing

to spend his or her hard earned cash on a new means of transport, probably the first mechanically propelled vehicle that they had ever owned. 'Rider manufacturers', that is people who not only sold the bikes, but who designed and rode them successfully in competitions, began to appear.

Second hand machines were said to be guaranteed and to ensure this was so, dealers had the equipment, spares and expert staff with, of course, every kind of facility for repairs. People who in an earlier life had traded horses, found new opportunities to make a few shillings.

By the end of the period the older and slower way of life was beginning to disappear, and the transport revolution was starting to have a serious effect on the way everyone's daily lives were being led. It is interesting to perhaps look at the reflections from contemporary writers.

First the ordinary motorcyclist, R K Battson from *The Land Beyond the Ridge*. "Perhaps it was the genuine openness of the road. There was so little traffic, and so much of that was motorcycles whose riders were brothers, always cheerful and ready to help or indulge in the odd scrap where the roads permitted; perhaps it was the unspoiled countryside, perhaps even it was the weather, maybe it was that we were, for the most part young and free........."

The Speed Merchant, T E Lawrence from *The Road.* "The extravagance in which my surplus emotion expressed itself lay on the road. So long as the roads were tarred blue and straight; not hedged; and empty and dry, so long was I rich......."

The Philosopher, Michael Fairless from *The Roadmender.* "I have attained my ideal; I am a roadmender, some say stonebreaker. All day I sit by the roadside on a stretch of grass under a high hedge of saplings and a tangle of traveller's joy, woodbine, sweetbriar and late roses."

Ixion, the curmudgeon, from *Motor Cycle Reminiscences*. "In spite of huge sums which are expended on roads nowadays, they are worse - probably much worse - than they were twenty years ago. The impressions of old-timers, like myself cannot be wholly trustworthy, of course. The prehistoric motor demanded ones entire attention, and no surplus facilities were available to criticize the road surface. Moreover a youthful body is composed of fencing wire and India rubber, so that it sustains tribulations that would be torture to a forty year old. Nevertheless, when all these allowances have been scrupulously made, I am convinced that the national road system has steadily deteriorated since 1900 or thereabouts"

Tools to be Carried on a Motorcycle Journey in 1920

Oil
Spokes
Spoke key
Spare engine valves
Grinding in paste
Grinding tool
Small phial of flux
Pocket blowlamp
Inner and outer Bowden cables
Cable ends and nipples
Rag
Coal Hammer
Three universal spanners
Screwdriver
Shifting spanner
Selection of nuts, bolts and wire

Oil squirt
Grease gun
Spare drive belt
Spare belt joiners and tool
Spare crank pedal
Circuit tester
Two spark plugs
File
Hand vice
Spare points
Inner tubes
Tyre levers and soap
Puncture repair outfit
Carbide and spare burners
Tow rope

Clothing

Minnehaha, Joy Rider

Or the sad tale of a maiden who went motoring with many men.

Taken from The Motor Cycle December 24th 1929

Dressed in nattiest of clothing
Plus-fours long and very baggy
Rode the mighty Hiawatha,
Sportiest of sporty laddies.
Far his scarf trailed out behind him
Gorgeous scarf of many colours,
Waving, flying in the West Wind,
In the wind that flows from Ealing.

Mounted on his sporting solo,
With a badge upon the mudguard,
Bearing these strange words upon it;-
"Speed on, Big Boy; Hell ain't full yet"
Blue his cap, as used for ski-ing,
Red the tassels on his hose-tops,
Pink and White was his complexion,
On his lip a Ronald Coleman.

The above extract was taken from a much longer poem that was a particular favourite of Jack Bacons. The poem reminded Jack of the time that he and Monica, whose nickname was Minnehaha, broke down whilst riding in a Windmill Rally and he was left to recover the bike on his own whilst she was picked up and taken to the finish. It is included because it gives a flavour of the required dress of the young man about town in the late twenties who chose to woo his maiden from the seat of a motor bicycle, but who in the end was thwarted by a cad on a 'two port pip-squeak with empty sidecar'.

Clothing was then, as it is now, very much a compromise between the practicalities of riding in the vagaries of British weather, and the sartorial elegance of the day.

Immediately after the first war there was much army surplus clothing around. You could equip yourself with lace up Cavalry boots, and leggings, a gas cape to go over the greatcoat, an RFC flying helmet and goggles together with a long silk scarf and rabbit fur lined gauntlets and still look reasonably fashionable At that time many of the cheaper low powered bikes were still fitted with devices that enabled the rider to give 'lpa', that is light pedal assistance, to their mount whilst ascending hills. In practical terms this meant that the poor rider was constantly overheating going uphill, then rapidly cooling as speed built up on the flat or descent. In oil skins you sweated, in lightweight clothes you froze.

By the end of the era things were improving and clothing became rather more practical. Manufacturers were producing garments that were designed specifically for motorcycling,

Miss Mae Ruffel (Mrs Lacey) on a 1928 350cc Grindlay. She gained the Wakefield Cup with a winning speed of 79.78mph (Photo: Jonathan Vickers)

and took into account the needs of riders who were not only unwilling to put up with unsuitable designs, but due to the faster speeds they were achieving needed to have some degree of protection in the unfortunate case of an accident. Leather was being used on the race track and helmets were becoming popular although still the flat hat seemed to be the most that some people deemed necessary as headgear. Rubber, or Gutta Percha was being incorporated into fabrics designed to be waterproof. Indeed it was at this period that certain n'ere do wells actually had the audacity to turn their caps around the wrong way with the peak at the back, thus becoming the forerunners of the modern day Rockers and Hells Angels.

So we can say that at the end of the twenties, the Promenade Percy would be dressed in Oxford Bag trousers, have gaiters or long socks and ordinary brogue shoes. A tie would be *de rigueur*,

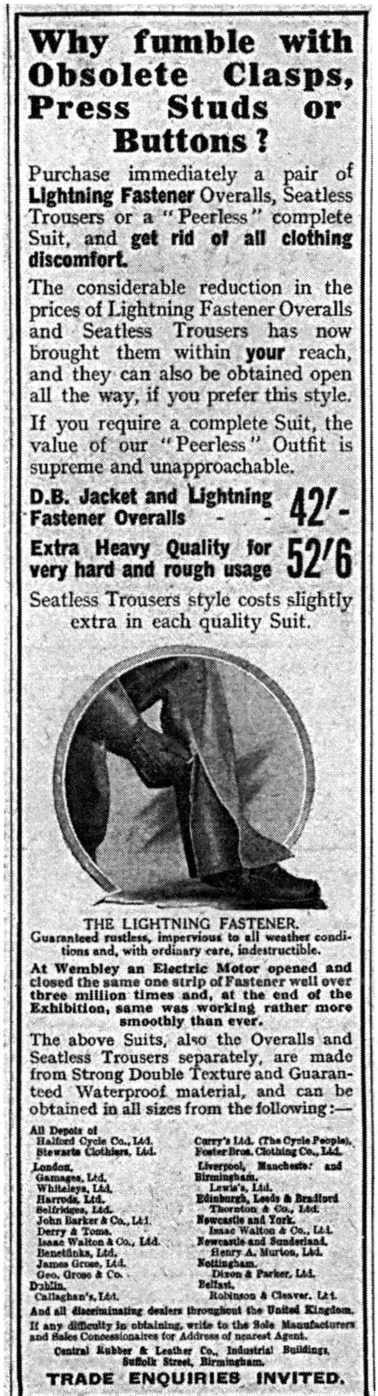

1927. The new lightning fastener now known as the zip.

as would a waistcoat with a watch and chain, probably a short sleeved Fair Isle jersey, and a large gabardine mac to keep out the rain and cold. Goggles and a flat hat would complete the ensemble with, it has to be said, a cigarette nonchalantly dangling from the lips. The ladies were not so well catered for, and this being the jazz age and an era of short skirts, cloche hats and stockings, female passengers were often perched on the 'Flapper Brackets', as the rear seats were called, or astride 'Ladies Models', that is to say ordinary machines whose frame had been cut down rather in the manner of a ladies bicycle. The alternative was to adopt clothes designed for men, and, if the lady wished to consider serious riding of her own machine - there were many who did - then this was really the only solution. One other great new invention that was only just beginning to make an impact on clothing at that time was the 'Lightning' fastener, the zip. In fact to prove how strong they were a length was mechanically opened and closed three million times during the 1925 Wembley Exhibition.

Incidentally, the poem refers to a 'Ronald Coleman' which was a very thin moustache: Ronald Coleman being a star of the black and white movie days.

BAKER

'My lad' said the staid undertaker,
'You'll soon need a smart coffin maker',
'Oh no', said the lad
'Don't think I've been had,
My bike is called 'Baker' not 'Shaker'!'.

This limerick which appeared in a press advertisement, is an allusion to the machine's handling qualities. FE Baker was the creator of the Beardmore Precision, the shortcomings of which included indifferent steering and road-holding and, so the legend goes, Mr. Baker vowed that good handling was to be the number one priority on any subsequent machine he designed.

These ideals were fully implemented in the Baker and were built-in rather than achieved by freak design. Correct steering geometry, scientific weight distribution and absolute frame rigidity were the open secrets of success. Indeed, throughout the period for which the marque was produced, friction or any other form of fork or steering dampers were never employed.

1927 Model BS (Photo: Terry Major)

1927

FE Baker of Alvechurch Road, Northfield, Birmingham, introduced their first machine early in 1927. According to an article which appeared in the Kings Norton MCC magazine, production started in a 'tin shed' which had earlier been the home of the Triple-H motorcycle. It was a pretty, if slightly dated-looking bike and would have looked even prettier had the control cables, etc., been tidied up. (Less scrupulous manufacturers were wont to 'eschew' these items from their press release and publicity illustrations!). The most eye-catching feature was possibly the colour of the mudguards and the wedge-shaped tank. They were finished in cellulose (for which claims of great durability were made) in 'a shade resembling primrose but more subdued' to use the words of a contemporary report. Black finish for these components could, however, be specified.

In the construction of the frame, brazing was confined to the two points at which the ends of the top-tube united with the seat-bracket and with the top of the steering head. Integral with the bottom of the steering head was a substantial flat member which continued downwards for a short distance at an angle corresponding to the line of the front down tubes. Its extreme end was then brought parallel to the ground and carried a transverse bracket, slotted at the ends, which supported the front of the tank. The two front tubes were joined to the bottom of the steering-head proper and their bottom ends formed the front engine mounting. Duplicated seat-tubes ran from the seat-bracket to the top of the rear engine plates at which point they conveniently picked up the front end of the gearbox platform. A pair of what would conventionally be called 'tank-tubes' extended from the seat bracket to the horizontal part of the flat extension from the steering head, at which point there were two additional clamps to ensure a rigid union with the front tubes. The rear mounting for the tank was provided by a second transverse bracket integral with the seat bracket.

The frame was completed by three further pairs of tubes, one pair from the seat bracket, one from the rear end of the gearbox platform and one from the bottom of the engine plates. Each pair met at the brackets which carried the rear wheel spindle, to form seat-stays, chain-stays and torque-tubes respectively. All tubes were perfectly straight and, except at the two points which have been specifically mentioned, 'pin-jointing' was employed throughout. Brampton-Baker front forks incorporated a single central compression spring. The construction of the fork girders completely eliminated brazing.

The engine was the then ubiquitous 172cc (86.4 x 95mm) Villiers two-stroke. The advance and retard lever extending from the back-plate of the flywheel magneto was held in the required position by a notched gate. Instead of being at the top of the mixing chamber, the needle control of the Villiers carburettor was brought up to the handlebar by Bowden cable. Automatic lubrication was by crankcase pressure via an adjustable sight-feed in the top of the tank.

Both exhaust pipes led into a transverse expansion box, which to prevent drumming and eliminate gas leakages was of heavy gauge, all-welded construction. From the centre of this box the final exhaust pipe ran unobtrusively beneath the engine and its flattened end emerged on the left-hand side just ahead of the rear wheel.

Transmission (as with but a solitary exception on all subsequent productions) was through an Albion three-speed gearbox with internal locking for each gear. In this instance the gear lever was directly mounted on the box and gear ratios were 6, 9 and 14 to 1. There was a guard over the top run of the primary chain.

Both internal expanding brakes operated on the back wheel. Beaded-edge (euphemistically described as 'flat base') tyres were 25 x 3 inch Hutchinsons. The tank held a gallon and a half of petrol and a half gallon (no less!) of oil. Varying sources quote the weight as 190 lbs and 175 lbs. The latter seems to be the more probable.

Direct electric lighting, in conjunction with the flywheel unit was standard. Other details which help to complete the picture included a 'pan' seat, a tool-box on the seat tubes, a small carrier-cum-lifting handle and adjustable footrests. The price was £36 or £38 10s 0d if supplied with a Villiers 247cc engine.

A Road Test of the 172cc Version appeared in *The Motor Cycle* dated 19th May 1927. No mention was made of petrol consumption but maximum speed was in the order of 50mph at which gait a little vibration, which was absent at normal touring speeds, became noticeable. Silence, docility, road-holding, top gear performance and the ability to climb trials-type hills all came in for favourable comment. The handlebars were, however, too wide for the tester's liking, a certain amount of mud escaped the front guard at about tank height and use of the foot brake required a little experience to prevent its locking the wheel.

The 172cc Model and its 247cc variant remained much the same for 1928 with the manufacturers now trading as Baker Motor Cycles Ltd. During the few months of its existence the Baker had notched up a few successes in events of doubtful importance such as a first place at the Addington Grass Trace Races, and oblivious to the fact that at least a couple of other manufacturers could have made the claim with more justification, the marque was being advertised as 'The first fine quality lightweight motorcycle'. As if to back up this slogan 53-55 mph was being quoted for the 172cc and 58-60 mph for the 247. 'Produced carefully' the makers said, '- and therefore in limited numbers - like all superfine work'.

1928-29

One important change for 1928 was the provision of an internal expanding front brake, with a commendable long anchorage. The position of the headlamp was lowered; there was the choice of Brooks or Leatheries soft top saddle, and the carrier which now had an added pair of vertical stays, extended further forwards.

The 172cc Model already described in detail in its 1927 form, with the aforementioned modifications, now became the 1928 Model A but with gear ratios of 6, 11 and 19 to 1. Endowed with two separate, plated exhaust pipes with black cylindrical silencers it appeared as the AS. A second alternative had its ground-clearance increased from 4½ to 6 inches and was offered as the Colonial A. In the same way the 247cc engined models became the B, the BS and the B Colonial respectively.

Finally there was the Special (obviously especially cheap rather than specially refined!) with a 147cc (55 x 62mm) two-stroke engine with petroil lubrication. It was of Villiers manufacture as were the engines of all Baker two-strokes. Tyres were of 2½ inch section and gear ratios 6, 11 and 20 to 1. It weighed only 155 lbs and was offered at £30.

At extra cost any model was available with facilities for charging the accumulator, thus providing an improved lighting system.

During 1928 the fairly regular visiting-card size press advertisements would be punctuated by the occasional quarter-page display, sometimes headed 'THE VERY FINEST LIGHTWEIGHT'. Further down in small print one gathered that was the opinion of a user from Merton Park - shades of George Brough?

With the advent of the 1929 season Bakers had modified their former somewhat extravagant slogan and substituted 'Leader amongst lightweights in its class'.

Baker 1928 247cc Model 60

All models now employed the 6 inch clearance Colonial frame and with saddle tanks almost completely universal, the marque took on a completely up-to-date and singularly handsome appearance. A Show report stated that a sturdy gear lever working in a neat gate alongside the front of the tank was in use on all models which was possibly correct, although a press illustration of what was now the 172cc Model 50 indicates otherwise.

Bakers were now represented in the cut-throat market with the 147cc Model 40 selling at £25. The wedge-tank was retained, likewise petroil lubrication and 2½ inch tyres. Front and rear brake diameters were 4 and 5 inches respectively. Two-speeds were standard but as an optional extra, three could be specified.

Rather more refined and using the 172cc Sports engine was the Model 50. Its saddle tank carried both petrol and oil. Tyres sizes were as for the Model 40, but the brake diameters were increased to 5 inches at the front front and 6 inches at the rear. The twin-pipe exhaust system as available for 1928 was standard.

A similar machine, but with a 247cc Sports engine, became the Model 58. However, in this case the mudguards were wider and 25 x 3 inch wired-edge tyres were fitted. Electric lighting was an 'extra' on the foregoing three models - £1 10s 0d for direct or £4 10s 0d with a charging set.

At the luxury end of the range were the 172cc Model 50 and the 247cc Model 60 with Super Sports engines. They were described by *The Motor Cycle's* man as being 'As good to look at as Olympia is likely to house this year' - a comment which did not pass unnoticed by Bakers' publicity department. These two models were supplied complete with direct lighting (with charging sets £3 extra), bulb-horn, air filter and speedometer.

Saddle tanks carried petrol only - in excess of two gallons - and oil was contained in a horizontal cylindrical separate tank below the saddle. The speedometer was recessed into the tank-top and was symmetrically balanced by a filler-cap of approximately the same diameter. Its drive was neatly taken from the rear hub with the help of a fibre gear ring inside the brake drum.

The programme was completed by a Grass Track racer (which had no model number). The wedge-shaped tank was used in conjunction with a separate oil tank. There was the choice of 172 or 247cc high-compression racing Villiers engine with an Amac carburettor controlled by a twist-grip. Both short exhaust pipes led into a transverse exhaust box which discharged via a long slot. The gearbox had close ratios and the narrow almost flat mudguards were plated. Either version was claimed to be capable of 70mph and cost £40.

1930

It is known that at some point in its history the Baker organisation passed into the hands of the James Cycle Co Ltd and by the time that the 1930 programme was announced this change may well have taken place since the producers now traded as Baker Motor Cycles, Tomey Road, Greet, Birmingham. The 147cc Model had been eliminated and if the Grass Track ('almost invincible in its class') continued to be built, it was no longer included in the *Buyers Guide*. 196 and 343cc models were now offered, thus somewhat widening the scope of the range.

Differences for 1930 were of a very minor nature such as the substitution of plated - but still cylindrical - silencers with fish-tails for black ones with trapped ends. Paint work was now black except for yellow tank panels. 25 x 3 in tyres were standard on all models.

Briefly then, the initial range for 1930 was:-

Model 55	172cc
Model 65	172cc (Brooklands engine)
Model 50	196cc
Model 58	196cc (Super Sports)
Model 60	247cc
Model 62	343cc

A little later, however, there was a break with tradition and a four-stroke model was added to the range. A 249cc (64 x 77.5mm.) side-valve engine, obviously of James manufacture, was installed in the standard Baker cycle with separate oil tank and there was provision for a tank-mounted speedometer. The engine was mounted with the cylinder inclined and parallel to the front down tubes. The magneto was sited forward of the crankcase and the long plated exhaust pipe passed behind the magneto drive-chain cover.

Lubrication was by the total loss system fed by a Pilgrim sight-feed pump. The carburettor was a Binks, an instrument which, following the formation of Amalgamated Carburettors Ltd. (Amal) from Amac, B & B and Binks a little earlier, had comparatively few adherents. Gear ratios were 6.5, 11 and 19.7 to 1.

An example with a separate dynamo behind the cylinder was road-tested by *The Motor Cycle* (29 May, 1930). Road-holding, steering and starting all received favourable comments and maximum speed was guesstimated at 52-55mph The manner in which the rear brake all too easily locked the wheel came in for comparatively strong criticism and the front brake was not considered to be sufficiently powerful.

With reference to fuel consumption, the tester reported 'With fast riding petrol consumption fell between the 90 and 100mpg marks, which while not being remarkable is very satisfactory in the circumstances'. He went on to remark philosophically 'A great deal too much is expected from a gallon of fuel by most riders'.

It so happened that there appeared in the same issue a Road Test of the then current 298cc side-valve Raleigh (also with separate dynamo lighting set). The Baker cost £42 10s 0d and the Raleigh was five shillings cheaper. Of the two machines, particularly taking into consideration the advantage of dry-sump lubrication and appreciably bigger brakes, the latter would have been the obvious choice for most people shopping around for a small four-stroke.

If the Baker, as such, continued to be marketed after 1930, it does not appear in the 1931 *Buyers Guide*.

Baker 1930 Lightweight

BERWICK

Introduced as it was in the depth of a depression, the Berwick could not hope to succeed due to its prohibitive price if for no other reason. Little about it ever appeared in the motorcycle press and casual enquiries made in Banbury where production, such as it was, took place proved unrewarding. However, an appeal for information which the *Banbury Guardian* was kind enough to print brought forth a couple of interesting replies from local residents, Messrs C Ayres and HR Sanderson. The latter also put me in touch with a former Banbury trader, Mr WE Kirkland, and to these gentlemen I am indebted for the background material they have been able to provide.

One of the first references to the Marque appeared in *Motor Cycling* for 18 September 1929 and the contributor seemed astonished that a motorcycle could have been produced in 'one extremely well equipped and neatly laid-out workshop' in the little Scottish border town of Berwick.

By November 1929 the manufacturers, varyingly described as The Berwick Motor Co and The Berwick Manufacturing Co - usually the latter - had moved to Banbury and taken over some works off Station Road, opposite, what is at the time of writing Banbury United Football Ground. These premises were formerly occupied by the Austin-Light Co, or a firm with a similar name, and were subsequently used by the Switchgear and Engineering Co.

The original caption reads:"The totally enclosed transmission unit, engine, gearbox, universally jointed cardan shaft and worm housing allow thousands of miles of running before it becomes necessary to make an inspection. The rider need not worry further than the necessary filling and supplementation of oil." (Photo: VMCC)

The interesting feature of the Berwick was that it employed shaft final drive. A contemporary described it as 'Britain's first shaft-driven machine with a proprietary engine' but in doing so either ignored or forgot the GSD which had been listed some six years earlier.

A high-fronted duplex cradle frame with a short, deep, saddle tank and extremely low saddle height housed a Villiers two stoke engine mounted with the crankshaft in line with the machine and the flywheel magneto facing forwards. Features of the frame were that the steering-head was of welded-up steel construction, there was no 'seat tube' and what would on a conventional machine be called 'chain stays' were upswept.

The unconventional method of mounting the engine meant that the cylinder head fins were across the machine, and had production ever reached a commercial scale complaints of over-heating may have resulted. Two short stubs from the exhaust ports were 'stabbed' into the horizontal front portion of a large bore exhaust pipe on the left hand side. The forward end of the pipe was blanked off. From what was now the rear of the cylinder the pipe swept downwards at an angle and then once more took a horizontal line before discharging into a silencer. Some illustrations show the silencer as cylindrical and black whilst in others it is an approximately rectangular, plated, proprietary Vortex with integral fish-tail.

Given the configuration of the engine, what would normally have been the auxiliary outside flywheel was facing towards the rear and accordingly it did duty as the driving member of a single plate clutch. On the clutch shaft was a skew gear which picked up the drive from a near-side kick-starter. The constant-mesh three-speed gear was arranged so that its housing formed a unit with the crankcase and the drive came out on the off-side. The final drive shaft had a universal joint at either end. It drove the rear wheel by means of an underslung worm-drive, the enclosure of which was rigidly bolted to the frame. The wheel had a knock-out or withdrawable spindle and was thus easily and quickly removable.

The transmission components were said to have been of Berwicks own manufacture, but it seems possible that they were of BMW origin since one of my Banbury correspondents informs me that in 1947 some Berwick transmission parts were sold by a M Shepherd to an advertiser seeking BMW spares.

Such descriptions as there are available mention the gear control being housed within the bounds of the petrol tank with only the knob visible, but at least one illustration clearly shows the lever to be directly mounted on the right hand side of the gear housing. Again a separate oil tank below the saddle is sometimes shown and presumably secured to the rear mudguard, but in other instances none appears to exist. Nowhere does any sort of provision for tools appear to have been made. Possibly it was considered that none was necessary since the manufacturers announced that the Berwick was 'Primarily designed for the minimum of attention and maximum of service'. One further point concerning which the designers do not seem to have been able to make up their minds, was the carburettor mount - sometimes shown with the air-intake facing directly outwards on the right hand side and elsewhere with it facing rearwards and to the left.

To complete the description as far as is possible, front forks were by Brampton and the saddle by Terry. Both brakes were of 7 inch diameter and the specification included a central stand. Mudguards (the rear devoid of carrier) were substantial, but they were supported only by rather inadequate-looking 'wire' stays. Tyres were of 3.25 inch section.

Models with 247cc and 343cc engines were listed at £55 and £57 10s 0d. Weights of 239 and 232lbs. respectively put them well outside the 'thirty shilling' tax bracket.

The Berwick looked to be a workmanlike job, yet somehow appeared to have been styled with a blunt pencil. In its Guide to the 1929 Olympia Show *The Motor Cycle* commended the machine to students of design, but ironically offered no such advice to prospective purchasers!

According to my correspondents, the frames of such machines as were produced at Banbury - possibly only three - were built up by a local mechanic, Fred Green. At this point the information becomes a trifle sensitive so I will not repeat it! Apparently the partners in the venture split up and local boys broke into the works, got out the bikes and were riding them around in the fields. Eventually the Police intervened and what was left of the machines subsequently came into the hands of, amongst others, the aforementioned Mr. Kirland, whilst certain jigs and tools are said to have gone to North Bar Garage, Banbury.

It is said that at least one enthusiast from Banbury was disappointed that the Berwick venture never came to anything for he visualised himself in the role of tester!

Berwick 1929 247cc

BLACKBURNE

What is probably the most authoritative account of the early history of the Blackburne is contained in an interview with CS Burney which appeared in *Motor Sport* for March 1948. The story opens in the early nineteen hundreds when the two Burney brothers, Cecil and Alick, were under training with the firm of Williams and Robinson, steam engineers of Rugby. It was here that they met Geoffrey De Haviland who was subsequently to earn fame as an aircraft designer. De Haviland had built himself a motorcycle, the engine of which had both inlet and exhaust valves mechanically operated, a distinct novelty in those days.

The Burneys were so impressed with this machine that they determined to build a similar engine. De Haviland was most co-operative and for a mere 'fiver' supplied them, not only with the necessary castings but with the patterns as well. The employers allowed the engine to be built in the firm's time and on completion, in 1904 it was built into a ready-made frame.

J Rance 1915 Blackburne

1921 range of engines

A second machine was built in 1905. Interesting though it would be to trace these engines through their steady process of development, suffice it to say that Cecil and Alick, who later went into the employ of Daimlers, rode their mobile test-benches in competitions for some years with considerable success.

In 1910 Cecil joined Rudge-Whitworth on the development side but in 1912 the two brothers decided to go into production of complete motorcycles on their own account. At this point Harold Blackburn, also of aviation fame, provided a couple of hundred pounds and Burney and Blackburn came into being.

The first three machines were built at Berkhampstead. AC Cars were said to have been involved in the manufacture of the engines. Mr. MG Wright, Sales Manager of that company informed me in 1974 that there was no record of this and that in any case, they would only have machined the castings. Two notable competition riders, the Roberts brothers, joined forces with the trio but after a short while Harold Blackburn amicably withdrew from the business. It was probably at about this time that Blackburn became Blackburne either deliberately or fortuitously. This was later to give rise to a confusing situation wherein a Blackburn aircraft was powered by a Blackburne engine!

Above, a 1918 gathering of Blackburnes for a 'paper chase' in Surrey

By 1913 a works had been set up at Tongham and the company was in the proud position of being able to exhibit at 'The Show' of that year. The machines were enthusiastically received, selling as they did at a most reasonable price fully equipped.

In 1914, when war broke out both Burneys and the Roberts brothers went on active service as despatch riders leaving the business in the hands of CQ Roberts, father of the Roberts brothers. All completed machines on hand at the time were taken over by the Military Authorities. Jack Holroyd became work foreman. By 1918 Len Heath and HJ Hatch were identified with the concern to which Cecil and Alick Burney never returned.

Circa 1920 Burney and Blackburne Ltd moved to Atlas Works, Great Bookham, Surrey, and control of the firm came into the hands of Gillett Stephens. The company acted as a Service Depot for the American 'Liberty' aero engine (many years later to reappear as a tank engine during the Second World War) amongst other activities. It was in 1920 that S Wilding Cole, managing director, was awarded an OBE. His foresight in making as many components as possible interchangeable from one model engine to another was later to pay valuable dividends. During 1921 he seems to have taken a step sideways acting as Blackburne's representative for the Midlands and the North and also as the UK agent for Burman gears.

From 1920 onwards it was obvious that Blackburne saw a greater future in the development, production and marketing of proprietory engines than in the building of complete motorcycles. Acccording to the serial numbers quoted, A101 to A141, it would appear that only forty machines were turned out for 1920.

By 1921 complete machine production had been farmed out to the Osborne Engineering Co Ltd of Gosport, and before the close of 1920, engines were available in five distinct capacity classes:-

HP	Bore & Stroke	CC	Single/Twin
2¾	71 x 88 mm	348cc	Single
4	85 x 88 mm	499cc	Single
5-6	71 x 88 mm	696cc	Twin
8	85 x 88 mm	986cc	Twin
10	85 x 97 mm	1100cc	Twin

The exact capacity of the 10hp works out slightly in excess of 1000cc. It will be noticed that with only one exception the length of stroke was constant and that only two bore diameters were employed.

Despite the fact that Burney and Blackburne were producing at the time a quite varied range of proprietory engines, only two models of Blackburne motorcycle were produced for the years 1920, 1921 and 1922, a single and a twin.

The 4hp single used an 85 x 88mm 498cc side-valve unit. A solid crankshaft ran in a compact crankcase and carried a steel outside flywheel of exceptionally large diameter. The plain big-end bearing was split, as in car practice.

A detachable cylinder head (which when removed brought the valves with it) was held down by three long studs. Lubrication was by splash via a hand pump and a drip feed. There was an ample area of finning to assist cooling of the head and the barrel. The magneto, driven by an enclosed chain, was in front of the crankcase. Carburation was by Amac and the magneto, initially of TB manufacture, was protected by a substantial guard. The exhaust system took the form of the familiar transverse expansion box, below the magneto, and a long tail pipe.

The frame was of the conventional diamond type and Brampton Bi-Flex forks were used. Transmission was all-chain and a Burman or a Sturmey Archer gearbox, in either case with three speeds, clutch and kick-start could be specified.

Whilst only a stirrup brake acted on the front wheel, the rear brake was of the external contracting type. Wheels carried 28 x 3 inch tyres.

Footboards actually were 'boards' covered with lino and edged with aluminium. For 1920 the tool-box was on top of the tank which held two gallons of petrol and three pints of oil and was coloured black with red panels. In that year it weighed 250lbs., and cost £115 which was about the norm for a 500cc machine of comparable specification.

The 8hp employed the firm's twin engine, the cylinders of which had the same bore and stroke as the 4hp The magneto was mounted behind the seat tube. Its necessarily long driving chain was enclosed in a housing which split to give a top and a bottom half. Most of the other 4hp details apply to the 8hp except that the tank top was sloping all the way from the front to the rear and that the frame was fitted with sidecar lugs - a feature curiously omitted from the 4hp.

The machine was usually listed in combination form and a Burman box with a gear change alongside the tank was general. *Fletchers* indicates otherwise, but there would appear to have been detachable wheels for a 'spare' included in the price of £190 for a sidecar outfit.

The most noticeable difference for 1921 was that the tank-top toolbox was replaced by the more conventional carrier-mounted type. During the season the brake pedal, which had been unduly high was lowered to a more convenient position. The rear chain on the 8hp was very thoroughly, but not completely enclosed. There was still a choice of gearbox on the 4hp.

During 1921 *The Motor Cycle and Cycle Trader* sampled a 4hp and after quickly getting used to the 28 inch wheels, the tester climbed every hill in the ACU One Day Trial without resort to bottom gear.

There were no changes in design for 1922. At the 1921 Olympia Show, Blackburne machines were exhibited on the stand of the Osborne Engineering Co Ltd, which suggests that this concern had now taken over the manufacturing rights. Be that as it may, the marque lost its identity as a complete machine after 1922.

Belts

Between the engine, the gearbox if there was one, and the rear wheel of the veteran or vintage motor cycle there had to be a connection. Chains could be used, there were designs that used shaft drive and even pedals and cranks following steam engine practice were tried. However it became apparent that the best compromise in terms of price, ease of manufacture and practicality was the belt. Belts had been around for a long time, their use with machine tools and in other industrial settings had been understood for many years, and their application to the driven wheel of a motorcycle seemed straightforward. However the conditions that the transmission encountered were far tougher than those previously experienced

A belt is most efficient when its surface contacts the largest area of the pulleys, a fact not at first fully realised by motor cycle manufacturers, who tried all kinds of engine, pulley and belt positions, including a figure of eight design to get most grip. Different materials

A selection of belts: John Bull, Whittle, Brammer together with clips and a belt punch

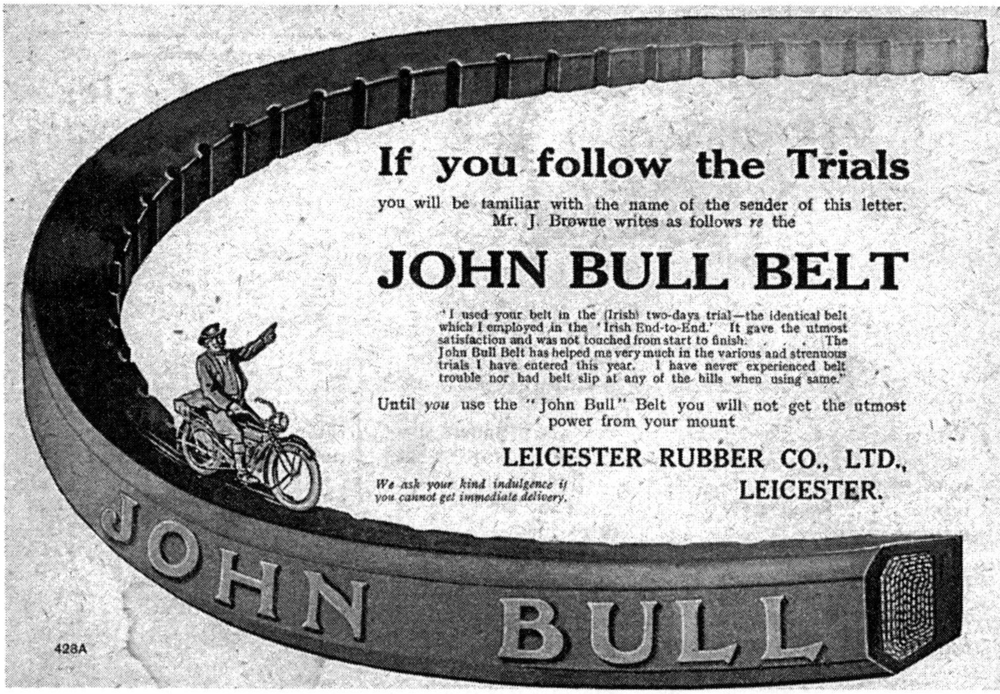

were experimented with. Twisted rawhide, canvas, leather and a mixture of all three were tried. The Whittle Belt for example was a complicated mix of rubber and canvas joined together with steel links. Flat belts were tried unsuccessfully, and as with tyres not all V-belts and pulleys worked on the same angles and sizes, so ill fitting or incompatible ones were inefficient. Rawhide needed frequent dressing and stretching, whilst simple rubber and canvas belts could be vulnerable to their links being pulled out. The belt had to run in mud and dust; it was spattered in oil and grease, and was often neglected and subject to all kinds of other abuse. When it slipped it could wear a groove in the pulleys, and could become glazed, thereby loosing much of its adhesive powers.

Although the belt made it through the First World War advances in technology during that period, and in particular through racing, spelt an end to this particular means of power transfer. By the early twenties the most common form of belt was the rubber and canvas mix and there were many manufacturers who claimed that theirs was the best design. By the late twenties however, the belt had had its day and was almost universally replaced by the use of the chain and sprocket. The days of the flexible transmission, the only sound of the machine in motion being the click of the fastener as it went over the pulley, had disappeared for ever. Modern Brammer style link belts of the rubber/canvas type and more recently of plastic construction can be made to work very well indeed and some recent motor cycles have reverted to the use of toothed belts in their final drives.

BROUGH SUPERIOR

Known as 'The Rolls Royce of Motor Cycles', the Brough Superior achieved legendary status during the twenties, fuelled by publicity generated by its charismatic rider/ manufacturer George Brough from Nottingham. The power for most of these machines came from JAP V-twin engines; later other manufacturers products were used. Trials, races, competitions all helped to sell the BS. The SS100 was guaranteed to do 100 miles an hour. Although these bikes were in the strictest sense assembled from other peoples component parts, they were never really beaten for finish, comfort and speed and to this day remain one of the most desired motorcycles ever produced.

Further Reading;
Brough Superior, Ronald H Clark, 1984, Haynes Publishing

1926 SS80 with 1000cc 4 cam JAP racing engine

BSA

The Birmingham Small Arms Company were armament manufacturers and made their first bicycles in 1880. They started making motorcycles in 1910, and produced a machine which was similar to the Triumph roadster. During the First World War they supplied the British Army with bikes, and post war supplied no nonsense, soundly built bikes for the sort of people who needed them for reliable transport in a safe and dependable way. BSA also engaged in a series of publicity stunts that included climbing Snowdon. They obtained contracts to supply the AA, the GPO and the Army throughout the twenties. In 1926 there was a six model range, from the two-speed round tank model up to the Colonial 986cc V-twins. In 1927 the 'Sloper' was introduced and by 1930 the range of BSA's on offer had increased to 16 different models.

Further Reading;
BSA, The Complete Story, Owen Wright, 1992, Crowood Press

BSA Model K ice cream outfit. Once the property of the Newlyn artist, Charles Simpson, who used it to carry his canvases, easel and paints.

CASTLE THREE

The Castle Motor Co Ltd, New Road, Kidderminster, produced the Castle Three which was probably the most elaborate three wheeler offered to the British public during the vintage period, and almost certainly the only one with a four-cylinder water-cooled engine.

In its 1920 form, when the price had provisionally been fixed at £250, the chassis was of channel steel and was reduced in width at the rear end where it accommodated the single back wheel. The four-cylinder water-cooled engine was conventionally mounted as in car practice.

The unit had side-valves and employed what was then described as 'forced fed' lubrication by plunger pump. The camshaft was driven by an enclosed silent (inverted) tooth chain and the magneto by spiral gear. A Zenith carburettor was mounted directly to the cylinder block and cooling was by the usual thermo-syphon principle.

Photo:VMCC

Widely differing sources variously give the bore and stroke at 63 x 88mm (1097cc) and 64 x 85mm (1093cc). The unit would almost certainly have come from an outside supplier, possibly Coventry Simplex but that is uncertain.

Two speeds and reverse were provided by epicyclic gearing running in oil. Since it was claimed that the system was protected by patents there can be little grounds for apocryphal stories that there were threats of litigation by Henry Ford. Final drive by shaft and bevel gears gave a top gear ration of 4 to 1.

The front axle, mounted well forward, was carried on quarter elliptic springs. A pair of long (40 inches between centres) semi-elliptic springs had the rear axle assembly mounted on top of them. There was an epicylic reduction gear at the bottom of the steering column. Contemporary reports that the steering was 'Ford type' suggest that the drop-arm would have been connected by a drag-link to one end of the track-rod. Wheels, shod with 710 x 90mm tyres, were of ten-spoke tubular steel construction and were fully interchangeable. There was a well for a spare on the right-hand running board.

The pretty two-seater body with car type bonnet and a tapering tail which effectively enclosed the back wheel, was available in cream, grey or blue, in each case with black wings. With blue went upholstery of the same colour, and on the cream and grey cars it was green.

Weight was quoted as approximately 8½cwt, the track 4ft 1in. Standard equipment included hood, screen and dynamo lighting set.

Had the manufacturers heeded it, the writing was on the wall for the Castle before the end of 1920. From the beginning of 1921, the Road Fund Tax was to come into operation with the effect that the Castle Three, due to its excessive weight, would be deprived of the considerable tax advantage which would shortly be enjoyed by its less ponderous competitors.

However, Castle Motors were at Olympia with their 1921 model. There may have been a change of engine, for the bore and stroke was now 62 x 100mm (1207cc) and the magneto was driven by silent chain. Lubrication was now being described as 'by pump and trough' which suggest that the big-end bearings, at least, relied on splash. The carburettor had been changed to a Solex and 40mpg was being claimed. Tyre section was marginally reduced to 85mm. The weight was now 10cwt.

The engine could be lifted clear from its sub-frame after the removal of four bolts; the gearbox was rapidly detachable leaving the lower half of the casting in-situ. The spare wheel could be brought out through the lid of the tail in under a minute.

The price, which specifically included a spare wheel, had risen to £295 in 1921. However the Castle Three was again at Olympia at the close of 1921 in its 1922 form when the price had been drastically reduced to £225. It was possible to have a dickey seat (which when not in use, folded into the tail) for an extra £5.

Several modifications were reported. The chassis was now of rectangular section and diagonally braced. Front suspension was by transverse spring (more shades of Ford!) and a Smith combined generator and ignition system dispensed with a separate magneto.

The transmission was somewhat modified. A new universal joint of the Hardy-Spicer type had all four bearing assemblies lubricated by a single screw-down grease cup and the back axle assembly now hinged on the springs to improve flexibility.

According to *Fletchers Motor Car Index*, production ceased after 1922. This work of reference also quotes for the vehicle in chassis form for the years 1920 - 1922. Serial numbers are given as:-

1920	001 - 103
1921	104 - 201
1922	202 -

It is, however, most unlikely that total production ever reached the levels which these numbers imply.

CLEMENT

Various machines of a type which in later years would have been called mopeds appeared during the twenties. Not the best known, but certainly the most interesting was produced by A Clement, 26 Albany Street, London W1.

The 1923 Clement was available two forms - ladies and gents; the basis in either case was a standard pedal cycle, but with a simple leaf spring front suspension. The engine was a tiny OHV affair of a mere 43cc (35 x 45mm) and contained the initial reduction gearing within the crankcase. This unit was mounted just in front of the bottom bracket where it was cooled by a curious air scoop built into the front mudguard. Final drive was by chain and there was also a second chain for the pedalling gear. For the 1924 season the bore and stroke were increased to 45 x 55mm (63cc). Even the carburettor and magneto were of Clement manufacture. A two-speed hub gave ratios of 8:1 and 18:1.

There were two types of frame and both retained the leaf sprung front wheel and the air scoop. An entirely new frame was built more on the lines of a conventional lightweight. The top tube was duplicated and was continued rearwards to form

1923 Clement motorcycle. (Photo: Mortons Media Group Archives)

the back forks or seat stays and there was a substantial rear stand. With 26 x 2 inch tyres the price was £26 5s 0d.

The other model was more like a pedal cycle in construction. It was lighter and cheaper than its less sophisticated contemporaries, but 1924 was the last year for which it was listed. Somehow, generally speaking, London does not seem to have provided an environment for successful motorcycle production.

The Clement can hardly have been short of power: in 1927 a correspondent to *The Motor Cycle* enquired what gearing he must use so that his own example would pull a sidecar.

COVENTRY MASCOT

The Mascot Cycle Company of 49 Gresham Street, Stoke, Coventry had over a period of years, built up an excellent reputation as builders of juvenile cycles. Then, in the early summer of 1922 they put the Coventry Mascot motorcycle on the market. Unlike the general run of 'assembled' machines of the twenties, the product did have one or two distinctive features, one of which made it almost unique; although the transmission was by chain and belt, both wheels had internal expanding brakes (but the front one was so tiny that it can hardly have been of any use).

The engine was the 349cc (70mm x 90.5mm) sleeve-valve Barr and Stroud for which 7bhp was claimed despite a compression ratio of only 4 to 1. The carburettor was a Vicy and the magneto a Fellows.

The primary chain case was panelled red-on-black to match the tank. The Burman two-speed gear-box had a clutch and kick-starter.

The frame had a divided front down tube which allowed the exhaust pipe to sweep with minimum obstruction to a cylindrical transverse expansion box. The front forks were Maplestone (Webb), foot boards were standard and a licence holder was incorporated in the front number plate.

1922 Coventry Mascot Model B, price £72. (Photo:VMCC)

This model was continued for 1923 when a three-speed all-chain version was also available. A somewhat more sporting machine with a 349cc OHV oil-cooled Bradshaw engine was also listed. This model had a long exhaust pipe terminating in a rectangular silencer mounted just to the rear of the gear-box and foot-rests replaced foot-boards.

A Bradshaw engined entry in the 1923 Junior TT was ridden by JL Brown.

The base chamber of the crankcase was of a new design, heavily finned at the forward end for cooling. Unusual for those days a four-speed gear-box was employed and it had a piped supply of oil. Two selector rods were used necessitating a gate change which was, of course hand-operated.

Success on the Island might have been just what was needed to put the Coventry Mascot 'on the map' but fate decreed otherwise. Brown retired and after that year the marque lapsed into obscurity.

COVENTRY PREMIER

Around 1920, when the number of makes of British three-wheelers was never greater, the Coventry Premier was without doubt the prettiest of them all. Like most of its contemporaries, however, it was hopelessly expensive.

The engine, rated at 8-10 hp, was a water-cooled V-twin with a bore and stroke of 80 x 105mm and a capacity of 1055cc. The cylinders had fixed heads and were inter-changeable, inlet and exhaust ports and top water outlets being arranged for flange connections. A Cox Atmos carburettor was used and the magneto (usually a TB) was bevel driven. Lubrication was by mechanical pump, the oil 'sufficient for 175 miles' was carried in the sump.

Transversely mounted, the engine was carried immediately behind a normal radiator. In common with the majority of tricars of the period, transmission was through a three-speed and reverse gearbox and final chain.

A substantial chassis had channel steel side members which were double-diagonally braced; cruciform construction the car people were to call it several years later. The rear wheel was carried in a frame which pivoted around the axis of the driving sprocket. The pivot incorporated eccentrics for chain adjustment. Rear suspension was by means of a pair of quarter-elliptical springs which consisted of a multiplicity of thin leaves.

A sliding panel in the rear chain enclosure allowed a 'knock-out' spindle to be withdrawn, thus making the rear wheel easily removable. Unfortunately, although

1920 Coventry Premier (Photo: VMCC)

this wheel was of the same wire type as the front ones and carried the same size (800 x 80mm) tyres, there was no interchangeability between front and rear.

No doors were fitted to the two-seater body. Forward of the scuttle (which housed a five gallon tank) it resembled that of a conventional light car of the period. Three pieces made up the bonnet. The top panel could be lifted clear; the side panels were hinged from the bottom and could be swung outwards.

The top half of the rear wheel was enclosed in a tail not unlike that of a Morgan on which was carried a spare rear wheel. Dynamo lighting was standard. There were two small head-cum-side lamps on the scuttle.

The 1920 version, marketed by Coventry Premier Ltd, of Read Street, Coventry, had flared wings and was listed at £260. By the time the 1921 model was shown at Olympia the front wings were more of the 'cycle' type and the price had risen to £288 15s 0d. Presumably the exhibitor, The Coventry Premier Co, had taken over some of the interests of Coventry Premier Ltd, which Company had gone

DALTON

For 1921 and 1922 The Dalton Motor Company Limited of 17-19 John Dalton Street, Manchester, marketed a programme of interesting models which offered excellent value for money. Since John Dalton Street was, as it is now, Manchester's 'Harley Street' it is not surprising that manufacture was actually carried out at works in Stretford Road.

The Dalton Model 'C' was a thoroughly impressive looking machine and used the Coventry Victor flat twin side-valve engine having a capacity of 688cc (75 x 78mm) equipped with an Amac carburettor and a TB magneto.

Straight tubes were employed almost exclusively in the construction of the frame. The front down tube was duplicated and between these two members lay the head of the front cylinder. This arrangement enabled the engine to be brought well forward leaving plenty or room for the gearbox immediately behind it on approximately the same plane, with a pleasing effect on the general appearance compared with most other horizontally opposed twins of that period. Bi-Flex type forks afforded vertical and reciprocal movement. Transmission was all-chain via a Sturmey Archer three-speed box operated by a disc type lever mounted

Blackburne engine in a 1920 Dalton frame

The Finest Value at Olympia.

STAND No. 15.

"DALTON" MOTOR CYCLES

INSPECT OUR THREE MODELS. — WE INVITE COMPARISON.

MODEL "A" 2¾ h.p. BLACKBURNE, **95 Gns.**
MODEL "B" 4 h.p. BLACKBURNE, **110 Gns.**
MODEL "C" 5-7 h.p. COVENTRY VICTOR, **£150.**

THE "DALTON" MOTOR CYCLE TAXI

HAS CREATED THE GREATEST SENSATION AT OLYMPIA DURING THE SHOW.
THE FINEST BUSINESS PROPOSITION EVER OFFERED.

Passed by the Authorities to ply for hire in London and many provincial and seaside towns.

MODEL "B" Sporting.

MODEL "C" and Touring Sidecar.

THE DALTON MOTOR CO., LTD.,

7-19, JOHN DALTON STREET, MANCHESTER.

Works: Stretford Road, Manchester.

TELEPHONES: Central 4733, 5990, 1023.
TELEGRAMS: "INLET, Manchester."

on the seat tube. Mud-guarding was thorough without detracting from the appearance and footboards did not look out of place.

A dummy belt rim rear brake was employed with the block operating internally and in common with the two other models a stirrup brake acted on the front rim. Unlike these, however, there were no inverted levers used on the handlebars. The tank was of a pleasant wedge shape rather deep in the front.

The Model 'B' was of normal diamond frame construction with a shallower wedge tank. It would have been really good looking, but as was the case with the Model 'C' the saddle looked as if it had been forgotten until the last moment. Mud guarding was well carried out and the forks had their lower shackles in the form of bell-cranks to permit the use of a horizontal spring. A feature that gave rise to favourable comment at the time was that items were attached to the frame by means of welded-on lugs rather than by loose clips wherever possible. Both footboards or footrests were available.

The already popular 499cc side-valve Blackburne engine was fitted with a TB magneto but could be supplied with any make of carburettor. Transmission was by a combination of chain and belt through a Burman three-speed box. The rear brake acted externally on the belt rim.

A 349cc Blackburne side-valve engine powered the Model 'A' and the Burman box had two speeds. Otherwise it was similar to the bigger single except that footrests were standard. Discs enclosed the wheels and the saddle looked less of an afterthought.

This was the range as it appeared at Olympia in 1920 and the leading particulars are confirmed in the 1921 *Buyers Guide*. *Fletchers* however, catalogues the same three models at somewhat reduced prices for 1922 and notes '1923 no longer being manufactured'.

Remains of a Dalton tank transfer

DANDY

One of the most unconventional three-wheelers ever to be constructed was the Dandy, introduced in 1921 by James Sumner & Son, 2 Latham Road, Southport. The price had been provisionally fixed at £195.

The chassis was of tubular construction, all joints being welded. The front was swept up to a steering head which carried a front fork. At the bottom of the fork was mounted a pair of full elliptic leaf spring assemblies and between them, running on roller bearings, was the front wheel. The rear axle was so arranged that it could very simply be reduced to half its normal length, for reasons which will be apparent later.

The engine, an 8hp air cooled twin JAP was mounted low and well forward with the valve gear facing towards the left side. A primary chain connected it to a two-speed gear-box and final drive was by belt to the right hand rear wheel.

The body was formed from what was basically a pair of touring side-car bodies mounted side by side and with the inner panel of each cut away. The driver sat in the right hand 'side-car' and steered by means of a wheel mounted on a sloping shaft.

The most ingenious feature of the design was that, for convenience of storing, the left hand 'side-car' could be swung up and over the other. This having been done, the rear axle was collapsed as previously described and the whole outfit thus folded had an overall width of only 2ft 8ins.

At the time, the Dandy was introduced, an experimental model had covered 3000 trouble-free miles and had competed in the Edinburgh Trial. Financial assistance was being sought to exploit production but little more seems to have been heard of the venture.

The Dandy folding cyclecar. Top, in running position and below, side and rear views of the Dandy in its folded position

DOUGLAS

The Douglas name is associated with the flat twin engine and the City of Bristol. The $2^3/_4$ Douglas was much used and much valued by Despatch Riders in the mud of the Western Front, and when war ended the company developed a new range of engines. Douglas was one of the few manufacturers that never used other manufacturer's products, at least up until 1932. They were one of the last firms to use beaded edge tyres and belt drive, but at the same time they produced many experimental models which used innovative engineering at their heart. The flat twins were gradually updated with overhead valves, all-chain drive and lower frames. Tom Sheard managed to win the senior TT on one in 1923. The basic military style side-valve twin was still available, plus a 600cc side-valve, and 500cc and 733cc OHV models. Despite providing one of the more successful speedway bikes at the end of the period, they hit financial trouble and were sold by the family at the end of 1931, but remained as a named manufacturer through to the fifties.

Further Reading;

The Douglas Motor Cycle, The Best Twin, Jeff Clew, 1981, Haynes Publishing

DUNELT

Firms such as Royal Enfield and BSA (firearms manufacturers) and Rudge Whitworth (ball and roller bearings) are examples of concerns which had to have had more than an average know-how with steel; their expertise in this area was reflected in the excellence of the motorcycles they produced. The same applies to the Dunelt, the manufacturers of which, Dunford and Elliott (Sheffield) Ltd, were (and at the time of writing still are) a firm of steel producers. The motorcycle side of the business was however based in the more traditional environment of Birmingham - at 96, Bath Street to be precise.

As far as Britain is concerned the Dunelt was the only unconventional two-stroke marketed throughout the twenties and the only 'big single' two-stroke ever to go into production on a serious scale. The feature which made the Dunelt engine unconventional was its truncated or double-diameter piston and consequent 'stepped' cylinder bore.

The purpose of the lower part of the piston having an increased diameter was to increase the volume of mixture drawn into the crankcase, compressed and transferred into the combustion space - for which reason the slogan 'The machine with the supercharged engine' was adopted.

1921 Dunelt

A 500cc Dunelt at the 2008 Stafford Show

The 'trunk' (or lower) part of the piston had a displacement some 50% greater than that of the 'working' part, thus an adequate charge of fresh mixture was available to more completely scavenge the remaining traces of burnt gas. Any loss of fresh gas which may have been occasioned by its egress through the exhaust ports while the piston was either near or at the bottom of its stroke was compensated for by an ability to run on a much weaker mixture than would otherwise have been possible. The theory behind the idea was well substantiated in practice. As early as 1920 a power output of 12bhp was possible and readers who have had experience with these units will doubtless agree that their willingness to two-stroke properly on light load and their torque at low speeds are features which have rarely been surpassed by any other make of two-stroke motorcycle engine.

1920-26 and the 500cc range

For a number of years only a 499cc engine was produced with a 'working' bore and stroke of 85 x 88mm. During the period 1920 to 1927 it was variously described as being 3 ½ - 7, 4 ½, 5 and 4.99 horse power, such was the haphazard practice of that era. Having been correctly designed in the first instance, the unit was but little changed throughout its production life. Invariably the exceedingly large outside flywheel was on the right-hand side and behind it the magneto at the rear of the cylinder was driven by an enclosed chain. The inlet port and consequently the carburettor, were on the left hand side of the cylinder. An inclined cylinder form of engine mounting was always employed not so much with a view to the appearance but more to do with providing the cylinder-head with the maximum possible benefit of air cooling.

The 1920 model looked sturdy and functional and it is difficult to think of any further complimentary adjectives with which to describe it. The general image was not improved by a large-diameter dummy belt-rim front brake, a tank-top tool box and a cumbersome rear carrier. A sloping tank held 2¼ gallons of petrol and 3 pints of oil. Specification details included Best and Lloyd drip-feed lubrication, a Thompson-Bennett magneto and an Amac carburettor.

Final drive was by belt and the 1920 *Buyers Guide* states that there were three speeds and shows an illustration depicting what appears to be a Sturmey Archer gearbox with the lever not on the box itself but alongside the tank. *The Motor Cycle and Cycle Trader*, published at almost the same time, lists 'own 2-speed countershaft' and 'expanding ring' clutch. *Fletchers* does not clear up the confusion since it does not start to list Dunelt until 1921!

1921 saw a less 'bitty' looking machine with a neater rear carrier and no tool box on the tank. The exhaust pipes now took a more pronounced sweep before entering the transverse cylindrical expansion chamber. Internally the engine had a split roller-bearing big-end and externally an optional Cox-Atmos carburettor and an ML magneto. Transmission was via Sturmey Archer three-speed gearbox with the gear lever mounted on the seat tube. As for 1920, foot-boards were standard. Since the Dunelt at that period was unusually offered as a sidecar machine it was an important feature that front, rear and sidecar wheels were interchangeable.

The single model for 1922 was almost unchanged. Alterations, such as they were, included a longer brake pedal and improved foot-boards. 28 x 3 inch tyres in place of the usual 26 x 2½ inch were an optional extra, and according to a Jardine advertisement the Dunelt was one of the makes to which their four-speed gearbox could be fitted, if specified.

The 1923 *Buyers Guide* indicates an increase of engine capacity to 799cc which was obviously a misprint for the bore and stroke figures remain unchanged. The newer type of Sturmey Archer gearbox with no extension of the casting to house a kick-starter quadrant, was now in use. There was a reduction in price if wheels were not interchangeable and all-chain transmission specified.

1924 models had a new frame with a sloping top tube and a more up-to-date looking tapered tank. The cylinder had now been redesigned with deeper and

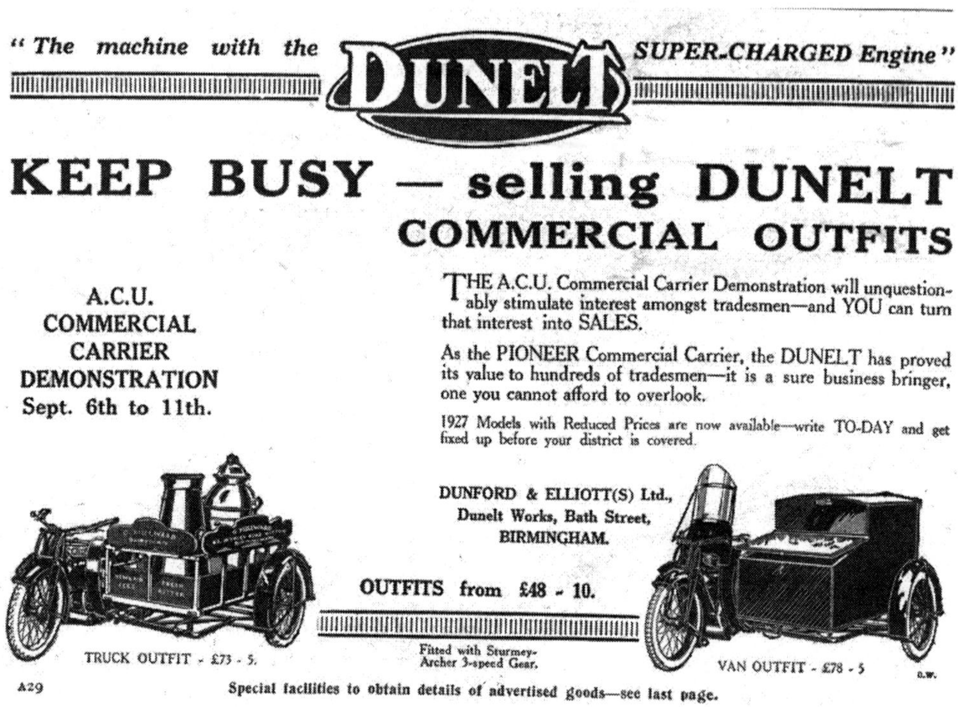

1926 commercial outfits

more widely spaced fins and an aluminium piston was internally ribbed. An extension from the inlet port brought the carburettor to a position at the rear of the engine. *Buyers Guide* and *Fletchers* both show a change to Burman gearboxes for all models but the manufacturers illustrations in their 'Show Time' advertisements are all of machines that are Sturmey Archer equipped.

A semi sports 'Solo' had all-chain drive, an internal expanding front brake and footrests. The rear brake operated a dummy belt rim on the right hand side.

Four sidecar machines all had foot boards. The 'A' had chain-cum-belt transmission, belt rim brakes and interchangeable wheels. A similar outfit without interchangeable wheels became the 'B'. An all-chain model 'C' had non-interchangeable wheels and belt rim brakes. Finally the 'D' had all-chain drive, internal expanding brakes and interchangeable wheels.

Sidecars were now listed in great variety: single seater, wide two seater, tandem two seater, 4 cwt van and 4 cwt truck. Dunelt probably did more than any other make to develop the motorcycle combination as a dual purpose passenger or commercial vehicle.

It was not until 1925 that the Dunelt became a tolerably pretty machine. A gradual process of tidying up culminated in recessing the top-tube into an even shapelier tank. Incidentally as a result of this change, the three point mounting was discontinued for the saddle. The engine by now had a detachable aluminium cylinder head and lubrication was by means of a Pilgrim mechanical sight feed pump mounted on the magneto chain cover.

The use of the belt final drive having been abandoned there was in consequence a reduction in the number of models and two very similar machines the 'G' and the 'H' formed the basis of the range, both with internal expanding brakes front and rear. No longer was there any question about the make of gearbox, for an advertisement announcing the 1925 programme contained the (possibly subsidised) insert 'All Dunelt models are fitted with Sturmey Archer 3-speed gears'. Perhaps the mention or possible adoption of Burman boxes for 1924 had been calculated to keep Nottingham on its toes!

Dunelt were still concentrating on commercial sidecar outfits and offered special bodies as milk-floats, ice cream dispensers and even fire tenders. Important users of Dunelt outfits now included Recketts, The Times Book Club, The Sketchley Dye Works and Avery Ltd, the scales and weighing machine manufacturers.

It was during 1925 that Dunelt made a modest bid for TT honours with an entry in the sidecar class. The most interesting feature of the engine was the installation of a second magneto which was mounted in a forward position. Each magneto was connected to it's own sparking plug and various accounts have appeared concerning the interesting behaviour of the engine as a result of juggling with the two separate ignition controls. Had there been any marked benefit through the use of two plugs it was not considered worth incorporating the scheme in production models.

The outfit was driven by OS Bridcutt who had never ridden in an Isle of Man TT before. He rode a leisurely and remarkably consistent race finishing sixth and last. His average speed of 49.34 mph would have given him an easy second place in the previous year's event. A dozen riders, most of them on machines with the benefit of an additional hundred cc, either retired or had not finished when the course was opened. To many people such a demonstration of high speed reliability by a comparatively unknown rider on a straight-forward machine cut more ice than a win by an ace on a mobile test-bench, the like of which was poles apart from anything that would ever reach the public.

Deliveries of the 1926 500cc models commenced in August 1925. Apart from modifications to the silencer and the fitting of stronger footrests the 'G' and the 'H' were unchanged. The 'G' was intended for solo or light sidecar use whilst the 'H' formed the basis of heavier sidecar outfits. 'H' models had leg shields as a standard fitting and had the advantage of interchangeable wheels.

A new model was the Super Sports with a guaranteed speed of 75 mph. It closely resembled the 'G' but had no rear carrier. Brakes were of 7 inch diameter front and rear and the specification included a steering damper, a Hartford friction damper for the front forks, a flexible top saddle and twist-grip controls. Initially the price was fixed at 70gns (£73 10s 0d) but by February 1926, when the *Buyers Guide* came out it had come down to a more acceptable £65.

1926-1930 and the rise of the 250cc Model K

The use of a sidecar outfit as a commercial vehicle never became universally accepted. Anxious therefore to secure a bigger market and doubtless foreseeing hungry times ahead, a 250cc model was introduced for 1926. Designated by the not very original title 'Model K' this was probably the wisest move that the manufacturers ever made, for not only was the 'K' a fast and powerful little machine but at £35 it was most reasonably priced.

The 249cc engine which closely followed existing Dunelt practice, had a rather off-beat bore and stroke of 66.7 x 71.4mm. The magneto however was driven by

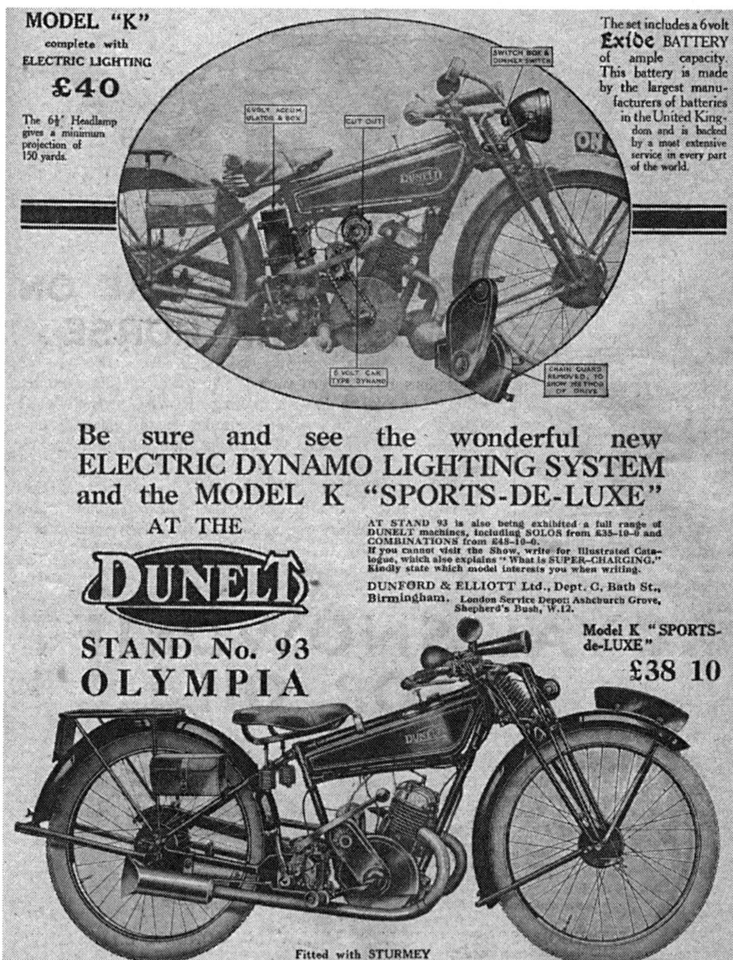

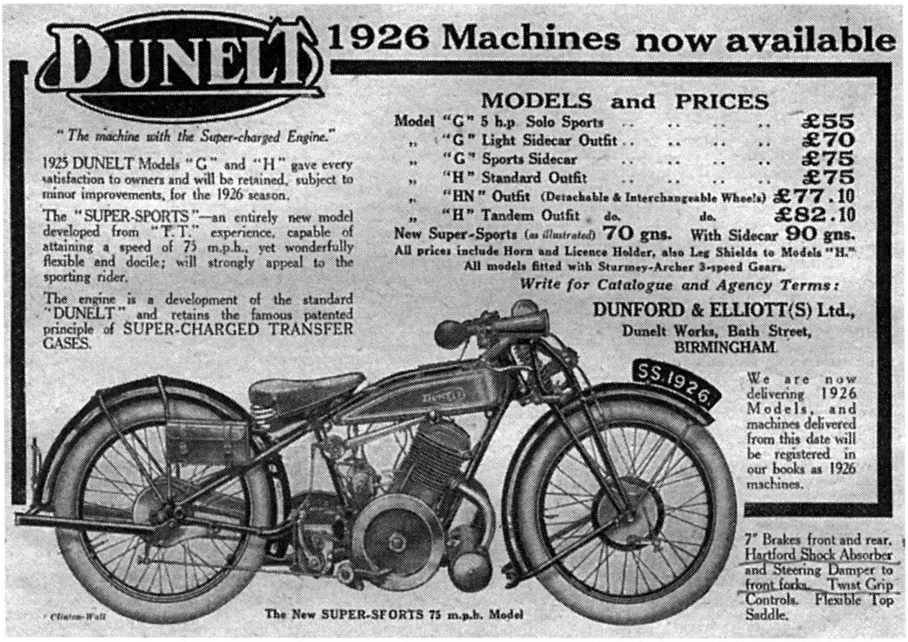

a chain running outside the flywheel guard which housed not only the chain but the top half of the flywheel as well. Initially a transverse cylindrical expansion chamber with a single left side tail pipe was employed. Later in the season however separate exhaust pipes were adopted terminating in cylindrical silencers with flattened outlets. Lubrication was described as automatic and the carburettor was usually a Binks.

Transmission (all-chain of course) was via a light-weight three-speed Sturmey Archer box with the gear lever mounted directly on the gearbox. It has been said that these particular boxes were the Achilles heel of these and subsequent small Dunelts. Brakes were 5 inch internal expanding front and rear, tyres were 26 x 2½ x 2¼ inch. A pan seat, pillar mounted gave a saddle height of 27 inches. During the 1926 season the material from which the magneto chain-cum-flywheel guard was made appears to have been changed from steel to aluminium and the price was increased by ten shillings on account of a rise in the cost of tyres. Some idea of the capabilities of the little machine can be gathered from a report by an owner to *The Motor Cycle*. After 5,000 miles of complete satisfaction he claimed 53mph and 115mpg.

It was at about this time that Dunford and Elliott expressed the view in the trade press that there was too much prejudice against two-stroke motorcycles. They blamed this state of affairs not so much on the public as on the retail trader. Their words cannot have fallen entirely on stony ground for in one five-week period 120 new dealers were appointed.

The 1927 season brought with it 'Professor Supercharge', a jolly, dapper little fellow with his body consisting of a partially sectioned Dunelt engine. He was for a time to become almost as much a part of Dunelt as the Scotsman was of Douglas. He probably owed his creation to Messrs Clinton-Wall who had been handling Dunelt advertising for some years. So instant had been the success of the 249cc 'K' that the 499cc models were lucky to be in the band at all.

The 'K' in its standard form was almost identical to the 1926 model as it was first introduced. There were a couple of slight alterations such as the addition of a silencer to the end of the tail pipe and the magneto drive and flywheel cover was once more of pressed steel. The specification was improved by the inclusion of a flexible-top saddle. The price was still a modest £35 10s 0d.

For an additional £3 the 'K sports de luxe' had a slightly larger tank, a saddle with three-point mounting and a Hartford type shock absorber. It also had two separate exhaust pipes with tubular silencers, the best shape for which the manufacturers never seemed to decide.

For only £4 10s 0d extra either 'K' could be supplied with Miller/Exide electric lighting. The dynamo was mounted on the tank tube and took its chain drive from a double sprocket mounted on the magneto. One contemporary report stated that a 'three-sided' drive was employed but such was not the case. Probably no manufacturer had ever offered a proper dynamo lighting set for such a small extra charge.

The 499cc Super Sports now became a most rakish looking affair by the simple expedient of fitting separate upswept exhaust pipes with tubular silencers and large fish-tails. Apart from having additional silencers the 'H' and the 'G' which were being, to use a more recent term, phased out, remained unchanged. Throughout the 1927 season the bigger Dunelts scarcely ever appeared in the Company's advertising. Some idea of their sudden increase in the share of the market is indicated by a letter which appeared in *The Motor Cycle and Cycle Trader* for 24 June 1927. It was from Glasgow dealers Messrs H Bairstow and Sons stating that, whilst not claiming to have set up a record, they had to date sold eighty 1927 Dunelts. Agencies now existed all over the country and Dunelt was being handled in London by George Clarke, Jarvis, Rowland Smith, The Service Co, and Pride and Clark and elsewhere by Hatton of Derby, and Huxham of Bournemouth, to mention but a few.

JB Anderson riding in the 1927 Colmore trial won the 200 guinea Calthorpe Cup for the best 250cc performance on a K Sports de luxe.

The 1928 Season opened in good time and by September 1927 the new models were available for delivery. All effort centred on the 249cc K models of which there were three variants. Common to all were such improvements as larger inlet and exhaust ports, mechanical lubrication and the provision of an air-intake silencer.

The details of the lubrication system were particularly interesting. A special Pilgrim pump was mounted on a bracket which moved with the magneto. A 'driver' on the pump spindle was pushed around by a peg on the magneto sprocket. Movement of the magneto in order to adjust chain tension had no detrimental effect on the drive. The pump was designed to draw oil from the tank and to deliver it in equal quantities to two outlets. One stream was taken to the engine and the other to the sight feed whence it gravitated back into the tank. The flow of oil through the sight feed thus indicated the amount of oil being delivered to the engine.

The air-intake silencer consisted of an elbow attached to the carburettor with an upward-facing tubular extension. The upper end was blanked off and air entered via a gauge cylinder and four large slots. A bell-housing covered the top end of the intake leaving a slight clearance. The more important use of the silencer however was probably to collect mixture blown back through the carburettor.

'Improved Silencing' was mentioned in connection with the standard 'K' which was substantially the 1927 model with the 1928 improvements already described.

A much more refined 'K Royal' had a saddle tank with a petrol capacity of 2 gallons. Tyres were 26 x 3 inch but due to a slight modification which had been made to the frame 26 x 3.50 inch replacements could be fitted. Some forty-four improvements on the previous years' production were claimed which included in addition to those previously noted, neat shock dampers built into the front ends of the top fork links, additional plates in the clutch, a tank-side mounted gear lever and a 7 inch rear brake. Twin exhaust pipes were very slightly upswept and the tubular silencers had their ends flattened to form miniature fish tails. A preliminary announcement said that the tool box would be moved from the right hand seat stay to the tank but actually it was mounted on the seat tube. At £41 complete with horn and licence holder or £46 with dynamo lighting the K Royal must have brought as much dismay to it's rivals as did the 'P' Triumph three years previously.

Offered at £38 10s 0d, the K Sports was a similar machine but equipped with 2½ inch section tyres, a 5 inch rear brake and the gear lever mounted directly to the box. Riding one of these N Anderson and JP Arrowsmith set up new 250cc seven hour, eight hour and 500 mile World Records at speeds of 64, 65, 64.16 and 64.22mph at Brooklands on 20th September 1927. The records were not to stand for long, but it is difficult to think of any other production two-stroke of the period which could have put up a comparable performance.

Unchanged 499cc 'G' and 'H' models remained available but at prices which must have put them completely out of the running, particularly since the 250cc 'K' models were being offered for serious sidecar work.

The Dunelt was going from strength to strength. Dealers were told 'The Dunelt, being in a class apart, does not interfere with any other agency you may hold' which was not much of a compliment to at least a couple of other Birmingham makes which immediately spring to mind. And on 10 March 1928, the Dunelt had a full front page advertisement in the *Daily Mail*. What a pity a few more manufacturers did not have sufficient faith in their machines or their future to 'climb a tree and holler' in like manner!

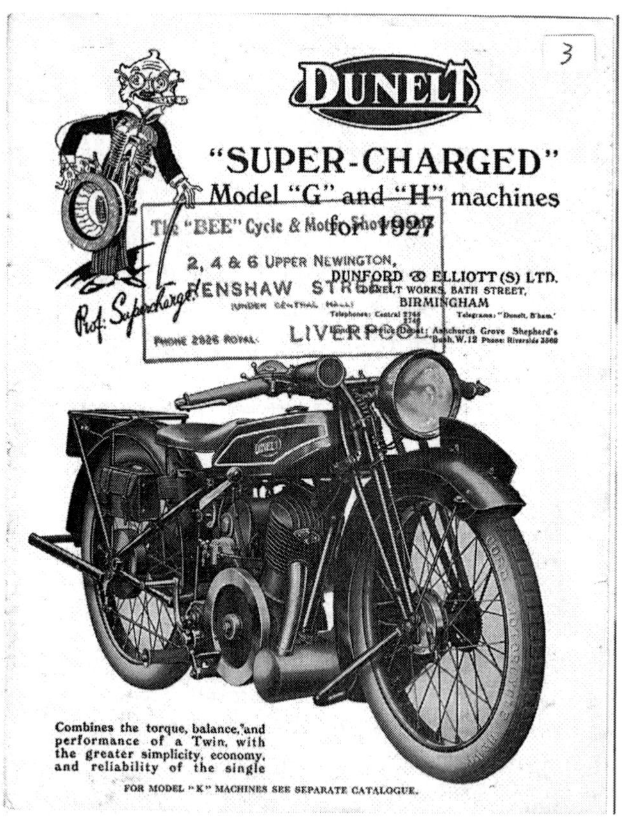

(Photo: VMCC)

Early in the 1928 season highly efficient leg shields and an under shield were offered for the K Sports and K Royal for £1 10s 0d. While an electric horn, mounted beneath the head lamp could be specified in place of the bulb horn for only five shillings.

Without resorting to a Works sponsored and organised 'pot-hunting' campaign, Dunelts were quietly making their presence felt on the Trials scene. In the 1928 Exeter seven Dunelts entered gaining seven awards. Amongst the three winners of Golds was AJ Pouncy the only 250cc sidecar competitor to do so. At the time of writing nearly fifty years later, Mr Pouncy still regularly competes in MCC events with an even tinier sidecar outfit. A little later N Anderson won the Calthorpe Cup in the Colmore. At about this time a firm of Chartered Accountants certified that Dunelt sales for the three months ending 31st January 1928 were more than twice that for the corresponding period ending 31st January 1927.

Success followed success. On a K Royal, G Stannard completed the Stock Machine Trial without loss of a single mark, whereupon the model was taken to Brooklands. With the lighting set removed JP Arrowsmith, M Anderson and RN Talbot riding alternately, proceeded to break - although not by a spectacular margin - the 'Double Twelve' World Record for the 250cc class covering over 1095 miles in 24 hours, an average speed of 45.64mph. The success of this attempt caused subsequent models to be supplied with an attractive plaque secured to the centre of the handlebar and reading 'WORLDS DOUBLE 12 HOUR RECORD BROKEN BY AN IDENTICAL MACHINE AT BROOKLANDS MARCH 1928'. Such a form of publicity was a welcome change from the more usual practice of adorning the tank with a 'coat of legs' or some other device to commemorate the fact that a machine bearing it's makers name had at some time in the past won a TT race.

On the 18th and 19th September of the same year, this time riding a brand new 1929 model selected from stock by the ACU, Anderson and Talbot again broke the 'Double Twelve' with an hour and a half to spare. Just over 1155 miles were covered and the average speed for the 24 hours was 48.13mph. For the attempt the chain guards were removed. No mechanical trouble was experienced but there were two plug changes and a worn out tyre had to be replaced.

The 499cc two-stroke models were omitted from the 1929 programme and the 240cc engine had a new bi-metal piston. Whilst the piston was still virtually an aluminium one, a ferrous annulus carried the top rings. The annulus was cast integrally with the piston and has variously been described as being of iron and of steel.

Cheapest model was the K Sports which corresponded to the 1928 standard 'K' but it now had a heavier and stronger tank. With 4 volt dynamo set and bulb horn it sold at a competitive £39 15s 0d And in this form it came within the 'thirty shilling' taxation weight limit.

The K Royal De Luxe was almost a new model. A modified frame gave a lower saddle mounting and the tank tube was raised to facilitate removal of the head and cylinder. A new type of saddle tank consisted of two separate welded steel panniers joined together at the top by four steel straps. The resultant gap between the two halves was covered by a plated strip, through a hole in which could be fitted a flush speedometer, driven from the gearbox. The carrier was of a new design and incorporated a tall tool box which tapered towards the bottom between its two right hand stays. In the event of the machine being electrically equipped the battery was now mounted on the seat tube. Heavier chain for the magneto and (where applicable) the dynamo drive was now employed and this drive cover was extended almost completely to enclose the fly-wheel. The size of the driving chains was also increased. A further improvement was the provision of a wider range of adjustment for the footrest and knee grips and a steering damper was also now standard equipment.

Slightly more austere, the K Royal followed the same general specification but had a 5 inch rear brake instead of a 7 inch, 3 inch tyres in place of 3.50 inch, and no steering damper or knee grips.

All three two-strokes used the new type piston and the air-silencer/air-cleaner/ blow-back trap was now fitted with an additional guard to prevent clothing being drawn into it.

In 1929 Dunelt entered the four-stroke market, initially with the 'Majestic'. The general layout was similar to that of the K Royal but the engine was a 348cc (71 x 88mm) two port OHV Sturmey Archer unit mounted in an inclined position. The gearbox was also a Sturmey Archer and of the horizontal type.

Oil was carried in a three pint tank on the seat tube. Large almost rectangular silencers with full fish-tails replaced the tubular type used in the smaller models, from which it differed in having both brakes of seven inches diameter and a spring-up rear stand. A gearbox driven speedometer recessed into the petrol tank was included in the list price. If electrics were specified the dynamo was mounted immediately behind the bottom of the cylinder driven by an enclosed belt.

1928 Dunelt Majestic

Of particular interest was an auxiliary oil pump operated by a pedal on the left hand side and the clutch control by means of an inverted lever. After the 1928 Show the mudguards were altered to give better tyre clearance but more protection, and the exhaust pipes were redesigned to give greater ground clearance. During the time that the model was current the oil tank was changed to one of rectangular section and moved from the right-hand side to the front of the seat tube.

The Majestic was a rather heavy machine. As road-tested by *The Motor Cycle* in touring trim which included dynamo lighting it weighed 345 lbs. The tester had very little fault to find and reported a speedometer maximum of 68mph. "Altogether" he said, "this new model is a notable addition to the Dunelt range, fully equipped it gives first class touring performance of great refinement".

For an extra thirty shillings, 1929 Dunelts could be supplied with the tanks 'crystalline finished' in black with green lines, green mudguards and cream wheels.

Whilst not strictly within the terms of reference of this book, it was during 1929 that Dunelt marketed an outboard marine motor (not to be confused with the Elto). It had a capacity of 249cc and employed the 'supercharging' system. Ignition was by Villiers flywheel magneto and carburation was by Amal. A special racing version developed 10.6bhp at 3,800rpm. The project did not end there for the manufacturers also produced a 10ft racing and a 14ft cruising hydroplane hull *and* a trailer for transport purposes. The complete equipage was light enough to be towed by a sidecar outfit.

During the 1929 season the Majestic won for its creators the Maudes Trophy thus proving that it was no ordinary 'assembly job'. 25,000 miles were covered in a period of just over twenty-three days (average speed 45.14mph) on the French Montlhery track. The machine was selected from stock by the ACU and it wore out two rear tyres in the process, so perhaps it can be forgiven for needing a new big-end bearing and two or three small items for the engine.

A 500 OHV was placed on the market in June 1929 which presumably can be described as a 1930 model. Designated the 'S' it employed the 79 x 101mm, 496cc Sturmey Archer two port engine. Apart from the exhaust system it was similar in appearance to the Majestic but in fact the main frame had been redesigned resulting, incidentally in a wheel-base increased by one inch. The silencers were deep and short, and almost square. Looking at the machine from the right hand side the exhaust pipe entered the bottom right hand corner and a short tail pipe with fish-tail emerged from the diagonally opposite corner, at a little over wheel spindle height. The horizontal type Sturmey Archer gearbox had a heavier clutch. A saddle tank was of conventional one piece construction and oil was carried in a separate tank on the right hand side of the seat tube, the arrangement being the same as for the Majestic when first introduced.

Lubrication was by Pilgrim mechanical pump using the total-loss system but for the 1930 season proper, a dry sump 'SD' was available, and it was this model which was most widely supplied.

The former Majestic was for 1930 renamed the Montlhery and had dry sump lubrication as standard. It was announced that the exhaust system would be as

1929 Montlhery

for the 'S' but if this change was in fact made it was not universal in its application. A detail change concerned the carburettor which now had a horizontal mixing chamber.

Completely new for 1930 and rather slow in getting into production was the Model 'T' a 248cc twin port OHC. The engine was built by Sturmey Archer and does not appear to have been adopted by any other British manufacturers - significantly not by Raleigh. It was not in the strictest sense an overhead camshaft engine and the manufacturers themselves were wont to refer to it as a 'camshaft'. The valve rockers were operated by face cams at the upper extremity of a vertical shaft, driven by bevel from the crankshaft. Arranging a magneto drive on this type of engine was always a problem and in this case the magneto, which was behind the cylinder, took its chain drive from the opposite end of the crankshaft. Lubrication was by the dry-sump system, oil being carried in a tank on the right hand side of the seat tube.

The engine was mounted in an inclined position in a duplex frame which incorporated torque tubes as well as chain stays. The exhaust pipes passed the front tubes on the inside and the system was completed by large silencers of an elongated diamond shape, the fish-tails of which ended well behind the rear wheel. A Sturmey Archer gearbox of the light-weight type was used from which there was a drive to a tank mounted speedometer fitted as standard. When Miller electric lighting was specified the dynamo was mounted in front of the crankcase.

On its first public appearance the model T got off to a good start by gaining a Gold in the 1930 Colmore but few examples ever reached the public: possibly it was not economic to sell such a machine at a mere £45 and it was discontinued for 1931.

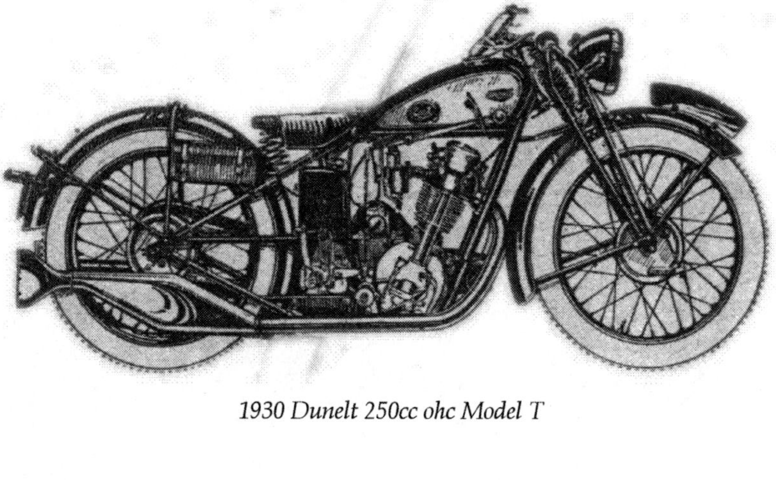

1930 Dunelt 250cc ohc Model T

The two-stroke side of the business was represented by a sole K Royal virtually unchanged from the previous year. The saddle was now however of more generous proportions and a built-in speedometer was standard.

In March 1930 one of the new 496cc OHV models covered over thirteen thousand miles in less than sixteen days and nights. The machine was taken from stock by the ACU and the exercise was intended to simulate fifty TT races. It took place over the TT circuit and despite snow storms and icy roads, the average speed worked out at 34.8mph. Apart from an inlet valve, replacements were minimal and the feat gained for Dunelt the Maudes Trophy - the second year in succession.

1930 is, as it happens, a convenient point at which to break off the Dunelt story for when the 1931 programme was announced the marque had become Sheffield Dunelt, although I can find no evidence that at this particular juncture, manufacture moved from Birmingham to Sheffield. Super-charged two-stroke engines ceased to be made giving place to modified Villiers units with two flywheels and coil ignition. Gradually motorcycle production ceased entirely by which time a healthy cycle and tandem business seems to have been built up with depots catering for the cycle trade generally in various parts of the country.

ECONOMIC

The Economic appeared in a number of different forms but the basis of them all was the little American Johnson flat-twin, two-stroke engine; the dimensions given as 52.5 x 38.5mm made a capacity of 165cc. Since it was American practice to quote bore and stroke in inches these measurements probably correspond to an actual $2^1/_{16}$ x $1^1/_2$ inches. The cylinders fired simultaneously, thus making possible a common crankcase. 2½ bhp was claimed. Ignition was by flywheel magneto and the carburettor was a Capac. Petroil, not unnaturally, provided lubrication. Subsequently the unit was made in Great Britain

Economic Motors Ltd operated from various addresses including 62 East Castle Street, Oxford Street and 2 Economic Corner, Wells Street both London W1.

In the very early twenties the Economic was sold as an attachment to motorize a pedal cycle and was mounted over the rear wheel. Later, circa 1921, pedal cycles were offered complete with this power unit. The rear wheel sprocket was attached by three springs to give a shock-absorbing effect. Some users employed this 'Auto-wheel' to propel tradesmen's delivery tricycles. By special dispensation such outfits were taxed at £1 10s 0d per year and not £4.

In 1922 there was a passenger carrying three-wheeler. This was known as the Buckboard and employed specially selected engines capable of developing about 4bhp the chassis was made of ash, the springy nature of which afforded a certain degree of (and the only) suspension. The engine, rear-mounted had a friction drive to a countershaft which drove one of the rear wheels by chain. One brake operated on one rear wheel and another on the countershaft.

The 1923 Economic had a 163cc flat twin two-stroke engine with friction drive

Also available in 1922 was a miniature motorcycle weighing only 94 pounds. The frame was of duplex construction and the engine was mounted with the crank-shaft across the frame. It was quite a pretty little machine and would have looked even better if the saddle had not been perched up so high. In its single speed form the engine was connected by chain to a countershaft immediately below it and final drive was by belt. A two-speed version was offered at a slight extra cost. Front and rear brakes were stirrup and belt rim respectively.

Probably the best known Economic was the friction drive model of 1922/1923. The machine was similar to the one already described, but with the engine mounted transversely. Cranked brackets from each cylinder head to the seat tube carried a countershaft keyed to a friction disc engaging at right angles with the flywheel. A pedal withdrew the disc from contact thus providing a clutch and a tank-side lever caused the friction disc to move laterally on the shaft giving overall gear rations quoted at from 6 to 19 to one. Final drive was by belt.

At £28 17s 6d this ingenious little machine marketed by Eynsford Engineering Co Ltd, Primrose Works, Eynsford, Kent, certainly did not price itself out of the market. Indeed it is difficult to believe that it could be profitably produced to sell at that figure - which may possibly account for the Economic's demise.

Royal Enfield

Royal Enfield is another marque to emerge from the Victorian bicycle manufacturing world. They produced their first motorised bicycle using De Dion Power around 1900. From the Redditch works they produced big JAP powered sidecar outfits for use as machine gun platforms in the First War. By the twenties they were using their own make of engines, notably a 350cc side-valve single in 1924 and a 500cc in 1927 which shared bore, stroke and piston with the companies own V-twin, alongside engines from Vickers and Wolseley. Production continued throughout the period, and for 1929 the range comprised 8 models, from a 225 cc two-speed two-stroke through various sizes of single cylinder four-strokes up to the 976 cc V-twins.

Further Reading;

The Story of Royal Enfield Motorcycles, 'Made Like A Gun', Peter Hartley , 1981, Patrick Stephens.

FRANCIS BARNETT

Francis-Barnett was one of the last makes of motorcycle of any consequence to start operations in Coventry and probably the last one to remain in production there.

For the early history of the marque, I rely on the writings of 'Handel Barr', which pseudonym obviously thinly disguised the identity of the late James Sheldon.

Shortly after the First World War, Captain Gordon Francis came out of the Army and with his father-in-law, Arthur Barnett, set up Francis and Barnett Ltd. Gordon was the son of Graham Francis of Lea-Francis fame and Arthur Barnett, formerly a director of the Singer Company, was already the producer of Invicta cycles and motorcycles and continued to do so for some years.

At some period during the firm's history Eric Barnett, son of Arthur Barnett, was identified with the concern and subsequently became sales director. Arthur died in 1939.

1920

Francis and Barnett's establishment in Lower Ford Street, Coventry, had until recently been a munitions factory and prior to that it had been used by Bayliss-Thomas, who produced the first Excelsior motorcycle and also by Hillman.

The 1920 Francis-Barnett, introduced in March of that year, was a 282cc model with a 70 x 76mm side-valve JAP engine and a CAV magneto mounted in front of the crankcase. The machine was described as being a 2¾hp although according to the convention of that period it was a 2½.

Chain and belt transmission was through a Sturmey-Archer two-speed box incorporating a clutch and kick-starter. The primary drive was enclosed in a well-fitting aluminium housing.

The aforementioned two units were mounted in a neat, sturdy diamond frame with Brampton Bi-Flex forks. The gear lever was attached to the seat tube. Other details which figured in the specification included a 'pan' seat, a well-valanced front guard, linoleum covered foot-boards with metal edges and a knurled nut adjuster for the parallel action belt-rim rear brake. Silencing was by the familiar transverse cylindrical expansion box and tail pipe and the front brake was of the almost universal stirrup type.

1920 Francis Barnett Standard Model

What lifted the model out of the rut was a particularly pretty tapered saddle tank with black panels on a red ground. The control cables neatly disappeared into recesses in the front of the tank.

The quoted weight was 'about 195lbs'. Apart from its saddle tank and more refined rear brake, it was virtually identical to its counterpart in the Invicta range. At £84, subsequently increased to £89 5s 0d, it was comparatively expensive.

Buyers Guide for 1920 also lists a 2½hp Villiers two-stroke engined version. If, in fact, it went into production it received little publicity and no mention of it appears in *Fletchers* for that year.

1921-22

1921 tanks had what can most easily be described as black side, nose, and top panels on a red ground. The 2¾hp model continued with minimum changes, but there was now a more expensive option with leg-shields and Maglilta electric lighting.

A similar 2½hp model was now being advertised equipped with 269cc (70 x 70mm) Villiers two-stroke engine. It came in either 'two-speed clutch and kick-start' or single speed (direct belt) form, although *Fletchers* does not recognise the existence of this machine. The two-strokes had drip-feed lubrication as distinct from a plain hand pump on the four-strokes.

For this year B and B carburettors were standard equipment replacing Amac. Tanks were all black in the 1922 range. The former 2¾ became a 2½ but was for all practical purposes unchanged.

A new Sports 2¾ used the longer stroke (70 x 90mm) 346cc side-valve JAP engine. The Sturmey Archer box in this case had three-speeds and there was an arrangement whereby the rear-control assembly, whilst not being integral with the box, moved with it thus facilitating primary chain adjustment. Final drive was by chain but a belt-rim rear brake was retained. For the front wheel there was a microscopic internal expanding brake. Fully adjustable foot-rests replaced foot-boards and the front guard had no valance. A specially prepared engine cost an extra £5 and the machine was also listed in competition form.

1923

The 269cc two-stroke was offered only with two speeds and without a saddle tank.

Until this point, only its saddle tank and its rather high price distinguished the Francis-Barnett from the products of various other assemblers. For 1923 however, there appeared a machine which represented a complete break-away from tradition, both as to design and price. This new model had a 147cc (55 x 62mm) Villiers two-stroke engine, with petroil lubrication, which was built into a pin-joined frame.

The new frame was reputed to have stemmed from an idea conceived by Gordon Francis some years earlier; it was almost completely triangulated. The top, seat and front tubes were duplicated and there were torque stays in addition to chain stays. It was built up entirely from straight tubes and thus could be cheaply produced and quickly assembled.

The front forks were of similar construction and relied for their resilience on a flat 'C' spring. An interesting feature of the design was that the forks rotated around a fixed spindle. This form of construction was to become synonymous with the name of Francis-Barnett and it was not long before the slogan 'built like a Bridge' was adopted and frames were being guaranteed against breakage 'for life'.

Final drive was by belt through an Albion plain two-speed box. Both brakes, on account of the fork design, operated on the belt-rim, one internally and the other externally. The saddle tank was replaced by a neat straight-sided wedge-shaped one, underslung from the top tubes. In its basic form as described, it cost £27 with a clutch as an optional extra.

For 1923 various alterations had taken place on the existing range of four-stroke models. The transverse-box and tailpipe exhaust system was replaced by a long plated pipe running into a flat, almost square, cast aluminium silencer bearing the legend Francis-Barnett. The same magic words now replaced JAP on the magneto chain cover. Tool boxes were now seat tube and not carrier mounted.

2¾hp (345cc) JAP side-valve models dominated the range, still with dummy belt-rim rear brakes. A 'Sports' model had foot-rests and a 'Standard' had foot-boards, polished aluminium leg-shields and a valanced front guard. A variant of the Sports was finished in mauve and grey, had no kick-starter and was called the TT model.

Francis-Barnett

Motor Cycles for 1923.

$2\frac{3}{4}$ h.p. STANDARD MODEL: BELT DRIVE.

With Two-speed Gear, Clutch and Kick-Starter.

¶ PRICE: With Two-Speed Gear, Clutch and Kick Starter - £58
With Three-Speed Gear, Clutch and Kick Starter - £61
Leg Shields fitted to order at 15/- extra.

SPECIFICATION.

ENGINE.—$2\frac{3}{4}$ h.p. J.A.P., air-cooled, 70 m/m × 76 m/m, 292 c.c. Silencer with extension pipe.
IGNITION.—High Tension Magneto.
CARBURETTER.—Brown & Barlow.
TRANSMISSION.—Sturmey-Archer two-speed Gear, with Clutch and Kick Starter.
TANK.—Saddle type; petrol capacity nearly 2 gallons; oil capacity 3 pints.
LUBRICATION.—Hand pump inside tank. Sight drip feed to order.
FRAME.—Specially designed with straight tubes.
FORK.—Brampton Bi-flex, as illustrated.
WHEELS.—26″ × $2\frac{1}{4}$″
TYRES.—26″ × $2\frac{1}{4}$″ Dunlop.
BRAKES.—Bowden hand applied to front wheel and specially designed foot brake on belt rim with quick-action adjustment.
BELT.—Dunlop.
MUDGUARDS.—$3\frac{1}{4}$″ wide; valances fitted to back and front.
CARRIER.—Strong tubular, as illustrated.
STAND.—Constructed with solid ends, "kick-up" type.
FOOTBOARDS.—Special design, furnished with metal toe shields.
SADDLE.—Pan Seat.
TOOLBAGS.—Two armour-plated with complete outfit of tools.
FINISH.—Best black enamel, bright parts heavily plated; tank specially lined; number plates fitted.
WEIGHT.—With empty tank and without tools, 188 lbs.

Telegraphic Code Words: Two-Speed, "ZARABAND"; Three-Speed, "ZARATRICE."

MANUFACTURERS:

FRANCIS & BARNETT, Ltd., COVENTRY.

Telegrams: "FRANBAR, COVENTRY." Telephone: 1359.

Buyers Guide refers to the TT as having 'disc' gear ratios. One assumes that 'disc' was short for discretionary - ie optional. The same source also lists a marginally cheaper 250cc version of the TT with no mention of engine make or type.

292cc 2½hp models continued in all-chain two and three-speed and chain-cum-belt two-speed forms.

Due if only to its absurdly low weight (approximately 110 lbs) and its modest price, the 1½hp 147cc model was an instant success and for 1924 the basic two-speeder could have a clutch for an extra thirty shillings or a clutch and kick-starter for £3. A carrier, leg-shields and direct electric lighting (from the fly-wheel magneto unit) were other inexpensive optional extras. Some illustrations show an additional pair of slender stays from the seat lug to the torque stays. Ixion, writing in *The Motorcycle* remarked 'It is indeed a miracle'.

1924-25

By about mid-1924 various competition successes had been notched up in various competitions including two Golds in the ACU 1,000 mile Stock Machine Trial, one in the Land's End and one in the Paris-Nice. Additionally there was the Hoffman Cup in the Johannesburg 100 Mile Road Race and the Walker Cup in the Colemore.

The 2¾ side-valve models were on their way out, but continued to be listed in Sports or Touring (leg-shields, etc.) form, somewhat pricey at £63 and £65 respectively. In either case the specification included three-speeds and chain final drive.

The conventional diamond frame no longer appeared in the 1925 range and the four-stroke engine was temporarily abandoned.

The 1½hp with plain two-speed gear and 2in tyres was still listed, virtually identical to the original production. Two slightly more expensive examples were available with clutch and with either two or three-speeds.

There was now the choice of all-chain drive. Since the design of the frame made no provision for doing so in the conventional manner, rear chain tension adjustment was effected by the movement of an eccentrically mounted jockey-sprocket acting on the lower side of the bottom run of the chain. The jockey had a further advantage in that it caused the chain to wrap around a greater part of the circumference of the gearbox sprocket. A clutch and kick-starter were standard with the choice of two or three-speeds.

The 1¾hp Sports was introduced in this year. It used the pin-jointed frame, and was powered by the larger and more efficient 172cc (57 x 67mm) Villiers two-stroke engine which had a non-detachable head but two exhaust ports. In this instance lubrication was by drip-feed and a three-speed Albion box with clutch

Brooklands Museum's 172 Super Sports Model showing its 'Oxford Bags'.

and kick-starter was fitted. Final drive was by chain and as in the case of the other all-chain models the tyre section was 2¼ inches. Direct lighting, carrier and leg-shields were all extras.

There were appreciable price reductions and fewer options for 1926, although price increases took place during the season on account of tyre costs.

The basic 1½hp designated Model No. 1 was down to £25 or £29 with clutch, kick-starter, and all-chain drive. A de-luxe version of the latter with direct lighting, carrier and leg-shields cost £31.

The Model No.5, the former 1¾hp Sports, was substantially reduced to £32 10s 0d. It was also listed with an eye to the Continental market, where it would enjoy a tax concession, with a 174cc JAP (sometimes quoted as AZA) side-valve engine at the home price of £34 15s 0d. which included a soft-top saddle.

Later in the season came the 172cc Super Sports, also with a soft-top saddle. A peculiar feature of this machine was the 'Oxford Bags' exhaust system. Each exhaust port discharged into a large vertical expansion chamber which merged into a horizontal exhaust pipe and a cylindrical silencer. Contemporary illustrations suggest that the system was not plated.

The 346cc side-valve JAP engine made a brief and unspectacular return in the now universal pin-jointed frame and with all-chain drive through a three-speed Albion box.

Both wheels, shod with 27 x 2.75 inch wired edge tyres had internal expanding brakes - with plated back plates - and were interchangeable. Due to the presence of an effective brake on the front wheel, the front forks whilst retaining built-up construction had a normal link action and a central compression spring. The exhaust system consisted of a plated exhaust pipe and tubular silencer and either a single-lever Binks or an Amac carburettor could be selected. The price was a reasonable £41 15s 0d plus a further £1 for Best and Lloyd mechanical lubrication if required.

1926-27

Francis-Barnetts had considerable competition successes during 1926, particularly in the Scottish Six Days in the hands of Messrs Meeten, Moxon and McQueen. Meeten and Moxon each gained silver cups and McQueen a Bronze. Moxon also won, for the second year in succession, the special award for the best performance on a machine under 200cc *The Motorcycle* referred to his performance as 'easily the finest of the week'.

The 1927 range was considerably tidied up as to the number of models. The Model 4, 147cc two-stroke now had all-chain transmission. To incorporate this feature must have been a last-minute decision because a manufacturer's advertisement which appeared in *The Motorcycle* 1926 Show Report makes no mention of this long overdue improvement and carried an illustration depicting belt final drive.

The machine was now offered in two-speed, clutch and kick-start form only at £29 17s 6d complete with leg shields, carrier and direct lighting. The weight had crept up to 142lbs. It was advertised as being 'suitable for town riding or long journeys' and its users included the Coventry municipality.

There were two 172cc Models each retaining the single dummy belt-rim for both brakes and the 'C' spring front forks. By now, however, the hollow of the spring had been filled in with a rubber block. Since rubber is said to be incompressible, one idly wonders what assistance to the suspension it provided. By far the more popular version was the Model 9 Super Sports. The Villiers engine had an aluminium cylinder head. Two separate, short, plated exhaust pipes each terminated in a long, plated, cylindrical silencer with the end of its tail-pipe flattened into a miniature fish-tail. Standard equipment included a steering damper, a Terry spring-top saddle and 25 x 3 inch so-called 'balloon' tyres. The quoted speed of 55mph was probably a conservative one.

The alternative Model 5 never got much publicity, although it was considerably cheaper (£32 10s 0d as compared with £38 10s 0d). In this case the engine had a non-detachable head and tyres were 24 x 2 ¼ inches (as on the 147cc Model). Included in the price of either the Model 5 or the '9' was direct lighting.

Also listed (£68) was a new Model 10 vertical twin It had a sort of 'Granville Bradshaw' air about it and was a great sensation when it appeared at Olympia in October 1926.

The Model 10 employed the well established pin-jointed frame but there were several departures from what had come to be accepted Francis-Barnett practice.

The forks had normal link action with a single central coil spring and both wheels were equipped with 7in internal expanding brakes with exceptionally long torque arms. The non-saddle type tank was conical instead of being wedge-shaped and the saddle was fitted with friction-type shock-dampers to check the activities of the suspension springs. Instead of being eccentrically mounted, the jockey sprocket was carried on an adjustable arm and there was a spring-up rear stand.

The most revolutionary feature of the machine was the vertical twin two-stroke engine which was built as a unit with a three-speed gearbox. It was the product of the Villiers factory.

More widely read writers than your humble scribe have stated that the unit was built especially and exclusively for Francis and Barnett, but there is room for doubt that such was the case. The development costs must have been considerable and moreover the unit was subsequently to be adopted for at least one other make of motorcycle, the Belgian La Mondiale.

Two cylinders with bores and strokes of 57.15mm (sometimes incorrectly quoted as 57mm) and 67mm gave a capacity of 344cc. It will be noted that these dimensions tie up with 172cc practice. Both cylinders were in a single block which had a common detachable aluminium head.

The three-bearing crankshaft was of built-up construction which permitted the continued use of roller big-end bearings. At the front end there was a Villiers flywheel magneto and at the rear end was a multi-plate clutch, the driven member of which transmitted power to a transverse gear shaft through a worm-drive.

A beautifully sculptured horizontal split cast aluminium base chamber served not only as a crankcase but also acted as an oil reservoir. It enclosed the clutch, the worm-drive, the transverse gear shaft, a layshaft and the necessary gear wheels, the kick-start mechanism and even an oil filter. The gear-lever emerged from the housing through a single oil retaining orifice.

Timed ports in the centre main bearing harnessed the crankcase compression and suction to provide automatic lubrication. The Villiers carburettor was mounted on the left-hand side of the cylinder block. Exterior to the right hand side of the base assembly was an auxiliary manifold which connected the exhaust ports to a single exhaust pipe.

The engine-gear unit was attached to the frame by the foot-rest bar at the point where the seat-stays joined up with the chain stays; it had its final drive sprocket coming out on the left hand side. A top-opening tool-box was tucked away neatly between the frame tubes and the left hand side of the engine-base casting.

The previously mentioned price was to have included electric lighting with battery charging facilities by the Villiers system but it is doubtful whether any examples of the vertical twin reached the public during the 1927 season.

It was during 1927 that Minnie Grenfell rode from London to Edinburgh under ACU observation in 19½ hours on a 147cc model. Mrs Grenfell, who at about that time had two sons, the younger one 'of but six summers' was 'quite capable of telling anyone of the advantages of a Villiers two-stroke over a common-or-garden four-stroke', to use her own words. One of the advantages must surely have been fuel economy, for in the course of the run, consumption of Pratts (now Esso) petrol was at the rate of one gallon per 214 miles.

1928 and The Pullman

When the 344cc Vertical Twin appeared as a 1928 model at the 1927 Olympia Show it was being called The Pullman. It looked more like a Francis-Barnett with its flat-sided, wedge-shaped two gallon petrol tank.

The power unit had undergone 'searching tests' and had now 'passed out of the tool-room stage'. One external difference was that the auxiliary manifold had disappeared and the single exhaust pipe emerged directly from the bottom-end casting. It was now possible to adjust the rear chain by moving the engine-gear unit forward or backward in the frame thus eliminating the jockey sprocket. Further constructional details were now released, some of which may or may not have been featured in the original design. The long internal bolts which held the

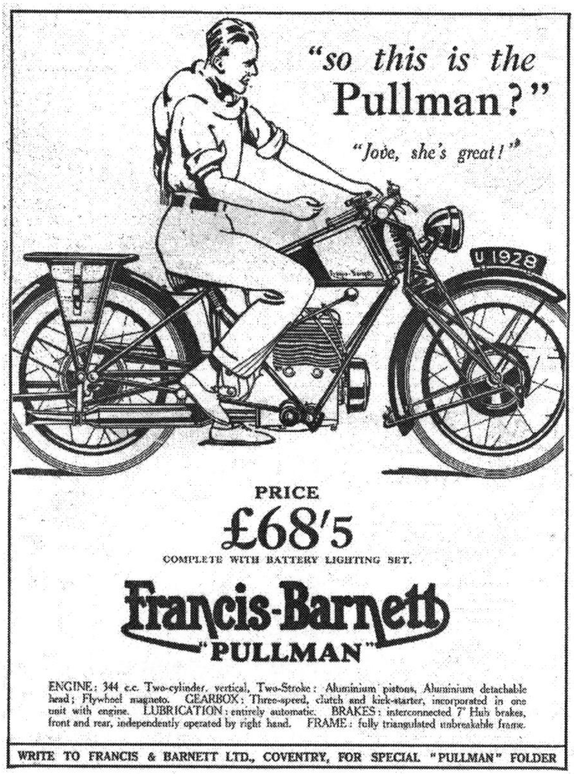

two halves of the base chamber together also served to hold down the cylinder block. The interiors of the cylinder-heads were shaped to conform to the piston deflectors. It was also made clear that there was ample cooling space between the two cylinders. The inserts of the five-plate clutch were of cork, since the assembly had to run in oil

The oil capacity of the base chamber was varyingly quoted as three or five pints. The latter seems to be the more likely. Each cylinder had an oil control screw which, when correctly adjusted, was secured by a lock nut. Due to the position of the filler cap it was impossible to over-fill. Once, on completion of the running-in period, the oil control screws were correctly set up, the only attention the lubrication system required was to ensure that the oil level was correct and that the filler-cap was properly tightened, with the special spanner provided.

The kick-start mechanism could be removed as a complete assembly. The cycle itself was much the same as described for 1927 except for the changes already mentioned, but the saddle was of the conventional spring-top type, with shock absorbers. Brakes were however interconnected with, contrary to the more usual practice, the rear brake being independently hand-operated. Twist grips were used for throttle and ignition control and in conjunction with non-inverted levers for the clutch and the brake. There was a small 'trigger' for the compression-release which all together made possible an exceptionally clean handlebar layout.

The spring-up rear stand continued and a front stand was added. Wheels with knock-out spindles carried 26 x 3.50 inch wire-edged tyres. Tools were now carried in tall, tapered pannier cases housed between the rear carrier supports. Gear ratios were changed from 5, 7.3 and 11.6 to 5.14, 7.7 and 12.6 to 1.

The overall weight was given as 280lbs, and no elaborate claims were made as to performance. Contemporary advertisements mentioned 55mph with 'occasional bursts' at 65mph being possible. At the time of the 1927 Olympia Show the impression was given that production would start almost immediately, but later it was announced that deliveries would start on the 10th March 1928. Little was heard of the Pullman during 1928 and only seldom was it mentioned in press advertisements. However, it secured Golds in the Lands End and the Edinburgh trials (with in each case the Silence award) and also a Gold in the Scottish Six Days. At Brooklands, in conjunction with Shell-Mex, TG Meeten coved the flying half mile at an unspectacular 59.18mph.

The Motorcycle road-tested the Pullman with the report appearing in the issue of 12th April, 1928 and gave the weight in touring trim including full (accumulator) electric lighting as 315lbs. The tester was at pains to point out that this was 'not designed as a super sports machine but as a luxurious touring motorcycle'.

The engine was delightfully smooth from 10 to 55mph in top gear and would run up to 40mph in second with a certain amount of fussiness, but no unpleasant vibration. Acceleration in the lower gears was 'extraordinary' and it was estimated that 60mph should be possible when the engine was fully run in

The rear brake alone, hand-operated, would stop and hold the machine on a 1 in 7 (approx.) gradient. On the practical side *The Motorcycle* man satisfied himself on the ease with which the drive chain could be adjusted and pointed out that it was possible further to quieten the exhaust note by telescoping the tail-pipe further into the silencer. Fuel consumption worked out at a little over 80mpg and with a generous setting rather more than three pints of oil were used in 250 miles.

The only criticisms were that the handlebars were too low and too wide and that the forks tended to clash on the rebound. The report ended with the simple comment, 'It is a true luxury machine'.

Even though the price included an accumulator charging set, £68 5s 0d was a lot of money and it seems possible that two-stroke enthusiasts sufficiently affluent to contemplate the purchase of a Pullman, decided to set their sights a little higher and to turn their attentions to a Scott.

Throughout the 1928 range, grease gun lubrication at the appropriate points on the cycle and, where applicable, for the jockey sprocket bearing, was standardised.

For some time there had been an off-centre inspection plate on the flywheel magneto cover on Villiers engines fitted to Francis-Barnett in order to give access to the contact-breaker points. This cover was now replaced by a much longer concentric one, held in position by a spring ring. On single cylinder models the Albion gearbox was of a new type with the lay-shaft to the rear of the main-shaft and not beneath it. Rear number plates ceased to be fixed directly to the mudguard, but were mounted vertically.

The 147cc two-stroke came in two forms, both with a more attractive plated exhaust pipe and silencer, but retaining the 'C' spring forks. A Model 3 was sold devoid of equipment and with 2¼ inch wire-edged tyres. With direct lighting, Terry saddle, 2½ inch tyres, a carrier, and leg-shields of new and improved design, it became the Model 4.

Mainstay of the range was the Model 9 Super Sports, almost identical to its 1927 predecessor except for the important fact that it now enjoyed 5 inch internal expanding brakes, with long torque arms and link-action central spring forks in addition to the general alterations already noted. One small difference was that an angled indication stub now enabled the carburettor to be mounted with its air intake facing rearwards.

A cheaper 172cc Model 5 continued to be available differing in having the all-iron cylinder and 2.5 inch as against 3 inch section tyres. It was seldom mentioned or illustrated.

Lubrication on both the 5 and the 9 was by the Villiers automatic system which used crankcase compression to pressurise the oil tank.

Since Francis and Barnett were among the most extensive users of Villiers engines, this seems an appropriate opportunity to record that 1928 units had their cylinder bores hardened and, without the use of abrasives, polished before boring. A new aluminium alloy was being used for the pistons. The bottom end of the connecting rod was of special channel section. Alternate bronze and steel rollers continued in use for the big-end bearing.

Electrically the contact-breaker arm was balanced to eliminate bounce at high rpm and the area of the fibre 'heel' was increased. An electro-mechanical device was available on engines which allowed the lighting coils in the flywheel magneto unit to produce direct current where battery-charging facilities were required. It was designed to work in conjunction with a nominal 5 volt four-cell 'Nipe' nickel-iron battery and 4 volt bulbs which, since they were being slightly over-run, provided an excellent light. Such batteries followed what text books call the Edison Cell principle. They had a tremendously long life and would withstand almost unlimited abuse provided that they were kept topped up and the alkaline electrolyte was not contaminated. Their use was not exclusive to the Villiers system, but due to their comparatively high cost they were never widely adopted for motor-cycle operation, although they were extensively used in other areas into the modern era.

At about the time these improvements were announced, Villiers claimed that there were 200,000 of their motorcycle engines in use whilst the staff of the repair shop consisted of one man and one boy.

1929

The 1929 Francis-Barnetts were already being advertised in early October 1928. Without drastic alterations to the fame all models now had saddle tanks. With but a single exception which will be mentioned later, the snub nose of a specially developed Terry saddle was recessed into the rear end of the tank. Initially there were to have been orange tank panels but by Show Time the colour had been changed to what the makers called Ivory White.

To an extent Francis and Barnett, and probably even more so Villiers, had doubtless burned their fingers on the Pullman. For 1929 it had been withdrawn 'pending further refinement' but it was never re-introduced. What was basically the Pullman frame now housed a 67 x 70mm 247 Villiers engine with aluminium head and twin exhaust ports. It was mounted in the frame in an inclined position with the cylinder parallel to the front down tubes.

The Pullman frame lent itself admirably to the adoption of this particular unit since there was room within the frame structure for the auxiliary outside flywheel. Clamps secured the front engine plates to the footrest bar. A separate gearbox now being necessary, there was a reversion to a jockey sprocket for tensioning the rear chain. The box, naturally an Albion, gave 'go anywhere' ratios of 5.25, 9 and 16 to 1.

It was on this model that the nose of the saddle over-lapped the rear end of the tank instead of being recessed into it. Knee grips were a standard fitment (as was the case for most other models in the range). This new machine was listed as the Model 12 or the Empire. The Empire also differed from the Pullman in certain other respects. Oil was carried in a separate cylindrical tank underneath the saddle, the brakes were not interconnected, and only direct lighting was included in the price - in this instance £39 10s 0d. Furthermore, in common with the remainder of the range the tyre section was 3 inch and twist grip control was an extra. Weighing some 236lbs, the Empire was well above the magic 200lbs, 'cheap tax' limit.

Before detailing the other models, mention may be made of an interesting feature of the new saddle tanks. They were of welded steel construction and the vertical sides were extended down past the bottom of the tank. Across the bottom edges were welded straps into which the fixing studs were screwed without actually penetrating the tank itself.

1930 Model 9

Only the petroil lubricated 147cc machines continued to use the C-spring front fork and the dummy belt-rim brake arrangement. A two-speed gearbox was still standard. The 'Model 3' was supplied without lighting, but on the 'Model 4' direct lighting and leg-shields were included in the specification.

It was still the 172cc Super Sports (Model 9) which received most of the limelight throughout 1929 and additional refinements included a Villiers air-cleaner, knee grips, a front stand and direct lighting. One contemporary mentions a spring-up rear stand, but the presence of such a feature is not apparent in that season's press illustrations. Oil was now carried (as on the Empire) in a separate cylindrical tank mounted below the saddle horizontally and in line with the frame. On the left-hand side was the filler-cap and on the right the sight feed assembly. There was thus no longer room for a tool-box in its accustomed position and so a rear carrier with two pannier bags - as on the Empire - was fitted. Also common to the Empire was a 6 inch head-lamp. The 172cc fixed-head Sports (Model 5) used the separate oil tank and the rear-mounted tool-bags but only a 5in head-lamp for the (inclusive) direct lighting. As in 1928 this model was to remain very much in the background.

A newcomer was the Utility 200. At the time of its introduction, it was listed as the Model 14 but *Buyers Guide* for 1929 calls it a Model 6. Villiers, in order to provide a more powerful work-a-day alternative to the 147cc unit, had introduced a fixed head engine of 196cc (61 x 67mm). Francis-Barnett was one of the first manufacturers to adopt it when they used it for this particular model. Lubrication was automatic and the general design followed the pattern of the remainder of the range. One particular advertisement contradicts itself as to whether or not electric lighting was a standard fitment, but it is reasonable to infer that it was. Like the Model 5 it received minimal publicity during the 1929 season.

Direct lighting (with 6 inch head-lamp) was standard on all 1930 models. If, at extra cost, an accumulator set was specified a Westinghouse rectifier replaced the earlier electro-mechanical device. With not a thought for the head-aches of Concours judges half a century later, chromium plate and/or cream wheels were optional extras. Common through the whole range were pannier type tool bags, knock-out hub spindles, 25 x 3 inch tyres and full-size fish-tails. On the larger models was a new type of gear lever approximately parallel to the bottom of the tank working in a vertical gate; the rear stands were of the spring-up type. Contemporary advertisements credit all models with these two features, but they are not apparent in *The Motorcycle* 1929 Show Guide illustration of the 147cc Model. There was only one machine of this capacity and it was usually listed as the Model 4. At last it had central coil spring forks and internal-expanding brakes. *Buyers Guide* for 1930 specifies three-speeds, but all other sources available indicate that there were only two. Leg-shields were standard and at £29 0s 0d it represented value for money which was difficult to beat.

The 172cc Super Sports (Model 9) was to remain the darling of the range and was unchanged from its predecessors except for (where they are applicable) the general overall details already outlined. Its fixed-head counterpart was no longer listed.

The 196cc engined machine which had been introduced for 1929 was, with detail alterations, listed as either a Model 14 or a Model 15 if powered by an aluminium head 2-port engine. On the Empire (Model 12) the nose of the saddle was recessed into the tank, thus bringing the machine into line with the rest of the range.

Early in 1930 the Dominion was announced. It was identical to the Empire except that it had an over-square 79 x 70mm 343cc Villiers engine (the capacity was frequently misquoted as 342cc). This particular unit was never widely adopted and was soon afterwards replaced by a long-stroke version.

It will have been gathered that for 1930 the Francis-Barnett range consisted of six models. A sign of the economic climate prevailing was that for 1931 there were only two. However, TG Meeten was still making unofficial 'fastest time of day' climbs of Hustyn and other MCC observed sections with his 172cc 'wedge tank' sidecar outfit - reputed to have a bottom gear of 25 to 1.

Francis and Barnett Ltd continued as a family business for several more years during which there were some returns to the four-stroke scene. Eventually, however, although it continued to trade under the original title, control of the Company found its way into the hands of the AMC concern.

GRI

Other workers have described some motorcycle engines in terms such as 'the most unorthodox ever built' but surely, at least as far as the period under review is concerned, this distinction must be afforded to the engine designed by GR Inshaw of 55 Cecil Street, Hill Head, Glasgow, and fitted to a GRI machine, a prototype of which was described by *The Motorcycle* in April 1920.

The most interesting feature of this 3hp single cylinder four-stroke engine (which incidentally had the curious bore and stroke dimensions of 83 x 79mm giving 427cc) was that it employed only one (overhead) poppet valve. Cast integrally with the cylinder head and sited transversely was a housing for a rotary valve. Flange fitted to this housing, and corresponding to their respective ports were stubs to accept the carburettor and the exhaust pipe. Made of cast iron, the rotary valve itself ran on ball bearings. The poppet valve, which was held closed only by a very weak spring, was operated by a rocker, the ball end of which was actuated by a cam integral with the rotary valve.

As to the general construction of the engine, both halves of the crankcase were symmetrical. The cylinder incorporated a boss facing rearwards for the sparking plug and one facing towards the front for a compression release valve. The cylinder head was screwed into the top of the barrel and locked in position by a threaded ring. Behind the cylinder was the magneto and this was driven by the same chain which drove the rotary valve from the right-hand side of the crank-shaft.

Without going into a mass of detail, the actual operation of the system can most easily be understood by accepting that the poppet valve was connected alternately by means of the rotary valve with either the inlet or the exhaust port. Various claims, some beyond dispute and others of doubtful validity, were made for the design which was patented both in Great Britain and overseas, but one cannot help thinking that perhaps the project was an example of misdirected ingenuity.

If the power unit was revolutionary there was nothing very exciting about the cycle to which it was fitted - an absolutely conventional diamond-frame machine with 26 x 2 inch tyres, aluminium foot-boards, the ubiquitous Brampton Bi-Flex forks and the all-too-common stirrup front and belt-rim rear braking system. Transmission was by chain and belt through a two-speed Sturmey Archer box with clutch and kick-start. Impressive, if not exactly elegant, was the length of flexible metallic tube which swept down from the exhaust port, behind the magneto, underneath the right-side foot board and into a transverse cylindrical expansion box in front of the crank case.

Tested on a short run and pulling a 4.1 to 1 top gear *The Motorcycle* reported little else than that it pulled well and that the valve gear was 'extremely silent in action'.

There has of necessity been a limit to the amount of research I can devote to any one make and I have failed to establish by whom the machine was actually manufactured, but in 1921 it was being advertised, now as the GRI by Macrae and Dick of Inverness who described themselves as Sole Distributors. The gear lever was now on the seat tube, not alongside the tank, and two models, a 349cc with two speeds and a 500cc with three-speeds were offered at 75 guineas and 90 guineas respectively.

These prices can hardly be described as excessive, but even with the implied petrol consumption of '150 mpg and over' the climate was not right for the wide spread acceptance of any such revolutionary ideas. The machine never found its way into the *Buyer's Guide* or into *Fletchers* so probably the venture was short-lived.

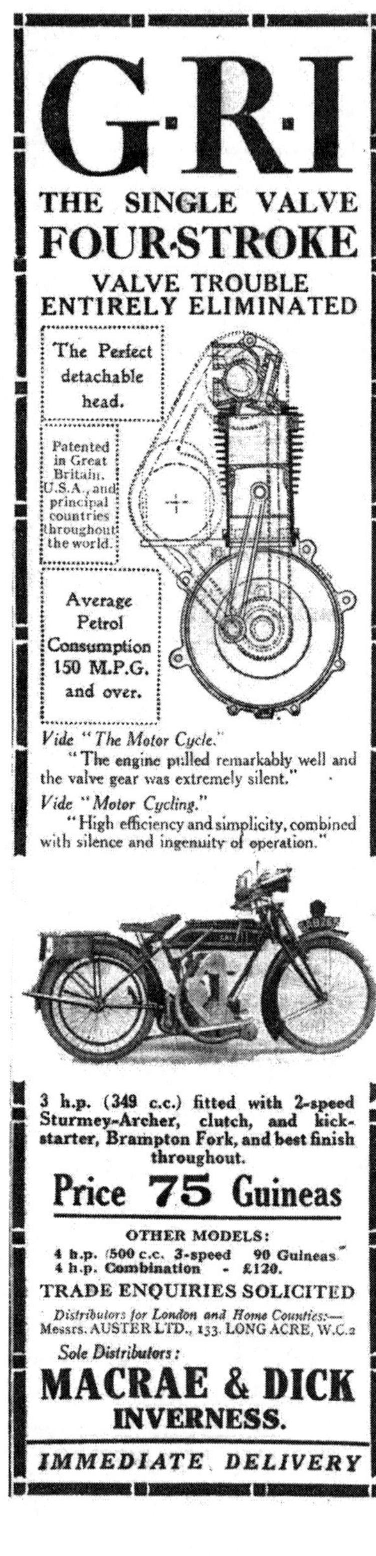

HACK

The Hack Engineering Co Ltd of Victoria Road, Hendon, London, NW did not enter the scooter field until most of the other manufacturers of these doubtful little machines had thrown in the sponge or were about to do so, since the Hack was not introduced until mid 1921.

If the manufacturers had learned anything from the shortcomings of those who had gone before there was little about the Hack in its production form to reflect it, save that the wheels, or rather the tyres were slightly larger than usual for this type of machine, having a diameter of 20 inches. The general construction can most easily be likened to that of a ladies cycle with an unusually long handlebar stem, a platform in place of the bottom bracket and upswept chain stays. At the bottom of the seat tube was the engine which drove the rear wheel by chain through a multi-plate clutch. There was only one gear and petroil was carried in a tank over the rear wheel.

In general the Hack did not vary much during the time it was in production although from year to year there are odd inconsistencies in the published details of the two-stroke engine. The 1922 model was said to be powered by a Hack engine with a bore and stoke of 52 x 52mm. Assuming this to be correct the capacity would have been slightly over 110cc and not 103cc as was quoted. The same particulars were given for 1923, but in 1924 the engine was described as a 'Simplex'. The capacity was still given as 103cc although the bore and stroke were now 51 x 51mm (104cc!).

The Hack engine of 1921. (Photo: Mortons Media Group Archives)

Forks and Steering Dampers

With the exception of some of the larger manufacturers, most companies bought in items from specialists to fit their own designs of machine. Carburettors, magnetos, seats, and forks were examples of these. Lucas, Bosch or Miller were prominent makers of electrical items, including magnetos. Similarly, Binks, Amac, and Senspray made carburettors, whilst Leckie, Brooks, and Lycett made saddles. Of course there were many others involved in this trade, as well as in the production of cables, wheels, tyres, carbide lights, oil pumps, speedometers, spark plugs and so on. Competition was fierce as to who would become the supplier of these items to the manufacturers.

In a similar fashion the front fork was a complicated object to design and manufacture, so it is not surprising that just a few firms became dominant with their products. Some fork makers such as Saxon believed that a rocking action would achieve best results, with the wheel going backwards and forwards so as to absorb the bumps in the road. Bramptons, with their Bi-Flex action combined up and down movement with a rocking action. Druid forks, made by Drew and Company, had springs at the side of the forks and simply went up and down. Other makers such as Webbs or Castle produced very successful versions of girder fork that were developed through racing and competitions throughout the period. There were also some innovative ideas that defied convention by using, for instance leaf, or coil springs, centre hub steering and swinging arm suspension.

Importantly on vintage machines, most of which had the magneto in a prominent forward position, mudguarding was seen as very important. The rain water could easily be

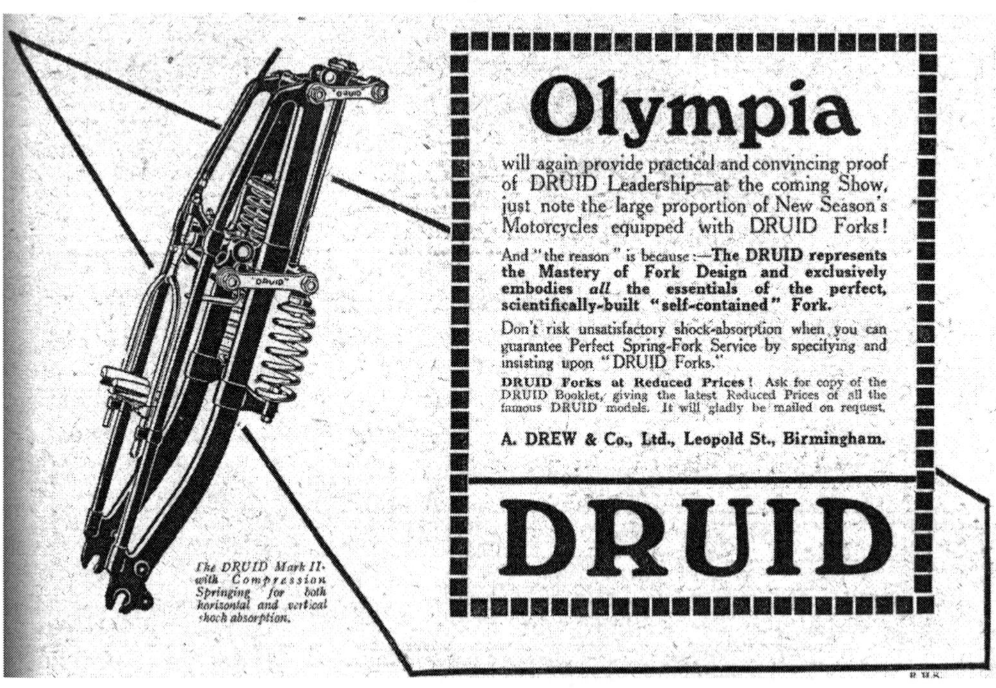

channelled straight from the front wheel into the magneto unless it was adequately protected. In the twenties the practicality of good mudguards overcame the aesthetic appeal of slimmer but less enveloping versions, although in particularly muddy locations, there was still the problem of clogging under the large valanced mudguards of touring or colonial machines.

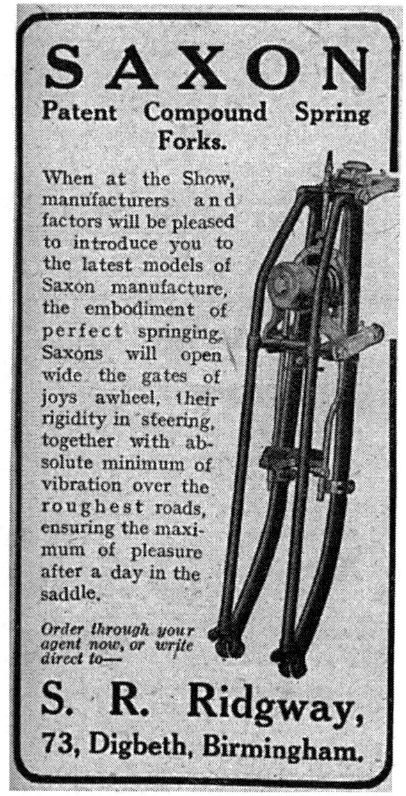

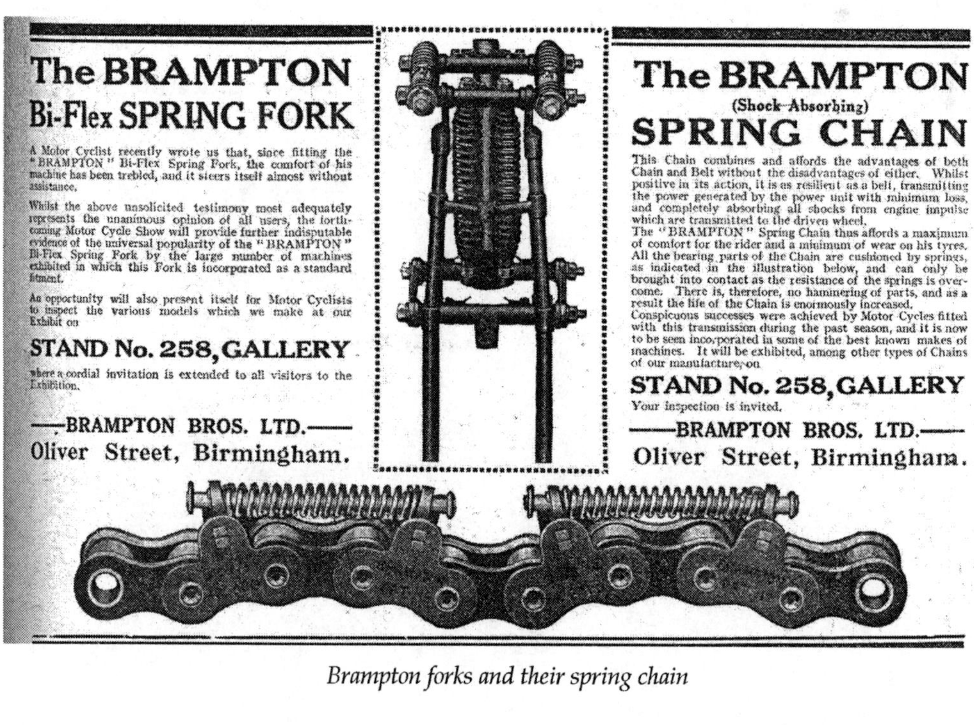

Brampton forks and their spring chain

Steering Dampers

In the early twenties the need for some form of steering damping became increasingly apparent. Some speedmen would even take out the lower row of ball bearings from the steering head and replace them with a ring of brass. In general motorcycle manufacturers were slow to standardise steering dampers fearing, no doubt, that to do so was an admission that handling was not all that it should have been. And so there appeared on the market proprietary steering dampers, the best known of which was probably the Andre.

For many years, those who were impecunious made their own with the material used for friction discs usually being plywood. In an old advertisement for Andre dampers their discs were claimed to be made of 'Aryuto wood'. I was intrigued and decided to try to find out more about this material, but a search through all the woodwork books at my disposal failed to reveal any mention of the stuff, let alone its origin and peculiar qualities.

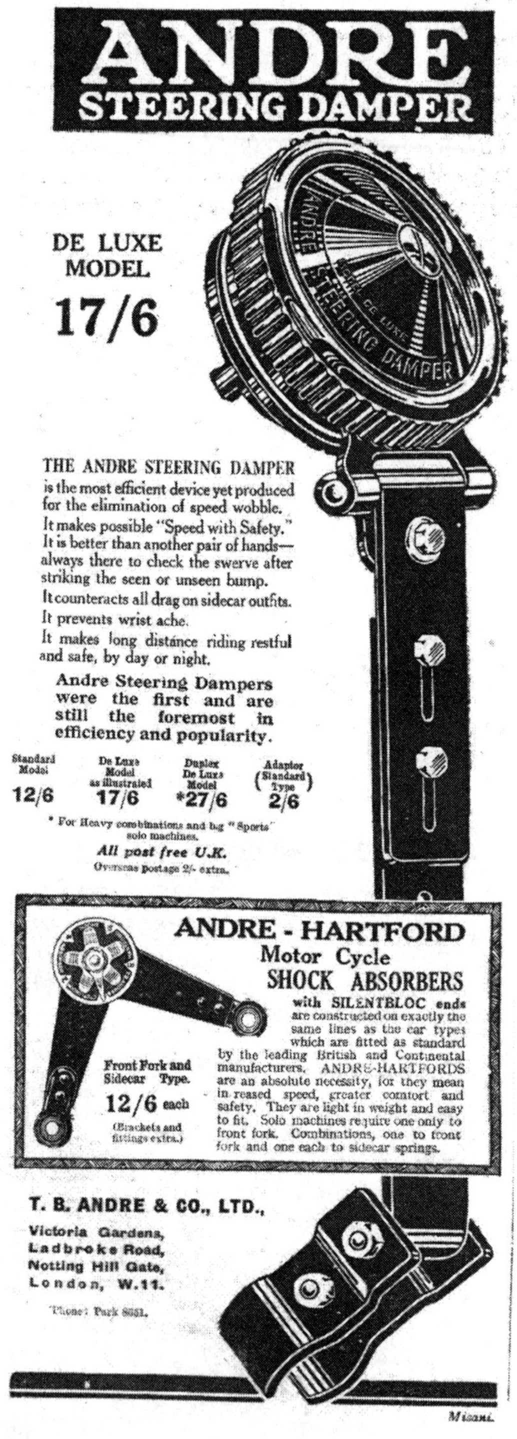

HARPER THREE-WHEELER

During the period 1922-1924 the Harper Runabout was marketed by the firm of RH Carlisle, 188 and 205 Deansgate, Manchester. Since their telegraphic address was 'Daracqrs' they were obviously motor car dealers of some importance.

'Not a camouflaged motorcycle and nothing like a scooter.... A real car de luxe but miniature in size..... Can be garaged in your hall' were the terms in which its sponsors described it at the time.

It was the creation of RO Harper who claimed twenty years' experience in the design and manufacture of leading makes of cars and it was produced under his supervision. From stem to stern the little vehicle owed nothing to convention, every feature was well thought out and construction was extremely sturdy. The rider or driver sat on a seat with a back-rest, his or her legs protected by the body-work which was framed up with ash and hickory clad with aluminium

Harper Runabout. (Photo:VMCC)

panels. Frontal protection was provided by an upswept extension of the front wheel cowling and by the windscreen. The windscreen was attached to a handlebar at the top of a steering column which was connected by linkage to the front wheel. This wheel was carried between a pair of quarter-elliptic leaf springs. A pillion seat for a passenger was augmented by a foot-rest which could also be used as a jacking point.

The 2½ hp engine, a 70 x 70mm, 269cc Villiers two-stroke with flywheel magneto and special Harper-designed cylinder, was mounted outside the body on the off-side. The carburettor, initially a special Zenith and controlled by both a hand lever and a foot accelerator, was fed with petrol from a tank beneath the seat. Starting was by means of a hand lever which could be operated from the driving position.

Drive was taken from the crankshaft to a transverse countershaft through a foot operated fabric-lined clutch. On the countershaft were three 'loose' sprockets. Locking any sprocket to the shaft by means of the gate-change gear lever selected any one of three-speeds for each sprocket which in turn was connected by roller chain to a corresponding sprocket permanently locked to the 'live' back axle. Sprocket diameters were of course worked out to provide the correct gear ratios, bottom being low enough to 'climb any hill'. The whole transmission system was totally enclosed.

The axle, also mounted on two quarter-elliptic leaf springs carried discs on which the hand and the foot brakes operated. Wherever applicable a single size of Hoffman journal ball races were used. Disc wheels, which were fully interchangeable, had detachable rims with 18 x 2 ¼ inch tyres. Wheelbase was 60 inches and track 33 inches. Standard equipment included a gas lighting set with large generator, waterproof apron and tools.

During 1922 and under ACU observation, RO Harper on a standard model but with an additional electric lighting set, covered 42½ miles in one hour at Brooklands - almost sixteen circuits - with a fastest lap of 43.16mph. The all-up weight which included spare wheel, tools and even a spare can of petrol was no less than 534lbs.

The foregoing particulars apply to the 1923 model. For 1924 certain slight alterations were made including a modification to the speedometer drive in such a manner that a spur gear attached to the end of the cable engaged with one of the countershaft sprockets. The compression release was now inter-connected with the starting lever and the carburettor had been changed to an Amac.

The price, although reduced from £100 to £80 17s 0d was still too expensive for the attractive little machine to be a commercial success.

HOSKISON

A feeling of complete inadequacy comes over me when I attempt to describe some of the lightweights of the early twenties, so devoid were they of individuality. Such a machine was the Hoskison as it appeared for 1920. Even *The Trader* in writing it up was forced to the conclusion 'There are no startling departures from what may be regarded as standard practice'.

The engine was the ubiquitous 292cc Union two-stroke with magneto coupled directly to the right hand side of the crankshaft. A B and B carburettor was fed via a long and rather vulnerable pipe since the petrol tap was at the very rear of the 1¾ gallon tank - presumably in the hope that fuel starvation would not occur when going uphill. There was the usual transverse expansion box in front of the crankcase, but the tail pipe with a slightly flattened end only extended to a point just beyond the right side footrest.

'The power of the engine' continued *The Trader*, 'is conveyed by an enclosed roller chain to a Burman two-speed gearbox combined with which is a handlebar controlled clutch, and a kick-starter'. No mention was made of the fact that the gear gate was mounted on the side of the tank in such a position that it could not fail to foul the rider's knee. Final drive was by belt and the ratios were approximately 5 and 10 to 1.

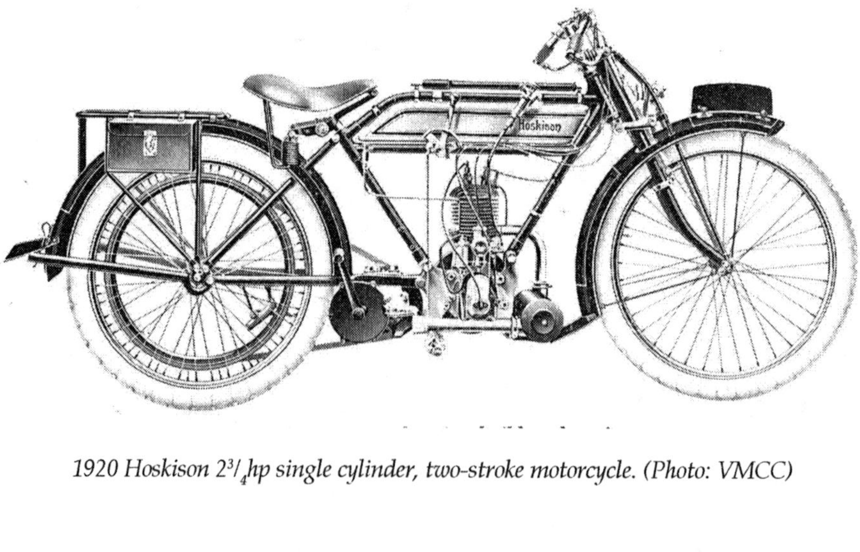

1920 Hoskison 2$^{3}/_{4}$hp single cylinder, two-stroke motorcycle. (Photo: VMCC)

Front suspension was by Saxon forks incorporating Terry spring links. Braking followed the usual pattern - a stirrup on the front rim and an external block on the belt rim. Mention was made of a low riding position but in fact, the saddle top was 31 or 32 inches from the ground which was the norm for the period.

The mudguards were 7 inches wide and these were decorated with thin lines of a contrasting colour in the manner beloved by builders of farm wagons, a form of adornment still indiscriminately practiced by some over-enthusiastic restorers of vintage machines.

The price, early in 1920, was 65 guineas, but by the beginning of March it had increased to 75 guineas and Hoskison Motors Ltd, 72 Lozells Road, Birmingham, regretted that no more orders could be taken for the time being. However, a month later the manufacturers were 'pleased to be able to announce improved deliveries', although no new agencies could be entertained.

As was the case with many small assemblers, Hoskison, having entered the field with a lightweight, soon turned their attention to more powerful machines and the 1921 models were offered fitted with larger four-stroke engines. The firm announced their intention of concentrating on these types, making much of the point that the 4hp and the 2¾hp versions were individually designed, not the same frame with a choice of two different engines.

Whilst at the time their appearance was described as 'rakish' they were somewhat unattractive machines. The oil plumbing was untidy, the exhaust pipe looked like the work of a none too cunning snake charmer, the saddle stuck out like the proverbial sore thumb and a dummy belt rim front brake never did much to enhance the image of any motorcycle. Features of these models were wedge tanks, vertical leaf spring saddle mounting and extremely wide mudguards. Each model had chain-belt transmission and Burman kick-starter boxes.

The 4hp was powered by the 499cc side-valve Blackburne engine with the usual outside flywheel and detachable head. Mechanical lubrication was by Best and Lloyd pump. A conflict of evidence exists as to the number of speeds. One contemporary report says three, but *Fletchers* and the 1921 *Buyers Guide* say two. It is rather curious that the 4hp at 175lbs was lighter than the 2¾hp (187lbs).

The 2¾hp used the 349cc Blackburne engine and a two-speed box, and it had 'disc' wheels. It was reported that both brake rims were practically the same size thus giving uniform retarding effect (ignoring the fact that one brake was applied by a foot pedal and the other by a handlebar lever!) Footboards, as on the 4hp were standard but a sporting model with footrests was also displayed at the 1920 Show. Also exhibited was the Union engined two-stroke, but such information as I have is divided as to whether or not it was in fact available for 1921.

Business, however, cannot have been very satisfactory for in 1921 on the 15th June a Mr FJ Cook was appointed receiver. During the following August it was announced that CS Spring of 24-52 Wilton Street, Aston, Birmingham, had purchased the stock of Hoskison Motors and intended to resume production of the 2¾hp model. The make however did not appear at the 1921 show, nor does it figure in the 1922 *Buyers Guide*.

Fletchers lists it as having been available in 1922, but with no prices given and for 1923 contains the laconic note 'So far as our information goes this Cycle is not being manufactured'. At the time that Hoskison Motors Ltd, were operating, there was another Birmingham concern call Hoskison Manufacturing Co Ltd, 20 Digbeth, Birmingham, specialists in 'Own Transfer' pedal cycles.

HP

Surrey provided a number of makes of three-wheeler; none really caught on, but one which deserved to do so was the HP built by Holton Pacey Motors, Broad School Lane, Woking. It was introduced at the 1926 Olympia Show where it was one of the few makes of tricar exhibited, and was enthusiastically received.

The two main chassis members were of ash. To the front end of these were bolted and clamped a pair of quarter elliptical springs which carried a simple front axle with direct steering for the spoked wheels. Behind a dummy radiator was the engine and behind this was the gearbox. The two units were mounted in a steel auxiliary sub-assembly. A pair of steel members ran back from this sub-frame to carry the rear wheel. There was no rear springing, it was considered that 700 x 80mm tyres and well-sprung seat cushions would compensate for this omission.

[Reproduced by kind permission of "The Light Car & Cycle-Car."]

PRINCIPAL DIMENSIONS.

Length Over All	11ft. 1in.
Wheelbase	6ft. 6in.
Width Over All	4ft. 8½in.
Track	3ft. 10in.
Weight Unladen	400lbs.

PERFORMANCE
and other details.

Speed	42 m.p.h.
Consumption—	
Petrol	65 m.p.g.
Oil	800 m.p.g.
Tax	£4 per annum.

PRICE with horn and licence holder but without lighting £65.

HP three-wheeler. (Photo VMCC)

There were two brakes, both on the rear wheel. One was an internal expanding brake of seven inches diameter applied by a pedal, the other was a band brake which operated on a dummy belt rim.

The engine was a 490cc side-valve JAP with mechanical lubrication. There was the choice of Binks or Amac carburettors with controls on the steering wheel, which of course had a minimum of movement. The silencer was well thought out. It was nearly 30 inches long and 6 inches in diameter at one point.

Some confusion exists as to the three-speed gearbox. One report describes it as a Sturmey Archer and another as of JAP manufacture under Sturmey Archer licence. The specification mentions hand starting, but a contemporary illustration shows what is clearly a kick-start pedal on the right-hand side. The clutch was foot operated. Transmission would appear to have followed motorcycle practice with a primary and a final chain

The two seater body, with no doors, had a pointed tail. This was framed up with ash and clad in fabric-covered plywood. In the tail was a locker and in the dashboard was a useful cubbyhole - but not much else. Other equipment included a three gallon tank (claimed to provide a range of over 200 miles) and a hood.

Despite the absence of any lighting there should have been a sale for this jolly little vehicle at £65, but little more was ever heard of it. It is difficult to look at a sketch of the chassis without feeling the urge to knock one up - perhaps potential customers at the time felt the same way!

HRD

Howard Davies was a successful motorcycle racer, winning the TT for AJS in 1921. By 1924 he became convinced that he could build a good machine by himself. Davies produced a 500 cc JAP engined machine for the 1924 Show which caused a sensation because it was the first machine to have a saddle tank. Production continued until 1928, with many racing successes along the way, but eventually HRD's became too expensive to produce, and the company was bought by an Australian named Phil Vincent, who moved to Stevenage where the machines became known as the Vincent-HRD.

Further Reading;

Vincent, David Wright, Crowood Press

Vincent HRD, Roy Harper, 1975, Vincent Publishing

1924 HRD

HUMBER

Humber Ltd, of Coventry who were also manufacturers of cars and bicycles, produced motorcycles of straightforward design, sound construction and superlative finish. Bearing in mind that during the period 1920-1930 there was only one year when engines of more than one capacity were available and that prices tended to be on the high side, the marque enjoyed a steady share of the market. The firm advertised extensively in the press, but unfortunately the matter contained in these advertisements was usually vague and did not give the sort of information the prospective buyer was likely to require, or which would have made my task an easier one.

1920-22

From 1920 until 1922 only 600cc horizontally opposed twin cylinder side-valve engined models were available. The wisdom of this policy is, in retrospect, questionable. The flat twin was not everybody's cup of tea; for solo use a 4½hp was somewhat powerful whilst the out-and-out sidecar man was not usually satisfied with anything less than an 'eight horse'.

1919 Humber flat twin

Humber. (Photo: VMCC)

These engines which varied but little during their currency, had a bore and stroke of 75 x 68mm and would have been described as over square in more recent times. The valves were arranged along the topsides of the cylinders and the valve pockets were detachable. A common induction pipe connected the two inlet ports and this was fed by an up-draught carburettor, usually a Claudel-Hobson. The air intake was sometimes extended in such a manner that the air was warmed by the rear cylinder. A mechanised pump, supplemented by a hand pump, kept the sump topped up. As was usual for this type of engine there was an outside flywheel on the left-hand side.

The engine was mounted on a duplex cradle and immediately beneath the rear cylinder sat the three-speed gearbox of Humber's own manufacture. It was of sound if somewhat agricultural construction and incorporated an enclosed kick-starter quadrant. The clutch which employed a quick-thread operating mechanism was of the multi-plate, multi-spring type and relied more on spring pressure than friction area to make it grip. An almost identical box was still in use on the last Humber to be made. Transmission as on all models for the period under review was all-chain, usually incorporating a shock absorbing rear sprocket.

Oil was carried in a horizontal cylindrical compartment let into the front part of the petrol tank. The right-hand end of this compartment was extended outwards to accommodate the oil filler-cap and the hand pump.

A dummy belt rim (with an exceptionally large block) was fitted to the rear wheel but the front wheel had to be content with a simple stirrup brake. Front forks were of Druid type with side springs.

For 1920 there was only one model which had footboards and touring handlebars. The weight was given as 290lbs, and the price £130. Came 1921 and two versions were available, a touring model with footboards and 'sit up and beg' bars, and a

TT style with footrests and dropped bars. The price in each case was £140 with 'all-weather' finish optional.

Whilst for 1922 the touring model remained much as before, the price had come down drastically to £119. By now it must have dawned on Humber Ltd that it takes more than dropped handlebars to make a sports machine and a new sporting model was introduced. It was initially said to have been timed at 75mph on the road but subsequent advertising modified this claim to 'upwards of 70mph'. This model had aluminium pistons, modified cams and a raised compression ratio. Each cylinder had its own straight-through exhaust pipe, both of which were brought out on the left-hand side where they ran for some of their length parallel and neatly clipped together.

An innovation on the Sports was that the saddle mounting gave a lower riding position. When first introduced a Brooks racing saddle was fixed direct to the frame, but the mounting appears to have altered slightly on the subsequent production models. To allow more room for the rider's knee, the gear lever and quadrant (and consequently the oil compartment) were brought further forward.

Either to increase the sporting appeal, reduce weight to 235lbs., or to bring the price down to £199, the tyre size was 26 x 2¼ inches (as compared with 26 x 2½ inches), mud guarding was minimal and the transmission shock-absorber was omitted. Originally chain guards were to have been dispensed with, but this does not appear to have been the case.

For this year electric lighting, with enclosed dynamo drive, and also the then popular Brooks Cantilever saddle were optional extras. All-black finish could still be supplied at no extra cost.

1923-26

1923 was the last year of production for the flat twins, listed at £99 and £89 for the Touring and Sports respectively and a 349cc single cylinder side-valve model was introduced. It was to change but little for some years to come. The dimensions were 75 x 79mm, an unusual combination probably adopted because it was expedient to use the same bore size as on the twin

The engine was simplicity itself with the crankshaft running on plain bearings. There were two separate cam wheels and these operated rectangular-footed tappets without cam levers. The tappets could not rotate and so valve clearance adjustment did not necessitate juggling with three spanners. Unfortunately, the exhaust valve lifter assembly looked like the work of a well-meaning amateur mechanic. A good feature was that the magneto, a 'round type' ML chain driven from the timing side, was placed out of harms way behind the cylinder. To clear it the Amac carburettor was mounted on a long induction pipe.

Chain guarding was close to total enclosure. On the primary chain guard was a cover which could be removed to reveal the clutch. It would have been really useful had it been a little larger so that its removal allowed the clutch to be dismantled. The tank, of pleasing wedge shape, retained the cylindrical oil compartment feature, but the extension to carry the hand pump and drip feed was now on the left-hand side.

The front forks were Druid with side springs; the front wheel had a minute internal expanding brake; the front guard had useful side valances and a front stand was provided. Neatly filling up the space between the seat tube and the rear guard was a tool box. A clumsy belt-rim brake with parallel wedge action was fitted to the rear wheel.

Designated the 2¾ hp Lightweight the model got off to a good start by winning the 350cc Team Prize in the 1923 ACU Six Days Trial. If the weight of 200lbs, as given in the *Buyers Guide* is correct, it must have been appreciably lighter than its successors.

A virtually unchanged machine remained the sole plank in the 1924 programme and was offered at £55, £55 7s 0d or £64. The main differences between the various versions were the shapes of the handlebars and whether there were foot-rests or foot-boards.

The most noticeable change for 1925 was that a tank of conventional construction was now standard. This modification probably crept in during the 1924 season. For the first time, as far as the 350 was concerned a sidecar was offered although no special lugs were incorporated in the standard machine for its attachment. Basically there were two models, the 'Six Days Sports' with 26 x 2¼ inch tyres and 4½ inch ground clearance (also available in Touring form) and the 'De Luxe Sports' (650 x 65 tyres and 4½ inch ground clearance), slightly lower geared, and which also appeared in Touring guise. The De Luxe model had extra-wide guards. Prices ranged from £47 10s 0d to £50 7s 6d.

Since 1926 was, as things turned out, a mini-depression year it was perhaps fortunate that Humber, who had for all practical purposes but one machine to offer, made no secret of the fact and came on to the market with a one-model programme. The machine was the Six Days Sports. At £48 and at a time when a 500cc side-valve could be bought for appreciably less, it was one of the most expensive machines in its class.

There were one or two departures from the previous practice, notably the adoption of Bi-Flex type forks and wired edge tyres. The latter innovation was a bold one since many riders of that period were prepared to put up with the disadvantage of the beaded edge tyre on account of the ease with which it could be removed and refitted. Less obvious was the introduction of grease nipples, stronger valve springs and an improved rear brake. Conservatively hand-pump lubrication was retained.

1927-30

In order 'to meet the requirements of the large body of riders who desire a speedier machine', the 349cc OHV Sports was brought out for 1927. The bore and stroke were the same as those hitherto employed. In fact the bottom half of the engine was almost identical to that of its side-valve counterpart which in turn differed little from its predecessor except that in either case a neat oil pump was now driven by an extension to the exhaust cam spindle.

1928 Humber 350 OHV. (Photo: VMCC)

Stout cast iron pillars were let into the cylinder head to carry the rockers. The top half of each bearing assembly consisted of a bronze cap fixed by four studs. The caps could be rubbed down in order to take up slack when wear developed. Each support embodied an ample recess to retain grease. An unusual feature on an otherwise straightforward engine was that the exhaust port discharged into a curious cast angle box to which the exhaust pipe was in turn attached. The silencer was finished in black and reduced in diameter towards the rear. It terminated with a longish tail pipe and a small fish tail. With a low riding position and rear guard devoid of carrier it was as pretty a bike as most and reasonably priced at £51 10s 0d.

A *Motorcycle* staff man who bought one for his personal use had little but praise for it. Tested by *The Motorcycle*, 90mpg and a cautious 70mph were recorded. Minor criticisms included engine vibration at certain speeds and heavy clutch operation, but generally the machine seems to have been most satisfactory.

Its Six Days success having become ancient history, the side-valve model was now called the Side-valve Sports and was still expensive at £46 10s 0d.

Both side-valve and overhead valve models now had internal expanding brakes of useful size, 6 inch front and 7 inch rear; Brampton centre spring forks with friction dampers; adjustable bars and B and B carburettors. The same rustic design of gearbox was retained with overall ratios of 6, 9 and 18.5 to 1 (SV) and 5.64, 7.75 and 11.59 to 1 (OHV).

When the 1928 programme was revealed it was apparent that the Side-valve Sports had scarcely altered at all. The OHV now had a saddle tank, black with blue panels, and a detachable carrier. The push-rods had enclosed return springs (which modification would appear to have come into effect during the 1927 season), there was a support from a point high on the engine to the front down tube, and the shape of the exhaust pipe had been altered. The silencer was now cylindrical and plated, with a tail pipe, the extreme end of which was cut off obliquely.

The sight feed was attached near the bottom of the left-hand side of the tank so that oil could flow by gravity all the way to the mechanical pump.

Possibly bottom gear had been found too high for some users and wide ratios were now optional.

A similar frame housed a new 349cc (75 x 79mm) OHC engine which must have been one of the first such units offered to the public with twin exhaust ports. The exhaust pipes were secured to the head by union nuts of the type which had, or were intended to be manipulated with a 'C' spanner.

The camshaft vertical drive shaft ran at engine speed with a reduction taking place in the cam box which was rendered somewhat bulky in consequence. Part and parcel of the cam shaft enclosure was a mechanical oil pump with integral flow adjuster. Two outlet pipes led to the camshaft gear and the crankcase respectively. Surplus oil from the former ran down the drive shaft tube to lubricate the lower bevels. It is indeed droll to note that such an outwardly sophisticated motor ran on plain main bearings and had no direct supply of oil to the big-end bearing.

There is little evidence that the OHC was appreciably faster than the OHV machines. Prices for 1928 were £46 10s 0d, £51 10s 0d and £60 in the order described.

Humber tank decoration had always tended to be restrained but the 1929 models had their tanks adorned in a most flamboyant manner. 'Humber' appeared in

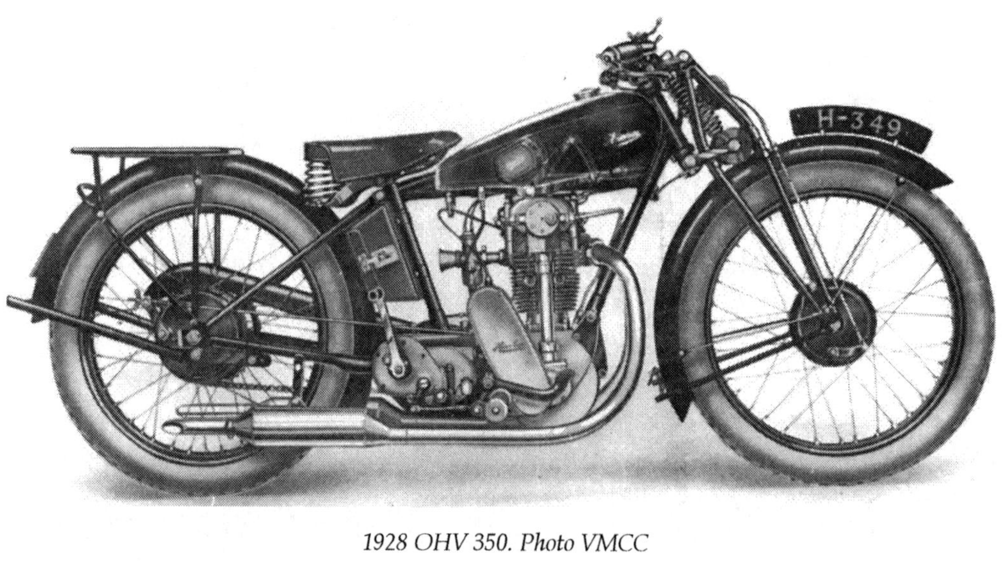

1928 OHV 350. Photo VMCC

blue on a silver panel which was flanked by a flash of lightning. The OHC had a new cradle frame but the most striking difference from the 1928 model was that the silencers now sloped upwards slightly giving a particularly rakish appearance. The side-valve model, still pricey at £48 10s 0d, used the same frame as its push-rod counterpart.

A novelty on the OHV and OHC but one which the manufacturers never bothered to publicise was that by a single flip of the operating toggle the steering damper could be brought into or taken out of action. For 1929 the push-rod model had the exhaust pipe flange-fitted directly to the cylinder head. Dispensing with the previously mentioned cast angle exhaust box considerably enhanced the appearance although the necessary new exhaust pipe must have provided the works 'snake charmers' with a headache since it was made up in three pieces.

At about this time both the OHV and the OHC models had the cylinder head holding-down bolts threaded not directly into the cylinder casting, but into (theoretically) easily removable cylindrical bosses inserted from outside the barrel. Any advantage which might have been afforded by this technique was negated by the fact that since the bolts were of a puny $^{5}/_{16}$th inch diameter and engaged with a mere half-inch or so of thread they stripped all too easily. Fortunately, this defect could be easily overcome even if the means of doing so seemed somewhat drastic.

At £48 10s 0d the push rod model was an excellent buy. Compared with, for instance, the corresponding Levis, steering and road-holding were in no way inferior. The Humber was a fast but perhaps not quite as lively mount, and

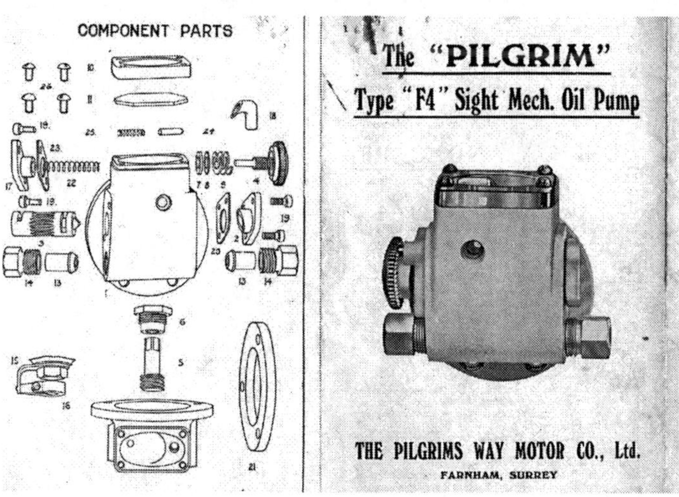

SPECIFICATION.

Part No.	Name	Price s.	d.
F 4	Body	6	0
2	End Cam	1	0
3	Plunger	3	0
4	Control Spindle	1	6
5	Driving Worm	1	6
6	Bush	0	9
7	Fibre Washer	0	1
8	Steel Washer	0	1
9	Spring Washer	0	1
10	Window Frame	1	0
11	Window	0	2
13	Nipple	0	3
14	Gland for Nipple	0	3
15	Driving Dog	0	2
16	Driven Dog	0	6
17	End Plate	0	6
18	Beak	0	3
19	Cam and End Plate Screw ...	0	1
20	Cam Washer	0	1
21	Distance Piece	2	0
22	Spring	0	3
23	End Plate Washer	0	1
24	Rachet	0	0½
25	Rachet Spring	0	0½
26	Frame Screw	0	0½

The Pilgrim oil pump

although the gear-change was inferior to that of the Levis the box itself was much more robust.

The SV, OHV and OHC appeared in much the same form for 1930 but the tank transfer was less elaborate, 'HUMBER' was now in block capitals instead of in the traditional cursive style, and Pilgrim sight feed oil pumps were adopted.

At £56 the OHC (or OCS as the makers were wont to call it) was the cheapest 'camshaft' on the market. A stay from the cylinder head to the front down tube cited in the press as an innovation, was in fact already established practice. A detail in which this model differed from its stable-mates was that rear chain adjustment was by means of 'push-studs' as distinct to adjusters of the pedal cycle type.

The OHV now had a degree of enclosure to the valve operating gear and on the side-valve model there was a cast aluminium valve cover.

In January 1930 it was announced that reorganisation of Humber's cycle and motorcycle divisions had been completed in order to expedite production, but times were highly competitive and the machines did not sell. It was no great while before Humber motorcycles were being offered at a vast reduction by a London dealer. After 1930 no more motorcycles were made, the cycle interest was taken over by Raleigh and during the mid-thirties the Humber car became part of what was then the Rootes Group.

Jack Bacon's 1929 OHV 350 Sports, now the property of Adam Mason.

LAD

In 1921 the LAD Manufacturing Company of Lower Bourne, Farnham, Surrey offered the LAD three-wheeler or 'runabout'. The layout, if not the exact construction, can best be likened to a belt-driven side-car outfit in which the driver sat in the 'chair' and steered by means of a long tiller which was an extension of what would normally have been the handlebar.

In single seater form with Villiers two-stroke engine (of unspecified size) and Chater Lea two-speed and kick-start gearbox it was to retail at £78. A speed in excess of 40mph was claimed. A two-seater propelled by a 3½hp Precision two-stroke unit was priced at £98.

The machine certainly seems to have been cheap and simple, but it must surely have been too unconventional to sell in any quantity.

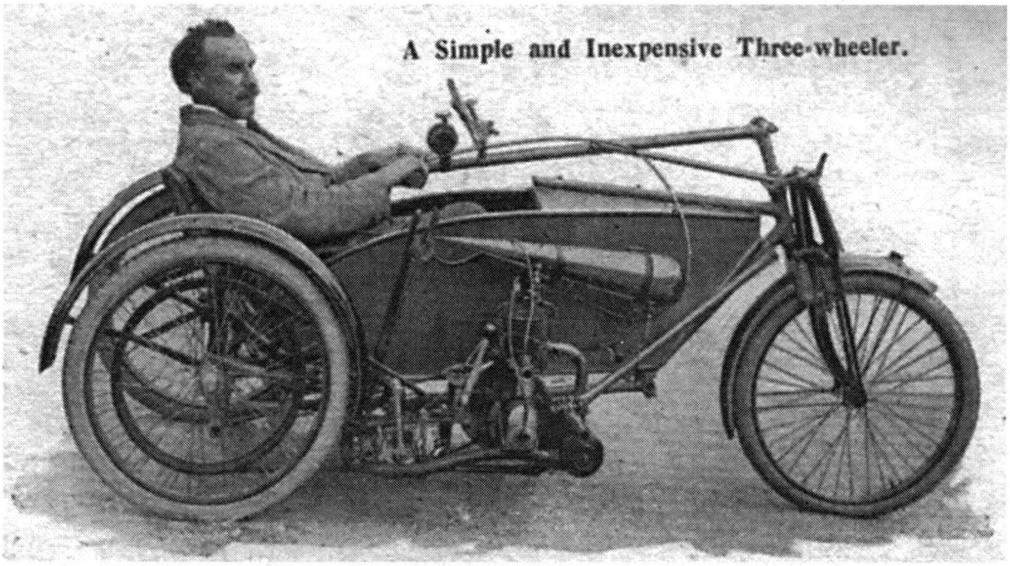

The LAD Runabout

Lighting

Early motor cycles were provided with very basic lighting, either oil or candle powered, designed to be mounted on a spring bracket, and destined to be shaken to pieces, lost or thrown over the nearest hedge in frustration at their lack of usefulness. Acetylene lighting was introduced at the beginning of the century and soon became popular because it produced it produced a white light and threw a good beam. The process of mixing the gas involved a container with two separate compartments, one mounted above the other. The top contained water and the bottom calcium carbide. The idea was that when the water was dripped onto the carbide it reacted and produced a gas which when lit produced a steady white flame. Put in front of a mirror at the correct focal length and protected from the elements behind a glass window, the flame gave out a powerful white light.

Such was the popularity and simplicity of the Acetylene lamp that they were still being made for bicycles in 1939. There were problems of course. They produced a disagreeable smell, and there was a constant need to clean the slaked lime residue from the lower compartment. The Carbide had to be kept dry, the jet burners clean and free from dust. The brightness of the flame was controlled by adjusting the amount of water allowed to

A fly-spattered P&H (Powell and Hammer) headlight

mix with the carbide, and water too could run out. It was all a bit of a messy business, but at the time was about all there was if you wanted to ride at night.

Most motorcycles were sold without any form of lighting, if you wanted to go out in the dark you had to buy the optional extras of lights. Many firms produced their versions of gas lights, but a few, Bosch and CAV, were experimenting with electric lighting. There was much need for movement of vehicles during the hours of darkness in the Kaiser War, and naturally much time was spent on research and development. Dynamos and batteries slowly gained a reputation for inexpensive reliability and do it yourself electric lighting sets were available from the early twenties, although these were still very expensive when put against a gas powered lighting set.

Electric lighting became commonplace on motorcycles after about 1928, although acetylene powered models continued to be catalogued. With the advent of cheap efficient dynamos, often combined with magnetos, it soon became almost universal, and designers treated the lights as an integral part of the design rather than as an add on extra

Further Reading;

Early Vehicle Lighting, Peter Card, 1987, Shire Publications.

Bonniksen Speedometers

On the later Bonniksen speedometers the time dial is calibrated from 1 to 12, as on a clock, and the pointer corresponds to the 'hour' hand when the machine is in motion, thus recording actual running time. The trip dial goes from 1 to 10 and each division equals ten miles. Later instruments usually had a 100mph speed dial, and the hands changed position at 2½ second intervals. For its time the Bonniksen was quite an advanced piece of instrumentation since it relied neither on centrifugal force or magnetic drag, but actually measured the distance traveled in a given time, i.e. 5 or 2½ seconds. Doubtless better grade present-day instruments exist which perform the same function in a less cumbersome manner, but those I have read about which have one hand indicating mph and the other average speed are beyond me - unless they involve the use of 'chips' - hardly likely in the vintage period! There was only one standard set of drive gear ratios, and any compensation for different overall wheel diameters had to be carried out within the instrument itself.

I think that I sold my last Bonniksen for £8 in 1940, complete with one-previous-owner 1928 Model 18 Norton!

The Bonniksen speedometer

Cockpit Trouble

I feel, and I am sure that there are many who will agree, that any reputation the 'Sloper' may have had for 'lying down', was founded on old wives' tales like for instance such myths as 'Scotts were always boiling', or 'Morgans easily overturned'.

I ran a 'Sloper' whilst in the RAF during the war and experienced no such trouble and neither did, as far as I know, the people who borrowed it, and they were numerous, for it was No.2 Station Bike. On the other hand, a 1929 OHV Levis, a model which had a marvelous reputation for handling 'lay down on me' - or 'under me' at least three times for no apparent reason - unless it was on account of what used to be called 'cockpit trouble'!

Cockpit trouble!

LEVIS

Butterfields Ltd, of Stechford, Birmingham, were among the very few motorcycle manufacturers who devised a trade slogan in Latin! Their trade mark (ignoring the jargon of Heraldry) was a shield bearing two crossed feathers. It was surmounted by a coronet and below it was a scroll with the words 'LEVIS ET CELER' meaning 'Light and Swift'. The Levis motorcycles were for a great many years exceedingly light which, rather than anything spectacular in the way of design, was the secret of the moderate degree of speed enjoyed by the production models.

It was claimed that the Levis was the first production air-cooled two-stroke motorcycle. The man who probably had the greatest influence on Levis development was Howard Newey invariably known as Bob. According to a miniature 'This is Your Life' which appeared in *The Motorcycle and Cycle Trader* for 11th June, 1926, Bob started his career with the General Electric Co in 1902. He took an interest in motorcycles at an early age and was one of the pioneer riders of the Midlands.

In 1907 he commenced experiments with two-stroke engines in company with Mr W Butterfield, joining Butterfields Ltd, in that year as Works Manager. He has been described as 'burly and genial' and at a considerably later date he admitted to a press-man that when 'filling in' on the turret lathe the ash and ends of his cigarettes tended to impede the flow of the suds. He was to hold the position of Works Manager for very many years. More recent sources of information which I have no reason to doubt, but which on the other hand I can not confirm, suggest that Bob was a brother-in-law to the brothers Butterfield and that in the early days the firm traded as Hughes Butterfield Bros.

As early as 1913 The Levis supported the TT and during the early twenties they were highly successful. Gradually they became hopelessly outclassed, their last year of any note being 1924 with a fifth and eleventh place in the Lightweight. Levis racing history however need not be recorded here since it has already been ably documented by the late LR Higgins in *Britain's Racing Motor-Cycles.*

Until 1927 Levis production models were all single cylinder two-strokes, the engines of which never had detachable heads or more than a single exhaust port. Petroil was never used for lubrication, there was always a separate piped oil supply. The usual arrangement was to deliver oil through an adjustable drip feed to the cylinder which also lubricated the small end bearing and to the main bearings whence oil passed via a drilled mainshaft to the big-end.

1920-21

During 1914 the Popular was introduced and although a variety of other models were listed for that and for each subsequent year, it was an almost identical machine which constituted the programme for 1920. The 2¼ hp engine had the familiar bore and stroke of 62 x 70mm giving a capacity of 211cc. The magneto was in front of the crankcase with an enclosed chain drive from the right hand side. Originally the magneto had been a UH but an EIC was now standard, as was an Amac carburettor.

The frame was of unusual construction, the top tube attached to the bottom of the steering head. A short tube from a point a few inches from the front of the top tube went up at an angle and supported the top of the steering head. The front down tube took the form of an inverted 'Y' and between the two lower members passed the exhaust pipe on its way to a transverse expansion chamber with a short tail pipe. The divided front tube became a typical Levis feature.

There was no gearbox or countershaft, the drive by ¾ inch belt being taken from a pulley behind the flywheel to the rear belt rim on which the rear brake operated. The brake block did not engage with the groove of the rim but on its convex inner periphery. The front brake was of the stirrup type. Tyres were 24 x 2 inches.

The Tom Davies Trio earned a living in the twenties riding their Levis machines on a Wall of Death

1923 Levis popular at a Bonham's sale

A tool box was built into the back of the rear carrier and opened outwards. Petrol capacity was 1½ gallons and oil was one quart. The saddle height was low for that period - 28 inches and the wheel base 50 inches. Weighing only 115lbs the Popular was one of the lightest machines on the market, yet it gave a comfortable riding position for *The Motorcycle's* tester who stood 'well over six feet'.

130mpg was guaranteed by the makers with 150mpg considered possible with careful handling which is not surprising since 320mpg at over 20mph had been returned under ACU observation over a fifty mile course.

For 1921 tyres were increased in section to 2¼ inches and there was a guard over the top run of the belt. Hitherto 'LEVIS' had appeared on the tank with letters of uniform size but the name now took the form of an oval. The rear brake was modified for this year so that the block entered the 'V' of the belt rim with a wedging action. It was heel operated avoiding the use of any rods or linkage.

A second and otherwise almost identical Sports model had a 67 x 77mm 247cc engine. These were the two models which were shown at Olympia 1920 but a two-speed version of the 211cc model appears to have been listed later in the 1921 season.

1922-24

A six model 1922 programme was introduced using two basic machines, the 211cc 2¼ and the 247cc 2½. The Popular continued in its single speed form. Equipped with a two-speed and clutch gearbox it became the 'S' and if (for an additional £2) a kick-starter was specified, the model was known as the SKS.

The 247cc engine now appeared in a much prettier frame with a sloping top-tube and a slightly tapered tank. Single speed, two-speed with clutch, and two-speed, kick-start variants were designated G2 and G2KS respectively. Throughout the range final drive was by belt, and gearboxes, when fitted, were Sturmey Archer.

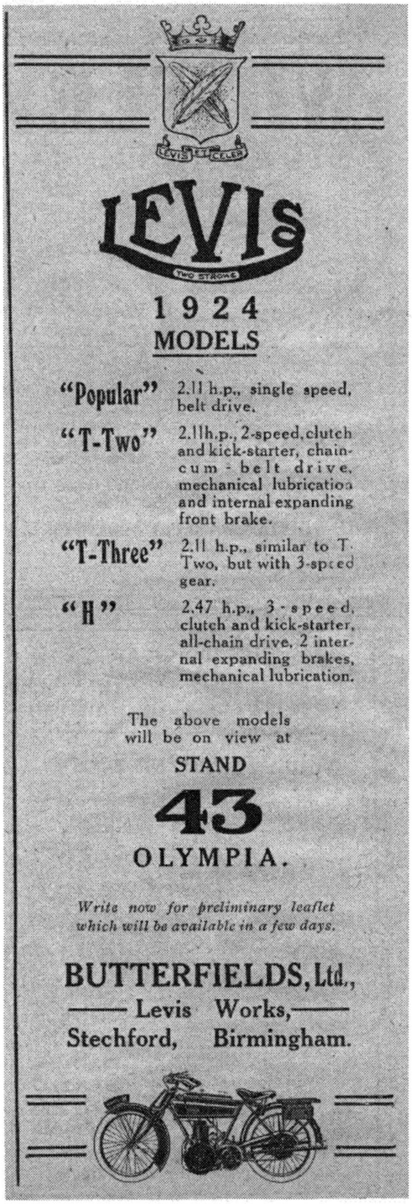

There were only four models for 1923. A substantially unchanged 211cc Popular was further reduced to £33. The other 211cc machines, both with two speeds, kick-starters and belt final drive were the 'S' which approximated to the previous years SKS and the 'T'.

The 'T' however, employed the new frame and had a Burman gearbox. It was at about this time that the manufacturers started to specify either a Burman or a Sturmey Archer gearbox in a quite confusing manner. Either they decided whose box they were going to use by the spin of a coin or else they bought from whichever of the two manufacturers would give them the better deal!

The sole 247cc example was the 'H'. Not only did it have all-chain drive but mechanical lubrication and three-speeds. In this case the gearbox was by Sturmey Archer. The price was a prohibitive £65.

1924-25

1924 models had their magnetos behind the cylinder. It must have been a sign of the times that the expressions 2¼hp and 2½hp were replaced by 2.11 and 2.47hp respectively. The new figures were arrived at by a completely un-realistic ACU Formula which alleged horse-

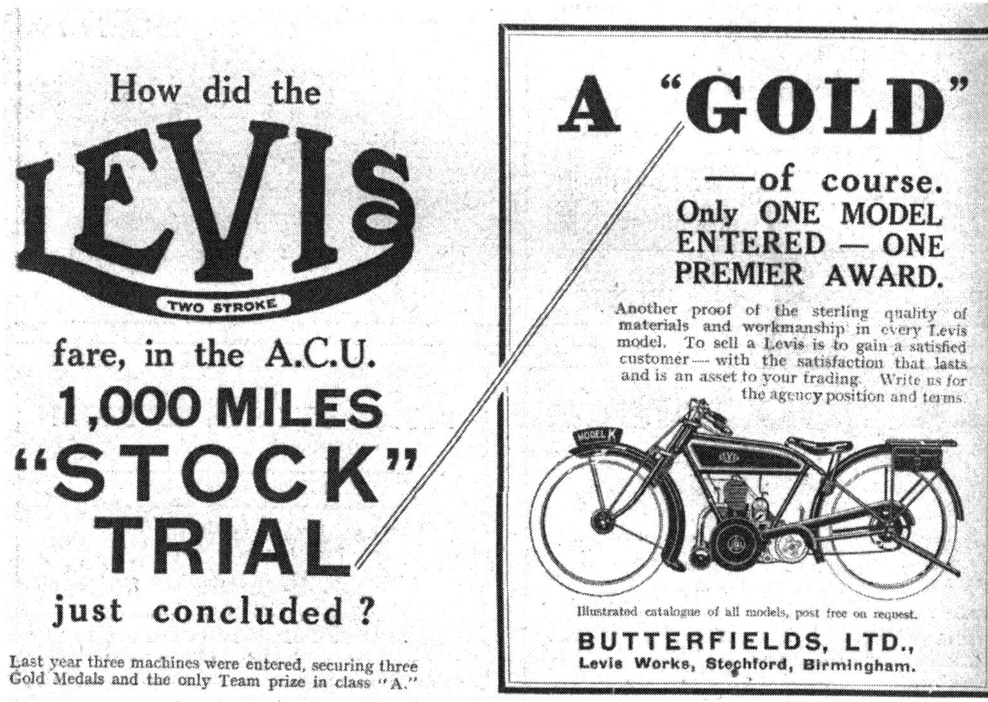

1925 Model 'K'.Photo VMCC

power to be cubic capacity in cc divided by one hundred. Little changed from the previous year, the Popular was one of the few single speed machines remaining on the market.

The 211cc engine, but with mechanical lubrication, was used in two less austere models with in each case internal expanding front brakes, clutch, kick-starter and belt final drive. They were labelled the 'T Two' with two speeds and the 'T Three' with three.

There was only one 247cc example, the Model H. Purchasers must have been ardent Levis fans for at £55 it was as expensive as a high grade 350cc four-stroke. Transmission was all-chain through a Sturmey Archer three-speed gearbox with clutch and kick-starter. Lubrication was by mechanical pump and there were two internal expanding brakes in the rear hub.

During this year if one really wanted to be up-to-date one could buy a three valve or four valve Levis - but it would be a radio receiver! 'Bob' Newey and WS (Stan) Banner are both reported as being extremely keen on wireless. Stan was for a number of years with a firm of patent agents. He joined Butterfields in 1915 as Head of the Spares Department. In 1919 he became Sales Manager, an appointment he held for a very long time.

1925 and the Popular was no more. The range was in fact considerably cut down and the 211cc engine only appeared in the T3 still with belt final drive through a

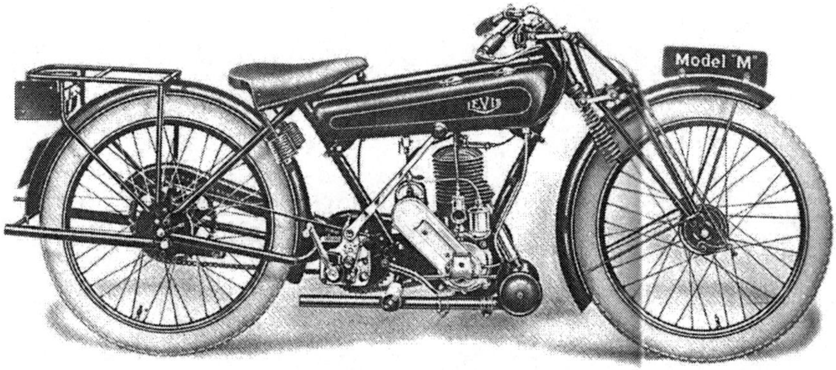

Levis Model 'M'. Photo: VMCC

Sturmey Archer three-speed box. Levis' 1924 'M' had a large rectangular aluminium silencer that formed a sort of under shield for the crankcase.

The Model K (a letter that seemed to have a great attraction for manufacturers of motorcycles) had the 247cc engine, a Burman three-speed box and all-chain drive. There was now a minute internal expanding brake in the front hub and the rear stand was of the spring-up type. The price was down to a realistic £40.19.0. - which looked even more reasonable when quoted as 39gns. A sidecar was now listed for this model and there was also a roomy box sidecar for trade use. Such an outfit took part in the ACU Commercial Sidecar Demonstrations held in July 1925, an event which caused a great deal of interest but which probably did not make a lot of converts. These were the only two models for 1925.

1926-27

The 1926 season opened with what was again a two model programme. The K2 remained at a casual glance unchanged, but a closer examination revealed a 5 inch front brake in place of the 3⁵/₈ inch previously fitted and a 6 inch rear as compared with a 5 inch for 1925. One detail improvement was the provision of a front stand and according to one contemporary report 'ignition was now variable'.

The 211cc engine was abandoned and the T3 was superseded by a 247cc Model M. The engine was similar to that of the 'K' but not identical for a difference in the design of the cylinder casting resulted in a downward sloping exhaust pipe. A three-speed Sturmey Archer gearbox was retained and the tyres were 24 x 2¼ inch as against 26 x 2½ inch otherwise the remainder of the specification closely followed that of the Model K.

During the 1926 season there was introduced what might be described as a Sports version of the K, and designated the Model O. The engine was claimed to be specially tuned. A break-away from tradition and one which probably did more for appearance than it did for efficiency, was the provision of a long plated exhaust

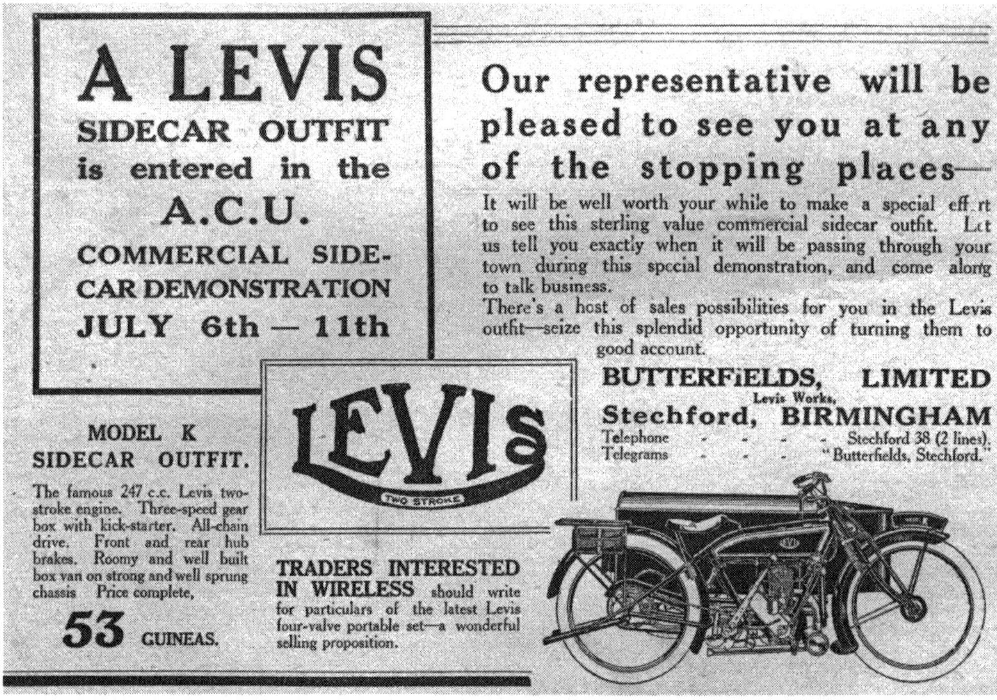

pipe, brought back along the left hand side, sweeping upwards slightly and terminating in a large diamond shaped silencer the tail pipe of which was above rear spindle level and still climbing.

Further to add to a sporting image the carrier was dispensed with and a tool box was now mounted between the seat tube and the rear guard. The front forks were described as being of 'Levis Druid' racing type with round tubes throughout and incorporating friction shock absorbers. A striking combination of yellow and black was employed in the tank finish.

The Model O, if it did not enjoy big sales, marks Butterfields first step towards establishing themselves as manufacturers of sporting motorcycles.

Keen rivalry existed between Levis and Velocette since both were the product of Birmingham factories which had for a number of years concentrated on smaller two-strokes. It was not surprising therefore that when Veloce Ltd, having broken with tradition by entering the four-stroke field, Butterfields should follow suit. Accordingly late in 1926 the Levis Model A was announced and whilst it was not an OHC it certainly looked like one - but was in reality a 350 pushrod OHV!

The Model A and its successors were examples of, (to borrow a phrase from the car world,) 'the triumph of workmanship over design' for such performance as they enjoyed was attributable to meticulous care in the individual assembly of engines rather than to anything revolutionary in their conception. Bore and stroke

1926 model 'O'. Photo: VMCC

were of the text book 70 x 90mm dimensions giving a capacity which it was customary to quote as 346cc

Both pushrods were enclosed in a common tube and there was reasonably effective closure for the overhead rocker gear. Total loss lubrication from a separate oil tank was via a Pilgrim mechanical pump with sight-feed. It was somewhat of a disappointment that the magneto was in front of the crankcase. Gear ratios of 5.5, 9 and 14 to 1 were provided by a Burman box.

The Model A had a conventional diamond frame with a curved top-tube which accommodated a rather pretty non saddle type tank which tapered to nil depth at its rear end. The Terry saddle was attached directly to the frame. A substantially finned union secured the exhaust pipe to the cylinder head. An approximately diamond shaped silencer had a short tail pipe and was plated overall. The front forks were of Druid pattern with side springs and friction dampers. Brakes were of 6 inch diameter and wired edge tyres were 27.2 x 2.75 inches. A good feature was the provision of a 'spring-up' rear stand.

The Model A rarely figured in the 1927 advertising, possibly few were built for that year although examples secured one Gold in the Colmore and two in the Victory - both important Trials in those days. However the mere introduction of the 'A' must have done many OHV owners a useful service since it caused Butterfields to place on the market a handy pair of tweezers for valve collets - price 4d including postage!

The recently introduced 'O' was improved in detail to the extent of having a stiffened frame, and a larger tank, whilst any alteration in the 'K' was difficult to detect. Neither the 'O' nor the 'K' were very widely publicised during the season either. In fact the 1927 sales effort seems to have centred around the Model M now with increased tank capacity, a larger saddle and larger (2½ inch section) tyres. At 28½ guineas it offered value which was difficult to beat. Towards the end of 1927 it was reported that since the Model A first made its appearance it had undergone thorough road and bench tests and that no modifications had been found necessary for 1928 although the design of the oil tank was being changed to give an improved appearance. There was however a further and extremely important alteration - the magneto was now behind the cylinder. At least three further detail points distinguished the 1928 model from its predecessor, the gear lever now worked in the new type Burman 'zig-zag' gate, the top tube was more angular giving a slightly lower saddle mounting and the bottom run of the exhaust pipe was no longer parallel with the ground but curved sufficiently to bring the top of the silencer level with the chain stays. Contemporary illustrations show a plated front brake plate which may or may not have been standard finish, and two different types of oil tank, one of which makes more use of the available space than the other. Gear ratios were now given as 5.25, 8.5 and 13 to 1.

Riding a 346cc OHV Levis, Percy Hunt completed four laps before retiring from the 1928 Junior Amateur Road Race (often incorrectly referred to as the Amateur TT). He covered one lap in 36 minutes 23 seconds, as compared with 35 minutes 20 seconds which was the fastest lap of the day, but his machine differed appreciably from the Model A for it had exposed pushrods wide apart, a saddle tank and centre spring front forks.

Although it was still seldom if ever advertised, a 1928 Model A was submitted to *The Motorcycle* for a road test and the report appeared in the issue dated 19th January, 1928. The tester certainly did not go into raptures about the machine but rather seemed to damn it with faint praise. Definite criticisms concerned the brakes which became inefficient in wet weather, and uncertain steering at speeds of from six to ten miles an hour. Acceleration was 'satisfactory' with a maximum speed of perhaps 65mph.

A statement from the manufacturers which appeared in *The Motorcycle and Cycle Trader* (9th September, 1927) mentions that so great had been the demand for the

1928 Model A. (Photo: VMCC)

two strokes during the 1927 season that it had been impossible to put the Model A seriously into production, and for 1928 the output would of necessity be limited.

1927 Levis Model M engine

1928-30

The two-stroke element of the programme suddenly became quite ambitious for 1928. At the cheaper end of the scale was the new Levisette offered at the time of introduction at £28 15s 0d. The name incidentally had been registered by Butterfields some fourteen years earlier. The 247cc engine was the same as that already in use in the Model M but it had a Pilgrim mechanical oil pipe and initially at least, a single lever carburettor, which judging by some illustrations, was a Villiers.

The Levisette can best be likened to a sporting version of the previous years 'M' and it retained the Sturmey Archer three-speed gearbox. The mud guards were however lighter, the rear being supported by flat strip stays, the carrier having been dispensed with. A tool box was mounted horizontally and somewhat untidily on the seat tube. Foot boards or footrests could be specified.

The price of the 'M' went up to £32 and had a flexible top saddle in place of the former pan seat. Round section tubes were now employed for the front forks and there was finger adjustments for the brakes. Lubrication was by Pilgrim mechanical pump.

A de luxe Model M was extensively advertised throughout the season. It was sold completely equipped with leg-shields, foot boards, and electric lighting and horn. The electrics were by Miller and the dynamo was mounted on the seat tube. It was driven off the magneto sprocket by a neatly enclosed chain

The Model K was replaced by the K2 which was the first production Levis to have a saddle tank, the frame having been slightly modified to suit. Alongside

Instead of the more usual single transfer port in the cylinder there were two, one above the other. They were covered by a recessed casting held in position with

the tank was the control for the Burman gearbox. The cylinder now used was similar in appearance to the 'M' type i.e. the exhaust pipe sloped away at an angle. There were however differences in both inlet and exhaust port shapes and sizes. As an alternative to the K2 the 'O' was still listed almost unchanged except for a slightly larger tank and the option of a spring-top saddle.

An interesting new two-stroke model was introduced during the 1928 season - the 247cc Six Port and for the first time there was a production Levis with twin exhaust ports and a detachable cylinder head. The bottom end of the engine was similar to that already in use but with a stiffened crank and a larger diameter big-end bearing.

four studs and thus the conventional transfer passage was eliminated. With the piston at the bottom of its stroke, both ports were uncovered and the lightly compressed mixture in the crank case passed through a port in the piston into the transfer passage and thence to the cylinder via the upper transfer port. Three ports have already been mentioned. An inlet and two exhaust ports make up the six which gave the engine its name.

The idea of a ported piston was of course by no means new and had been employed by various other manufacturers notably Clyno and Cedos with the same object in view - helping to keep the piston cooler.

Since the cylinder head, which incidentally was of aluminium, was detachable it could be more accurately shaped internally and the opportunity was taken of matching it to the contour of the piston crown thereby invoking turbulence. Adopting a practice borrowed from Villiers, the exhaust side of the piston head was divided by a rib, hopefully to balance the exhaust gases equally between the two ports. Much credit must be accorded however to the designer of the Six Port piston for it incorporated an internal baffle further to assist cooling and the slope on the exhaust side of the head was such that it took the same line as that of the front ends of the exhaust pipes. Not unnaturally the bore and stoke followed normal Levis practice ie 67 x 70mm.

The engine was installed in a business-like frame similar to that of the existing Model K2 with a low riding position and having an attractive welded steel saddle tank. Short exhaust pipes engaged with the cylinder by means of ribbed aluminium union nuts, and terminated in long cylindrical plated silencers with fish tails. Initially a Sturmey Archer three-speed gearbox was used. Other specification details included 5 inch front and 6 inch rear brakes, a Lycett Aero saddle, 25 x 3 inch tyres and Druid forks with side springs. Gear ratios were 5.25. 8 and 14 or 5.57, 9 and 16 to 1.

Tested by *The Motorcycle* (Report 5th July, 1928) the Six Port weighing 197lbs in touring trim was said to 'devour gradients with consumate ease' (it is difficult to imagine a present day tester using such an expression!) and the maker's claim of a possible 60mph was not considered to be very wide of the mark. Steering called for nothing but praise and the spring-up rear stand was much appreciated. The tester criticized the lack of sensitivity of the rear brakes; the carburettor air intake since clothing could be drawn into it, and the rather pronounced exhaust note (that was before the day of Japanese two-strokes) - but in his summing-up he says 'an altogether different Levis with new characteristics and a performance quite unlike anything associated previously with the name'.

It is indeed remarkable that as far back as 1928, when the TV as we know it was little more than a pipe-dream, Butterfields incorporated LEVIS in an advertisement headed 'TELEVISION'. Television makes everyone far-seeing was the theme and what does it show you more clearly than Levis? .

In its 1929 form the Six Port had a Burman gearbox. The Pilgrim oil pump was moved so that it took its drive from the magneto sprocket instead of from the end of the crank shaft. Knee grips were now standard and a tank mounted speedometer driven from the gearbox was an optional extra.

A new model, the 'Z' used the normal three port 247cc two-stroke engine fitted to a machine which otherwise closely resembled the Six Port but it still had a front mounted transverse exhaust box and short tail pipe.

The OHV Model A for 1929 had a frame modified to accommodate a 2$^3/_8$ gallon saddle tank. Apart from bringing the machine up-to-date there was the distinct advantage that the tank could very quickly be removed since its design necessitated no balance pipe, which made access to the rocker box cover when valve clearance adjustment became necessary much easier. Front forks were of the excellent but never widely adopted Druid enclosed central spring type and the rear brake was now 7 inch diameter. A modification which had crept in took the form of a stay from the cylinder head to the front tube.

It was during the 1929 season that the Model A won its spurs. Representing Great Britain it completed the 1929 International Six Days Trial without the loss of a single mark.

The 1930 programme was large and varied but only now was the 346cc OHV coming into its own. It appeared in two versions with both having larger brakes and tank and tyre section increased to 3.25 inches. The engine had changed little from the previous year and still used a big-end bearing with a single row of rollers. Lubrication continued to be the total loss system. A model corresponding to the 'A' of 1929 but with the aforementioned general improvements was designated the A1 but little was seen of it, the more popular choice by far being

1930 Levis A2

the A2 which had a two port cylinder head, and other such adjuncts to an up-to-date appearance as a chromium plated tank and a clean rear guard.

At least two different styles of low-level exhaust system for the A2 were depicted at the time. A press photograph shows rather angular pipes and a diamond shaped silencer but in publicity illustrations the pipes are more sweeping and the silencers long and four sided with a smaller fish tail - high level compression pipes were made available as optional extra equipment.

Various other options were offered. Standard gear ratios were 5.4, 8.7 and 13.75 to 1 but it was possible to specify a close ratio gearbox or one with a lower bottom gear. A high compression piston could be chosen giving a ratio of 7.2 to 1 instead of the normal 6 to 1 and there was the choice of a 3 inch ribbed front tyre. Competition tyres were offered at slight extra cost.

'Quite the nicest 350' was how *The Motorcycle* described the A2 and *Motor cycling* said 'Nothing but a joy to ride'. The Manufacturers, (and I have in the past been guilty of doubting that they ever made such a claim) called it 'The Fastest Standard 350'. A maximum speed of 80mph has often been mentioned which suggests an engine speed in the order of 5,500 rpm in top gear - not bad for a machine weighing 270lbs and an engine depending on wet sump lubrication.

Chromium plating was general on both the A1 and the A2 and twist grips and knee grips were standard.

That other sporting favourite the Six Port, now had single centre spring forks and sold at an attractive £37 10s 0d. It differed from its predecessor in having a swan-neck induction pipe which allowed the carburettor air intake to face rearwards thus overcoming *The Motorcycles'* objection to the earlier arrangement. Whilst it is a matter for regret that few Six Ports survive it is perhaps fortunate for concours judges because there was a choice of four colour schemes for the tank or it could be chromium plated if required.

The 'Z' now became the Popular Z , the price of which, £31 10s 0d included leg shields and can have left little profit margin for either manufacturer or dealer. The carrier had been dispensed with and a plated exhaust pipe was brought back along the left hand side into a tubular silencer. Completely new productions were a trio of 247cc four-strokes. The Model C had a side-valve engine using the familiar bore and stroke measurements of 67 x 70mm. The head was fixed and the plug threaded into the inlet valve cap. A plated cover held in place by a knurled nut enclosed the valves. The magneto was behind the cylinder and inclined backwards. A Pilgrim sight-feed mechanical oil pump took its drive from the magneto sprocket and had its window inclined forwards. This unit was mounted in a machine otherwise almost identical to the Six Port. The exhaust system consisted of a long plated pipe, secured to the cylinder by a 'C' spanner union nut, leading into a four sided silencer with integral fish-tail. It was not until the late thirties that a model with a similar engine was listed again.

The Model B was listed as a 247cc, 67 x 70mm two-port OHV machine. It is not illustrated in the 1930 Levis catalogue which publication describes it as a 'smaller replica of its bigger brother' ie. the A2 and also a similar machine to the 'C' – but it cannot have been both! The B Special is listed as a specially tuned high compression version of the 'B' with plated tank, steering damper and shock absorbers.

Miller dynamo lighting was available on all models for 1930. On the Model Z there was the choice of either a 4 volt or a 6 volt system. Electric lighting on the Six Port brought with it de luxe equipment including chromium plating, electric horn and tank mounted speedometer. A tank mounted speedometer for the 'Z' included in its cost the provision of a larger tank.

After 1930 two-stroke models were discontinued and additionally 500cc and 600cc models were introduced, all individually built to tool room standards, always with the aim in mind of not 'how many' but 'how good'.

1930 Levis Model Z 247cc at Banbury 2008

LGC

By 1926 most of the small assemblers who had commenced operations immediately after the War or in the early twenties, had retired from what in more recent times would have been called the 'rat race'. But around this period various new makes were starting to appear, most of them with nothing very revolutionary to offer. During June of that year, the LGC was announced and was still in production in 1930. Excellent mud guarding and good ground clearance were characteristic of the range throughout the period.

The Leonard Gundle Motor Company (the manufacturers of the LGC) were already well known, particularly for their tradesmen bicycles and tricycles. At this time their works were at Unett Street, Birmingham. The more interesting of the two models which comprised the initial programme was the '0/1' intended to appeal to the sporting rider.

The engine was the 346cc (70 x 90mm) 'Standard' OHV JAP in the form which carried the magneto in front of the crankcase. As was usual (but not universal) with these engines, the exhaust pipe was attached to the cylinder head by a union nut. The pipe swept around the front down tube to the near side of the machine. The gearbox was a Moss, a make which was only being used by two or three other British manufacturers. The gear lever was mounted on the box itself and the ratios were rather wide - 5.5, 8.53 and 15.6 to 1.

1926 LGC 0/1 with 350cc OHV JAP engine

A straight forward diamond frame was stated to be light in weight, but possessed of immense strength - there is a familiar ring about this description. The front forks were Bramptons with a single spring. An almost wedge shaped tank was not of the saddle type. Oil was carried in a separate tank on the seat tube.

Mud-guarding was thorough without being obtrusive. The front guard was of sufficient width for the fork blades to have to pass through holes in the guard. No carrier was fitted and this did much to give a sporting appearance.

The other model, the S1 followed much the same lines, but was powered by a 300cc side-valve JAP engine, and employed 'semi TT' forks, whatever that may have meant.

The same two models continued without much alteration for the 1927 season, although on the 0/1 a soft top saddle replaced the pan seat, a toolbox appeared on the tank top and the licence holder was no longer integral with the front number plate. The price was £52 10s 0d which was more or less in line with other 'component' machines of similar specification.

By the time the 1928 range was announced, the Company appears to have become 'Ltd', (although this may have been a misprint) and the address was 174 John Street, Birmingham. There were two OHV models both using 346cc standard JAP engines, but in single and two port versions and designated 0/1 and 0/2 respectively. The distinctive 'wrap around' exhaust pipe was still used on the former and it trailed in a rather unlovely fashion along the left hand side to a cylindrical silencer with a large fish tail. Burman boxes were now used on the OHV's with the change lever at the side of the tank. Overall gearing was high with ratios of 5.1, 8.2 and 13 to 1. A new saddle tank, finished in brown had a capacity of 2½ gallons and a separate oil tank held half a gallon. Strapped to the top of the petrol tank was a tool box. There were plenty of other places where it could have been accommodated so one can only assume that it was meant to look like a tummy rest. The front guard was now 'trapped' where it passed between the fork girders, and the forks themselves were Bramptons with central spring and integral shock absorbers.

The 300cc side-valve JAP engined 'S1' appeared with a new and smaller frame giving a 2 inch lower riding position, but had a flat petrol tank holding 2½ gallons, and a four pint oil tank on the seat tube. In the case of this model an Albion three-speed box replaced the Moss as in the case of the other two models. 27 x 2.75 inch wired tyres took the place of the 650 x 65mm beaded edge type previously used.

1929, and the home of the LGC was 41-42 Smith Street, Hockley, Birmingham. All models had welded steel tanks. Standard tank finish was black with orange nose, but to special order a crystalline finish was available. Four-pint separate oil tanks were still used.

The 350cc OHV 0/1 and 0/2 were fitted with the new JAP engines with enclosed push rods. The main difference between these two machines was that the former had a single port engine and the latter a twin port. The exhaust pipes on the 0/2 were impressive, if somewhat angular and terminated in rectangular silencers with fish-tails. The tool box had found a new home. It was of new design and helped neatly to fill the space between the off-side seat and chain stays. These models were fitted with Burman gearboxes.

New for 1929 was the TS1 of completely 'up-to-the-minute' appearance having the popular high-fronted look and a short deep 2 gallon saddle tank. The assembly which united the seat stays with the forward part of the frame was a particularly fine piece of work to which the saddle springs were directly attached.

The engine was the 247cc (67 x 70mm) two-port Villiers two-stroke. The exhaust pipes blended well with the rest of the machine and terminated in rectangular silencers with fish tails. Lubrication was by the Villiers pressure system from a separate tank on the seat tube. In this case an Albion gearbox was used. Weighing 198 lbs, it came within the 'thirty shilling' taxation class. With a price tag of £39 17s 6d, there cannot have been much of a profit margin although the prospective purchaser, even by dint of foregoing wine, women and Woodbines would have been lucky to save enough in a year to buy one!

The S1with 300cc side-valve JAP engine and Albion box was still listed in 1929.

LGC rarely advertised and they were not at the 1929 Show. It is therefore difficult to provide much detail concerning the1930 range. According to the *Buyers Guide* all four models remained in production with unchanged specifications.

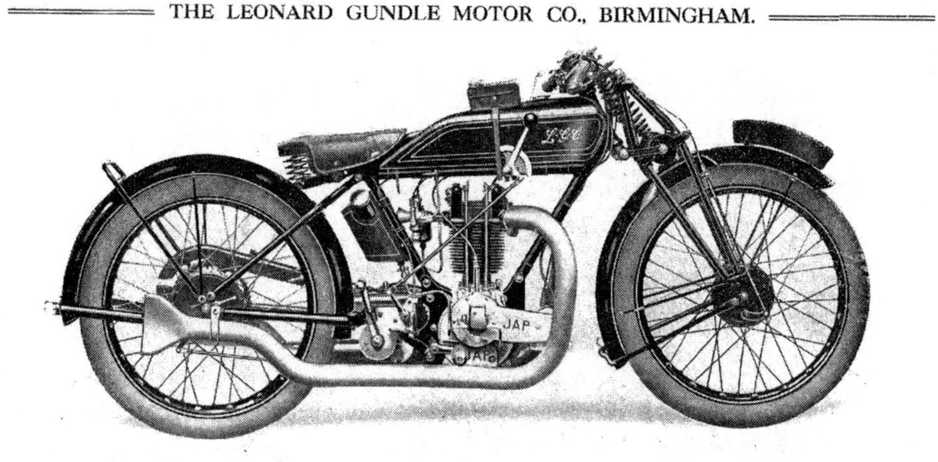

1929 LGC 0/2. (Photo: VMCC)

MACKLUM

'Sooner or later the lightweight open frame machine will come. Of this we are convinced'. Thus spoke *The Motorcycle* (22 January, 1920). F MacCallum of Guildhall Buildings, Navigation Street, Birmingham, took comfort from this prophesy and used the quotation in the advertisement for his scooter.

The 1920 Macklum was not a particularly handsome effort. The engine was mounted rather high over the front wheel; considerably above it was a horizontal cylindrical tank. A seat which looked something like the old 'Tan-Sad' pillion was fixed to a tall box. The handlebars were so high that the machine was obviously meant to be ridden in the standing position. It is difficult to know if the seat was to enable the driver to take the weight off his feet or to carry a passenger.

The well known 292cc Union engine was employed in its less familiar form - i.e. with chain-driven magneto. Transmission was by chain, direct to the front wheel.

By comparison the model announced for 1921 was of quite passable appearance. This 'Motorette' was designed to be driven in the seated position with a less unsightly seat mounting, the handlebars were much lower and the tank was closer to the engine. The front wheel was well guarded and the rear one semi-enclosed. A sort of bulkhead separated the driver from the engine.

At this time the Pero Works Co, 10 Anderton Square, Whittall Street, Birmingham, were turning out the particularly neat little 70 x 70mm (269cc) 'Pero' two stoke engine and this was the power unit employed (one of its few applications). Drive was carried out via a Brampton 'spring chain'.

If the day of 'the lightweight open frame machine' ever came, it certainly did not do so in time to be of any help to the Macklum judging by the fact that it did not figure in the Spring 1921 *Buyers Guide* or any subsequent issues.

MATCHLESS

The Collier Brothers produced their first motorcycles in their factory in Plumstead in 1899, and went on to achieve great success in early races. Although production came to a halt in 1916, post war there was a period of massive growth for Matchless at their London home. Many extra workers were taken on to meet the demand for their products. The motorcycles ranged from 246cc singles to 1000cc twins. They also supplied their engines to other manufacturers including OEC, Morgan and Brough. By 1928 Colliers had stopped using other peoples proprietary engines in their own machines (they had used MAG and JAP motors for their twins) and became self sufficient. In 1930 the range consisted of seven singles and three twins, and a year later they took over AJS of Wolverhampton.

Further Reading;

Matchless, The Complete Story, Mick Walker

MEREDITH

According to one of my correspondents, 125 George Street, Erdington, in Birmingham is a house in a residential area but it was from this address that Hubert A Meredith announced in the Spring of 1921 a composite lightweight.

So devoid of any special features was this machine that in describing it a trade journal was forced to resort to such phrases as 'ignition of the explosive mixture which is supplied by a B and B carburettor is effected by a handle-bar controlled CAV magneto' to pad out its story.

The engine was the ubiquitous 70 x 70mm, 269cc Villiers two-stroke lubricated by a Best and Lloyd drip feed and it drove via a Burman two-speed box with clutch and kick-start.

Footboards were fitted and the mud guarding was ample. 26 x 2¼ studded tyres shod 'extra strong' wheels. The front forks were Maplestone (later to be known as Webb).

There was a stirrup brake on the front wheel and the rear brake operated externally on the belt rim.

It is highly improbable that a machine ever appeared with Meredith on the tank since this motorcycle was offered to dealers to adorn with their own transfers.

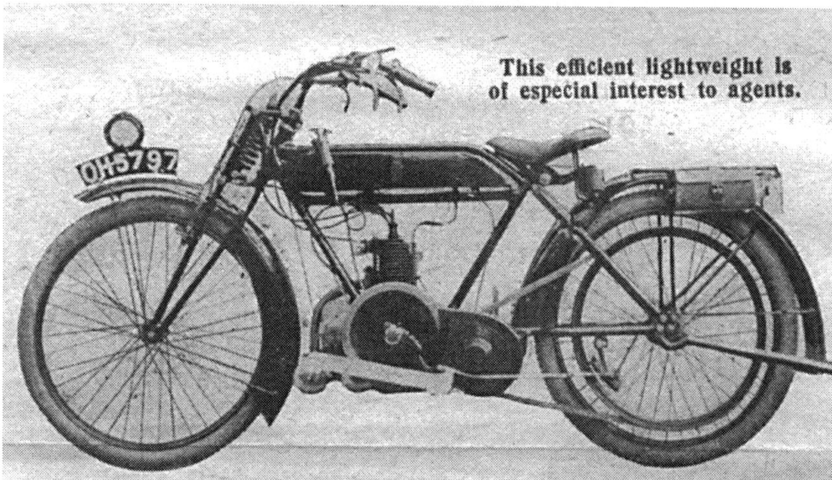

This 1921 Meredith was offered to dealers to adorn with their own transfers

MERRALL BROWN

Throughout the twenties the Morgan was the yardstick by which all three-wheelers were measured, both in price and general acceptability. Any manufacturer who thought that there was a market for a more refined vehicle at greater cost found, usually too late, that there certainly was not. The same fate befell the remainder of Morgans competitors who for the most part imagined that any outlandish tricar would sell provided it was sufficiently cheap.

Various examples are cited in this book of products which were doomed to failure from the start on account of their being over-priced, if for no other reason, and the Merrell Brown three-wheeler provides just one more example. It was introduced in 1919 by the Premier Engineering Company of Georges Road, Bolton, when the price was tentatively fixed at £250. By 1920 however the makers now styling themselves as Merrall Brown Motors were asking £300, which figure contrasted sadly with £175 for a Morgan.

There is no doubt that the Merrall Brown was of exceedingly fine design and construction, if one is prepared to overlook the bobbin-and-cable steering. The chassis was formed from a steel channel with tubular cross members. Two angle

10hp Merrall Brown three-wheeler fitted with water-cooled Precision engine of 1096cc. (Photo: Mortons Media Group Archives)

section cross members at the rear end provided a mounting for the bevel box and to the underside of the rear one were clamped two quarter elliptical springs. Between these springs and located more precisely by a pair of radius rods was a twin-tyred wheel with a brake on either side. The front axle was carried on semi-elliptical springs.

At least one Merrall Brown was fitted with a Coventry Simplex four cylinder engine, but standard equipment was a 1096cc V-twin Precision with water cooling. Power was transmitted through a fabric lined clutch and a prop-shaft to the bevel box which was also the two-speed and reverse gear. Final drive was by open chain.

Viewed from the front, the vehicle with its conventional bonnet and honeycomb radiator, looked much the same as an orthodox light car. From the rear it was not unlike a Morgan. The two-seater body was made of aluminium and there was a door on each side. Aluminium, but in this case highly polished, was also used for the front wings, bonnet and wheel discs. The wheels were detachable. What would have been a striking appearance was somewhat marred by gas headlamps rather untidily mounted on the front wings and a spare wheel carried just forward of the passenger door.

How many of these vehicles actually found their way on to the market, I have not the faintest idea, but by April 1921 the concern was in bankruptcy.

NORTON

One of Britains most famous marques, James Lansdowne Norton produced his first motorcycle in 1901. By 1907 a V-twin Peugeot engined Norton was entered for, and in fact won, the twin cylinder class of the first ever Isle of Man TT race. Pre-war production was based around 490cc and 630cc engines of their own manufacture, and found considerable favour with military buyers during the conflict. Post war domestic production was resumed using the slogan 'The Unapproachable Norton'. They gained a considerable reputation for reliability and build quality for everyday use, and this was only topped by their phenomenal racing successes at home and abroad. Nortons side-valve's held many Brooklands records, and when the 490cc ohv went on sale in 1922 it too gained a considerable reputation , Graham Walker used one to win the sidecar TT in 1923. 1927 saw the introduction of the Walter Moore designed overhead camshaft model on which Alec Bennett won the TT. In the 1930 catalogue ten models were featured, all singles, of 348cc, 490cc, 588cc, and 630cc. The flat tank model 18 was said by some to be one of the prettiest machines ever made, and the ohc Nortons were successfully adapted from road racing to street use.

Further Reading;
Flat Tank Norton, George Cohen, 2006, Norton George Publishing

1928 Norton 16H

OEC

During the period 1920-1930 and, in fact, until 1930, no concern turned out a greater variety of interesting motorcycles than the Osborn Engineering Co Ltd, makers of the OEC. The products included not only a bewildering range of catalogued machines but all manner of specially built ones as well. These included 'one-offs' for particularly arduous duties overseas and projectiles for world speed record attempts. Small batches of motorcycles built to rigid specification for government departments abroad were produced as a matter of course and in fact if you wanted a special motorcycle built, OEC were the obvious people for the job.

The house of Osborn was in business before the turn of the century and had occupied, in its time, factories at Coventry and Southall. In 1916 the firm became The United Aircraft Co Ltd with a factory at Lees Lane, Gosport although early in the twenties the address became 'Atlanta Works, Gosport' . The trading style was subsequently changed to Osborn Engineering Co Ltd, but it is interesting to note that as late as 1930 the telegraphic address was 'Planes, Gosport'.

The Lees Lane premises consisted of a modern three-bay factory, a two storey building and a collection of wooden sheds. The complex incorporated a comprehensive machine shop, a wood-working department and paint and plating shops. During the peak of war time activity as many as five hundred people were employed there.

With the end of hostilities the firm found itself in need of other outlets for its production capacity and turned its attentions back to the motor trade. Soon they were turning out car bodies and before long arrangements were made whereby

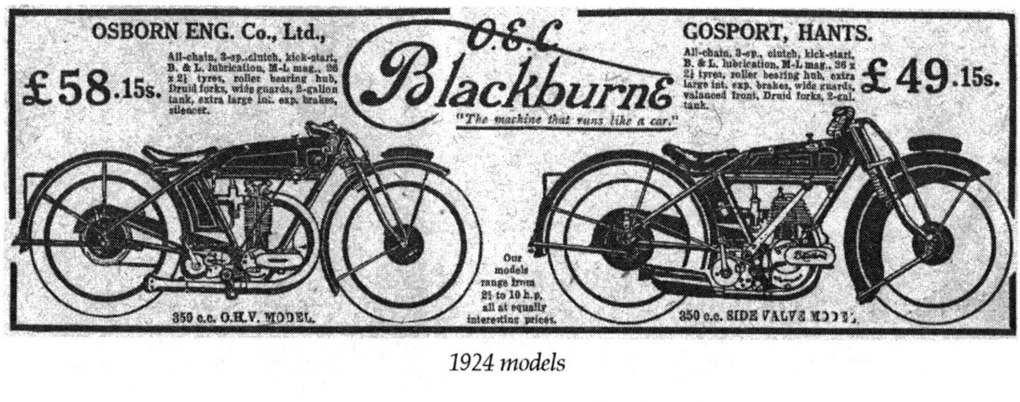

1924 models

1923 OEC Blackburne 998CC (OHV to special order)

they undertook the complete construction of Blackburne motorcycles around this firm's engines, using proprietary gearboxes. Among the wartime hands were a number experienced in pipe bending and other special skills and their services were retained.

The Blackburne range was displayed at the 1921 Show on the OEC stand. This seems to mark a transition period where the Blackburne becomes the OEC, since there was on show an 'Osborn' for taxi sidecar use and fitted with a steering wheel. (The effect was described by *The Motorcycle* as grotesque.) the firm obviously had its own ideas about sidecars. As VAC it produced a special chassis for taxi work and at one period experiments were carried out with sidecar wheel steering.

The OEC was first listed for 1923 and the offerings for that year inherited a distinct resemblance to the Blackburne. Whereas Blackburne had contented themselves with a limited range, OEC each year offered a wide choice of models and sometimes the programme was most complex.

1923-25

For 1923 there were three basic models all with side-valve Blackburne engines, Burman gearboxes and all-chain drive.

They had capacities of 348, 548 and 998cc, two singles and a twin all with mechanical lubrication. The '350' weighed 198lbs. and thus was within the then 'thirty shilling' taxation class. The two larger models retained the 28 inch wheels of the Blackburne. This would seem to have been a straightforward enough programme, but also available were a 250 side-valve, a 250 OHV, a 350 OHV, 700cc twins in SV and OHV form, and a 1098cc side-valve twin.

1924 saw a vast pruning of the range and a two-stroke model was listed. This had a 147cc Villiers engine but with Amac carburettor. The price when it went into production was £36 which was on the high side, but direct lighting was included together with chain transmission via a Sturmey Archer three-speed gearbox. Both brakes operated on the rear wheel.

The 350cc class was represented by a very rakish OHV Blackburne-cum-Burman ensemble known as the TT Model. Lubrication was 'semi automatic' (a euphemism used to describe a spring loaded hand pump). A long graceful exhaust pipe

1927 OEC TT Model

discharged direct into the atmosphere save that its outlet end was compressed to form a tiny fishtail.

The most interesting model was the '5/7 HP' twin which had a 696cc, OHV Blackburne engine with mechanical lubrication. Each cylinder had its own plated exhaust pipe and these pipes extended back to a point just behind the centre of the rear hub where they terminated in a common silencer. As to general construction, a saddle tank was incorporated as were such other refinements as adjustable handlebars and detachable and interchangeable wheels with internal expanding brakes. Forks were by Webb with side springs. Somewhat similar machines, but fitted with Brampton forks and either 550cc or 1000cc side-valve Blackburne engines were also available.

New for 1925 was the 198lb, 350 Atlanta. This must have been one of the first overhead cam-shaft singles offered to the public. It was expensive at £80, but could be supplied at £5 less with hand pump lubrication. Unusual for OEC in those days it had a Sturmey Archer gearbox, as did the 1096cc side-valve twin which could still be obtained with 28 inch wheels, if required. The 696cc OHV twin was retained but the 550 single seems to have been dropped, although doubtless the works would have obliged with one if requested.

1926-30

Around 1926 a rather piquant situation existed. OEC, always well abreast of current trends, and Ariel who had only just emerged from a state of complete stagnation in design, were both using the slogan 'The Modern Motorcycle'. This state of affairs did not continue for very long and OEC became 'The most Modern Motorcycle', which left Ariels little choice but to 'soft-pedal' on 'The Modern Motorcycle' theme.

The 1926 programme was ambitious to the extent of being unwieldy. No less than ten basic models were listed and where the new duplex frame was not standard it was usually offered as an optional extra. There was a general swing away from Blackburne engines in favour of JAP and more extensive use was made of Sturmey Archer gearboxes. The title OEC Atlanta was no longer reserved for the 350 OHC but was applied to various other models in a seemingly haphazard manner.

Using two or three standard frames one had the choice of:-

350cc	OHC Atlanta, SV and OHV Blackburne, SV JAP and OHV JAP in 'cooking' and hot-stuff' versions.
500cc	OHV Anzani and SV JAP
550cc	SV Blackburne
700cc	680 JAP SV and 696 Blackburne OHV twins
1000cc	SV and OHV JAP and eight valve Anzani
1100cc	1096 SV Blackburne

Typical of the range was the £95, 350cc OHV two port JAP model which, but for its side-spring forks was certainly 'three years ahead in design'. The frame was of duplex construction and triangulated from steering-head to rear hub. A continuation of the engine cradle tube met up with the extreme ends of the chain stays to form torque arms and the complete engine could be withdrawn after the removal of four bolts.

A Burman gearbox was used and other features included interchangeable wheels with taper-roller bearings. The engine was lubricated by a mechanical pump via a sight feed in the tank; a hand-pump was also fitted.

The two gallon-plus petrol tank was finished in black with red panels. An Amac racing carburettor and straight through exhaust pipe set the seal on what was a mount 'designed primarily for the sports enthusiast'.

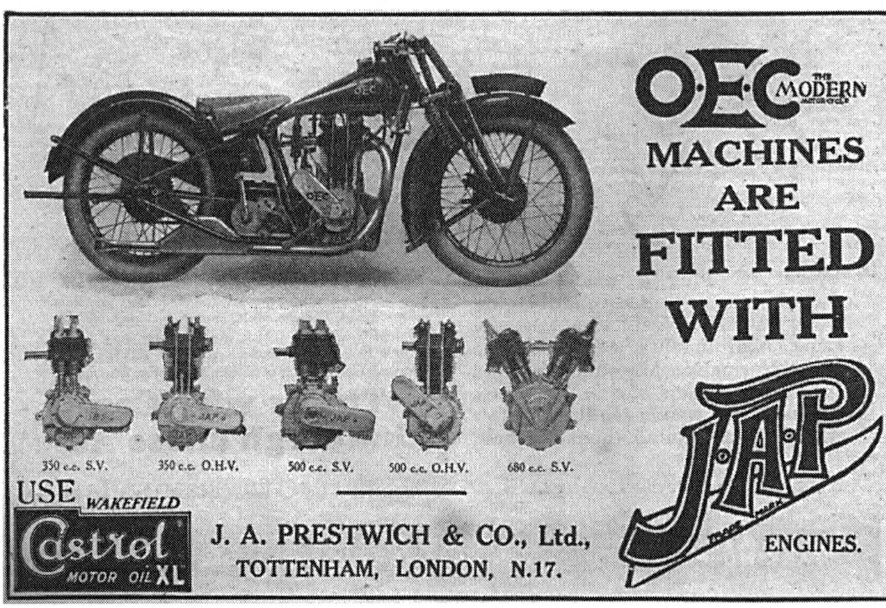

There were twenty-one models for 1927 all of which had Burman gearboxes. Common throughout were taper roller hub bearings, interchangeable wheels, seven inch foot-operated brakes, adjustable handlebars, armoured control cables and spring-up rear stands. Lubrication of the engine was in all cases by mechanical pump and an oil supply was included to the primary chain. The machines had, however, lost a little of their sporting appearance due to the use of heavily valanced mudguards.

Powered by JAP there was the choice of a 346cc SV, a 346cc (70 x 90mm) OHV and two 344cc (74 x 80mm) OHV's. Then there was a 490 SV, two 490cc OHV's and a 596 SV 680cc and 980cc twins each appeared in SV and OHV form. There were five Blackburne models, a 348cc SV, two 348cc OHV's and a 498cc SV and the 696cc OHV twin.

An assortment of OEC Temples (more or less!) completes the list, a 350 and a 500 with OEC Temple OHC engines and a 496cc single and a 996cc twin powered by OHV Vulpine units.

OEC were regular supporters of the TT. They entered openly without expecting a win. With a view to improving the breed and following this policy they prepared for the 1927 Senior and Junior a completely redesigned machine incorporating the new duplex steering system which can best be described by quoting *The Motorcycle and Motor Trader* for 3rd June, 1927: '*...the duplex frame terminates at the front in two long steering heads, one on each side of the front wheel extending from the top of the front mudguard to some inches below the wheel spindle. Inside both steering heads are tubular members in bearings carrying links at the top and bottom which swing at right angles. The forward ends of pairs of the links being connected rigidly to a bar carrying the wheel spindle lay between the load and rebound springs. The wheel has no trail and the system utilises the weight of the machine as a definite righting or stabilising force*' Both Senior and Junior entries retired but the layout proved itself and was put into production for 1928 although in a somewhat tidied up form.

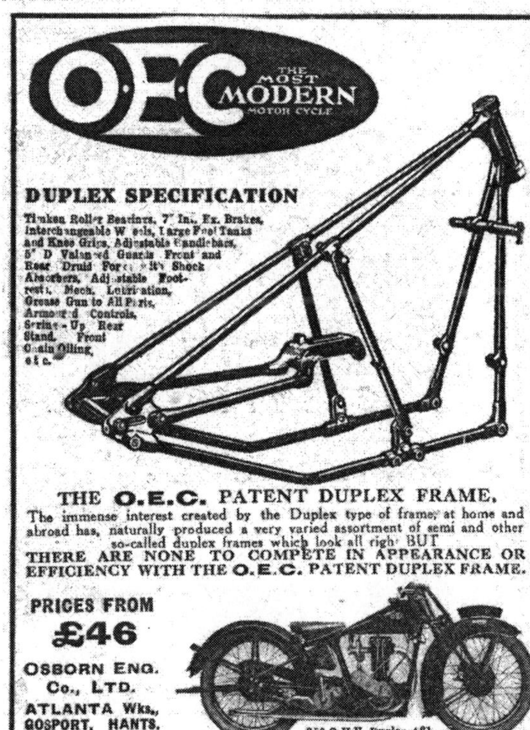

The basic range embodied some two dozen models and was further complicated by the option of duplex steering on more than half of them. All capacities from 175 to 1000cc were represented in most cases with a wide choice of engines including JAP, Blackburne, MAG, Bradshaw, Vulpine, Villiers and Atlanta. Burman gearboxes were, however, standard equipment throughout.

There were two extremely novel machines at the 1928 show. Named the OEC Tinkler, the unit construction 490cc single cylinder OHV engine was housed in the duplex steering frame with pivoted suspension both front and rear. Every part of the water cooled engine, three-speed gear and accessories was housed in an aluminium box fronted by the radiator and covered by the petrol tank. A jockey pulley controlled the tension of the primary chain, which served as speedometer drive, chain adjuster and chain lubricator. This model was said to be the centre of attraction at that years show on account of its novelty. The other outstanding machine was an open frame model with enclosed mechanism and duplex steering that was designed very much as a utility motorcycle. These were powered by Villiers 172cc, 343cc or Blackburne 300cc engines. Also introduced at this time

Water-cooled OEC Tinkler has the engine and gearbox combined in one unit. (Photo: Mortons Media Group Archives)

was a duplex framed speedway machine fitted with a 498cc JAP engine, although this was not successful and only sold in small numbers.

OEC were a group apart from most manufacturers. Although their output was not as prolific as some, the range and scope of their ideas was vast. The duplex frame created a new standard in stability when it was introduced in 1927. It proved its worth in 1930 by housing a supercharged 1000cc V-twin JAP engine to briefly take the World Speed Record at 137.2mph. The same team upped the record later in that year to 150.736mph, although in time the word leaked out that the record had actually been taken on a spare machine with ordinary girder forks! OEC supported an epic round the world journey by two of their outfits driven by

Geoffrey Mallins and his friend, they designed a military half-track utilising the rear of a production Triumph to incorporate a set of inline bogie wheels and track. The steering wheel taxis and the persistent, if largely unsuccessful TT support all served to emphasise the idiosynchratic nature of their business. In 1930, OEC like so many manufacturers was feeling the effects of the depression and production at the Lees Lane factory came to a halt.

Later, manufacture re started at Atlanta Works, Highbury Street, Portsmouth where the tradition of producing machines which were often at odds with more traditional ideas continued right up to 1954 when the factory finally closed for good.

Above, 1928 open frame 172cc OEC. Below, the 1930 OEC JAP record breaker at the Brooklands Centenary Motorcycle Meeting

ORBIT

Orbit Motors Ltd, operated from Orbit Works, Sedgeley Street, Wolverhampton. In 1921 this concern brought out at a retail price of £17 10s 0d, a complete, seemingly sound, two-stroke engine, but it was not adopted by many motorcycle 'manufacturers'. This unit had dimensions of 68 x 72mm giving a capacity of 261.5cc. It was of straightforward three-port design with particular attention paid to efficient cooling.

Forged from high grade steel, the one-piece crankshaft carried a plain big-end bearing which was split 'in order that any wear at this point may be taken up with minimum of trouble' - the fact that to do so meant stripping the engine and splitting the crankcase was conveniently ignored. The drive side of the crank carried a boss to which was bolted a forged steel flywheel and the right hand side drove the forward mounted magneto, with the chain enclosed in a neat aluminium housing.

A tube led gas from the compression release to the exhaust pipe. A Senspray carburettor was clipped on to a readily detachable stub. The whole package was supplied complete with engine plates, plated exhaust pipe and transverse cylindrical expansion chamber 'ready to drop into the frame'.

Orbit Model A. (Photo: VMCC)

The Orbit two-stroke engine.

In 1923 complete 'Orbit' motorcycles were marketed using this engine. They had chain and belt transmission and sold at £40 and £45 according to whether the kick-start Burman gearbox had two- or three-speeds.

Also offered was an all-chain 2¾, 8hp oil-cooled Bradshaw powered model. At this time the 350cc OHV Bradshaw designed engine was produced by Walmsley of Preston. The 8hp obviously refers to the bhp and seems to have been a rather conservative figure since, when the manufacturer of this unit was taken over by Dorman, every engine which left the factory was bench-tested to show almost double that output.

This was quite a distinguished-looking mount, although in appearance it could hardly have been described as sporting. Against a background which included footboards, a heavily valanced front guard and touring handlebars (incidentally celluloid covered) the upswept exhaust pipe looked, to say the least, incongruous. It discharged into a curious little silencer with the outlet flattened to form a slot. Both brakes were of the internal expanding type; the gearbox was by Burman.

Advertising by Barr and Stroud during 1923 indicated that their 350cc sleeve valve engine could be fitted to Orbit motorcycles.

The Bradshaw model was continued for 1924 but with an Amac carburettor instead of a Binks. The toolbox was moved from the carrier to the saddle tube and the front forks were Swan with enclosed spring.

Known as the TS 24 the two-speed two-stroke sported an upswept exhaust, but the silencer had quite a long tail pipe. Final drive was by belt, the belt rim being of rather large diameter on which a heel brake operated externally. The carrier was of massive construction and closely resembled the type traditionally associated with Zenith.

The other model powered by the same two-stroke unit was designated the TS 12 and was unique in that it had an endless belt primary, and chain final drive. This was because a 'Philipson Gear' replaced a conventional gearbox. As the engine pulley expanded the countershaft pulley contracted thus giving twelve 'speeds' ranging between five to one and fifteen to one. The layout incorporated a clutch and kick-starter.

These three models were those which were exhibited at the 1923 Show. However, when the *Buyers Guide* appeared in the spring of 1924 only the two-speed two-stroke was listed. At about this time the Company's affairs were in the hands of a liquidator which is probably why, after the year under review, the make seems to have faded out.

P&M

The name P&M, laterPanther, is synonymous with sloping engines and the County of Yorkshire. Produced by Phelon and Moore from 1904, the machines were almost from the start chain rather than belt drive. The big 499cc single cylinder engine was the mainstay of the P&M range, with occasional experiments with a 771cc V-twin engine. The first war saw P& M machines being used by the Royal Flying Corps. Sales to the domestic market resumed in 1919 with much the same models as pre-war. In 1927 Granville Bradshaw designed a 246cc V-twin Panthette which was supposed to do 60mph. By the end of the twenties a 600cc engine was introduced, mainly for sidecar work, but was not a huge success.1930 saw a six model range that included a147cc Villiers powered Panther that sold for a mere £25.

Further Reading

The Panther Story, Barry M Jones, 1999, Panther Publishing

P&M OM 451 'Queenie'

P&S

Pearson and Sopwith Ltd was formed in September 1919 as 'Dealers in motor cars, motorcycles and accessories' in Mortimer Street, West London. Early in 1920 motorcycle 'manufacture' was commenced and premises consisting of a couple of floors were leased at 8 and 9 Long Acre, London W1, at what was then an astronomical rental of £2,500 a year.

The actual construction of the machines was entrusted to the Nottingham Engineering Co to whom engines were supplied for incorporation in complete P&S motorcycles

Unfortunately Nottingham Engineering went into liquidation and the receiver seized all the engines which were on the premises. Fresh arrangements were made for assembly to be carried out at Worthing, but few, if any machines were completed.

By may 1921 the situation was such that it was decided to 'wind up' the company 'voluntarily' and at a meeting of creditors held in June a deficit of something in the order of £14,000 was disclosed. Since the corresponding figure at the previous October meeting was £4,000 this came as a bombshell; angry noises were made and there was a feeling in some quarters that the company should be compulsorily liquidated. However, a Mr Groves was appointed as Liquidator. The concern remained on the official list of Companies for some time, certainly until 1927.

Just about the only notable feature of the 1920 model was that it must have had an exceedingly large tank; it was quoted as having two gallons of petrol and two quarts of oil. No make was given for the 3hp engine but the dimensions (70 x 76mm equals 292cc) suggest a Union.

Transmission was by chain and belt through a two-speed box of unspecified make with kick-start. This model, fitted with footboards, weighed 170lbs. An alternative version had a 2³/₄hp JAP engine, but weighed ten pounds less. The prices were £74 and £81 respectively.

On paper at least there were three models for 1921 all supposed to have Sturmey Archer kick-start boxes and chain driven. They consisted of a 499cc Blackburne, a 292cc JAP, and a 318cc Dalm two-stroke. The Blackburne had three-speeds, the others two. It is indicative of the climate at Pearson and Sopwith at the time that the picture supplied to illustrate the make in the 1921 *Buyers Guide* was that of the 1920 belt driven machine.

Those versions, if any, of the P&S which were actually produced for 1921 can only be a matter for speculation but it may be significant that when the list of creditors was presented at the winding up proceedings, Dalman, makers of the Dalm, was the only engine manufacturer included. Details of the 1921 models are in accordance with the *Buyers Guide,* although the Dalm and JAP engined models shown at the Olympia Show employed Burman boxes and chain-belt transmission.

PARAGON

FK Portway and BW Cooper set up as the Paragon Motor Manufacturing Co at Manningtree in Essex in August 1919. Paragon machines were shown at the 1919 Show and orders were taken for nearly 500. About £650 was collected in deposits, which cannot have worked out at very much per machine, but this money helped to keep the business going.

Unfortunately a moulders strike had a serious effect on production and when it was finally resolved the price of the castings had risen considerably. The result was that when machines were at last available for delivery they had cost appreciably more to manufacture than was anticipated, and moreover in many cases the prospective customers were no longer interested. About four months of the selling season had been lost and the trade was going through one of its all too frequent slumps. The firm had started off with limited cash backing, loans from friends helped to ward off the day of reckoning, but by the end of 1920 the partners were in bankruptcy and a trustee was appointed.

However, it would appear that someone was at hand to pull the chestnuts out of the fire and in the spring of 1920 the 'New Paragon' was being advertised by the Motor Works, Cressing Rd, Braintree. According to an enquiry from a subscriber the following September in the *Trade*, the manufacturer was FM Cooper. At about this time BW Cooper was discharged from bankruptcy but later on in the year FK Portway successfully applied for the bankruptcy of the original partnership to be annulled, all debts having been paid and provided for. The foregoing serves to provide a reminder that the lot of the small manufacturer in the twenties was an extremely precarious one.

PETERS

Most motorcycles of this period were little else, basically than a bicycle which has been adapted to house an engine. A few, however, were built from first principles, a traditional example being the Scott. A lesser known one was the Peters from the Isle of Man.

Exhibited at Olympia by Peters Motors Ltd, Parliament Street, Ramsay, it was one of the most novel designs at the Show, every bit as unconventional as an ABC albeit less sophisticated and accordingly falling into a lower price bracket. There was no frame as such, a nicely shaped pressed steel tank holding 2¾ gallons of petrol and a quart of oil replaced the usual top tube and tank rail. The 3½hp two-stroke engine with square dimensions acted as a front down tube. These two members were formed into a triangle by a saddle tube which did duty as a petrol

sump. Behind this tube was carried a large metal tool box and this also housed the battery.

A large diameter vertical tube encased in the nose of the tank enclosed the steering head and a leaf spring. The pivoting front forks consisted of a pair of blades with no additional stays. The rear frame, with suspension springs below the saddle was hinged on the bracket which would have carried the gearbox on a conventional machine. These were coil springs, not leaf as has been stated elsewhere. The mudguards were steel pressings, the front one being stiff enough to need no separate stays. The rearguard was shaped out to form a platform carrier and a number plate. Leg shields were standard and designed to assist engine cooling, and the ample footboards had Peters embossed on them.

Both brakes were heel operated with one acting internally and the other externally on the belt rim. Tyres were of a generous 2½ inch section and a central stand was fitted.

The engine had roller bearings throughout. A little confusion exists as to its exact bore and stroke since this has been given as 3 inches by 3 inches (ie 76.2 x 76.2mm) and elsewhere as 76 x 76mm. Supposing the latter figure to have been correct, the cubic capacity would have been approximately 350cc, not 347cc as was usually quoted. A flywheel magneto provided ignition and also supplied current for the lamps. A Cox carburettor was controlled by one twist grip and another operated the compression release. There were no other controls on the handlebars. The lubrication system was interesting, oil being forced into the crankcase by pressurizing the tank from the cylinder (not from the crankcase in the manner adopted by Villiers). Transmission was by belt and ratios of between 3¾ and 11 to one were obtained by closing up and opening the convex faced flanges of the engine pulley. A tank top crank handle performed this operation and at the same time varied the wheel base to maintain uniform belt tension.

This remarkable motorcycle, every detail of which bore the stamp of a rider-designer, sold for £63 including electric lighting. For 1923 the Peters does not figure in *The Motorcycle Buyers Guide*, although *Fletcher's* lists it as manufactured in that year. In 1924 the model with its somewhat out-moded transmission was still marketed, now down to a mere £42. There was also a chain-cum-belt version with Burman three-speed gearbox, for which a sidecar was offered.

A Blackburne engined 350cc side-valve Mark 4 was part of the programme. It had all-chain transmission and was listed with a three-speed Jardine gearbox, but a Burman box was also available. The two-stroke model following the same broad principles of the original, was now known as the Mark 1 and came in variable belt, chain-cum-belt and all-chain form.

The Peters does not appear to have been listed after 1925 which is a matter of regret since it was truly 'The Motorcycle of Practical Simplicity'

PRIORY

Probably the most interesting thing about the Priory was its rather improbable place of origin since its producers, The Priory Engineering Co (who claimed to be 'Motorcycle Experts') operated from Kenilworth, Warwickshire, the author's home town! Unfortunately, the makers did not seem exactly to go mad in the matter of advertising and so any information about this machine is hard to come by.

However, the Priory did appear at the 1920 Olympia Show where it was exhibited by Derry and Edwards of 1 Great Easter Street, London E1. *The Motorcycle,* with whom I sympathise in having to make some sort of a story about a multiplicity of 'nothing' machines, referred to it as 'an attractive little mount' and a little further on as 'a thoroughly practical little mount', but they did not seem to think it worth a picture.

The construction was absolutely straightforward except that the front forks were by Arden with pressed steel blades.

The engine was a 269cc (70 x 70mm) Arden two-stoke with chain driven forward mounted CAV magneto and B and B carburettor. Transmission was by chain and belt. The two-speed Albion box was available with or without kick-starter.

There were aluminium foot boards and a neat aluminium case enclosed the primary chain. Braking followed the usual pattern, a stirrup acting on the front rim and a block operating on the convex surface of the belt rim. The model shown at Olympia had Ace wheel discs and an aluminium casting to connect the two exhaust ports and lead them to an expansion box, but a picture in a contemporary advertisement does not show these features.

It seems possible, however, that no Arden engined models were produced, for according to a last minute entry in the 1921 *Buyers Guide* the engine was now a Villiers of the same dimensions as previously quoted, while the gearbox had been changed to Burman, still two-speed but with kick-start as standard.

The 1922 model had conventional front forks and for this year the engine, still a two-stroke, was the 292cc (70 x 76mm) Union in its chain driven magneto form. The dead straight and most impressive looking exhaust pipe extended from the front expansion box to a point level with the circumference of the rear tyre. Transmission was as before, but there was also a single speed model.

The single speeder sold for £39 18s 0d which suggests that Priory had been able to buy the engines 'right' for scarcely any other assembler was standardising the Union.

If Priory had a programme for 1923 they did not bother to let the *Buyers Guide* have details of it.

1924 was the last year that the Priory appeared in the *Buyers Guide* and the 147cc (55 x 62mm) Villiers two stoke engine with flywheel magneto was being used. Whilst its predecessors had been tolerably good looking machines, the 1924 model was not beautiful to say the least.

The front forks consisted of a pair of single blades, the tank was of almost the same depth throughout its length and the exhaust pipe was thoroughly ugly but would have looked less so had it been another eighteen inches longer. A heavily valanced front guard and 'sit up and beg' handlebars added the final touches in a sorry picture.

There were two versions, both with belt final drive. One had petroil lubrication, an Albion plain two-speed box and 24 x 2 inch tyres, and the other employed a drip feed, a Burman box and was fitted with 26 x 2¼ inch tyres. At prices of £27 10s 0d and £38 0s 0d respectively, they would probably be in greater demand today than they were at the time!

QUADRANT

During the twenties Quadrant was being described as 'Britain's Oldest Motorcycle'. Certainly its origin dates back to the very early 'nineteen hundreds' and in 1903 Tom Silver broke the 'End-to-End' record on a 3hp model. It has been stated by no less authority than Ixion of *The Motorcycle* that Quadrant, along with Excelsior did more to demonstrate the practicability of the motorcycle than any other makes.

From the year 1911 onwards the manufacture of Quadrants was in the hands of March Newark and Co Ltd, of Lawley Street, Birmingham, who on occasions styled themselves 'Quadrant Motorcycles' of the same address. Originally founded in the days of the Klondike gold rush, the firm in the early days exported timber appliances and various types of wooden wheels to Africa. The latter activity possibly inspired their telegraphic address which was 'Spokesmen'. Later, manufacturing capacity was extended to cover the production of wheels of all descriptions, enamels and lubricants, and for a number of years the concern enjoyed a near monopoly in the manufacture of steel bands for solid tyres.

By the mid-twenties the Lawley Street works was a model of its kind and largely self-contained with its own artesian well and a beautifully maintained electricity generating plant powered by two suction-gas engines of 95 and 135hp respectively.

Ixion describes the early Quadrants as being 'beautifully made and finished' but the products of the twenties although of sound construction were 'agricultural' to say the least. Wrought iron, a material which at that period was losing favour even with blacksmiths, was pressed into service where it was expedient to do so and the pitted state of the few surviving examples I have seen indicates either poor quality steel or minimal attention to detail in the matter of stove enamelling. Quadrants were invariably 'bitty' looking machines and the extensive use of nuts and bolt heads of full Whitworth dimensions did nothing to help appearance. Examples of extreme thoroughness in design are occasionally apparent, such as the practice of screwing the rear sprocket to the hub (left hand thread) and further securing it by studs threaded through the hub-boss, with lock nuts and spring washers to finish the job off.

Despite the impression which may have been conjured up as a result of the foregoing paragraph, Quadrant was probably, during the twenties, the most robust machine on the British market, the simplicity of its designs rendered it almost

fool-proof and it sold at a remarkably low price. Whilst I am in no position to verify the theory, I would imagine that the manufacturers were, at this particular period too pre-occupied with other 'irons in the fire' to care over much if they sold any motorcycles or not. There was nothing aggressive in their advertising and they would let a year lapse with scarcely an advertisement in the motorcycle press.

1920-22

Supposedly to assist 'streamlining' of the ports the single cylinder engine in use for 1920 was unusual in that the exhaust valve was at the side of the cylinder and the inlet at the rear. The exhaust cam wheel drove a second wheel of the same size on the end of a short inlet cam shaft. This second wheel engaged with a third to provide the drive for the magneto which was mounted behind the crankcase.

The engine fitted to the sole model for 1920 had a bore and stroke of 87 x 95mm which was, with commendable accuracy described as having a capacity of 565cc and less precisely as being of 4½hp. The magneto was ML and the carburettor an Amac.

All-chain transmission was via a three-speed Sturmey Archer gearbox with its control mounted on the seat tube. The frame gave a moderately low saddle height of 29 inches and what was technically a saddle tank had a capacity of 2½ gallons of petrol and two quarts of oil. At £95 the 1920 Quadrant offered more cubic centimetres per pound (sterling) than most of its contemporaries.

An even bigger single was introduced for 1921, the 6hp with a stroke of 110mm which gave a capacity of 654cc. The new model closely followed the design of the 4½hp which in turn differed but little from its counterpart of 1920. For 1921 however, on either model a Senspray carburettor in place of an Amac was optional and chain-cum-belt transmission could be specified by anyone sufficiently conservative to do so.

There was a reversion to only one size of engine for 1922 and some doubt exists as to its capacity. At Olympia in December, 1921 the bore and stroke of 85 x 110mm (624cc) was given, but the *Buyers Guide* which appeared in April 1922 lists 87 x 110mm (654cc).

The curious valve arrangement was retained and such items as aluminium footboards, dummy belt rim rear and stirrup front brake arrangements remained as previously. There were however several changes, the front mudguard no longer had valances, the saddle tank was now rounded off and stout aluminium covers protected the chains. Hitherto the exhaust system had consisted of the familiar cylindrical expansion chamber in front of the crankcase but there was now an aluminium 'double expansion' chamber on the right hand side just below the footrests. It can most easily be described as two approximately cube shaped chambers, one behind the other linked together with a restricting passage. Belt final drive was available at £80 as compared with £85 for all-chain transmission.

1923-25

1923, and the big single is quoted as having a capacity of 654cc. There is a return to the original silencing system and the tyre size had changed form 26 x 2½ inches to 700 x 80mm. The other important alterations were the adoption of an internal

Jack Bacon's 1923 6hp Quadrant

expanding brake for the front wheel, and the newer more compact type of Sturmey Archer gearbox.

A machine of traditional Quadrant conception had a new engine with a conventional side-by-side valve layout. On this engine the cylinder head was detachable and when removed it brought with it the valves and their associated seatings and ports as with the more familiar AJS. The method of securing the head by means of a yoke across the top pulled down by two long rods from the crankcase also closely followed AJS practice. Gear drive was retained for the magneto which was mounted behind the cylinder. The capacity was 490cc (79 x 1000mm) and so the introduction of the machine marks Quadrants first post-war '500'. Both models for this particular year were listed at prices which included electric lighting.

In the 1924 programme the capacity of the big single was reduced to 624cc (85 x 110mm), and an orthodox arrangement was adopted for the valves as in the case of the previous years smaller model. The head was secured by the yoke and two long rods method, but the barrel also had a four-stud flange.

The 624cc model was now being called the 'A' and the 490cc the 'B'. How much midnight oil the publicity department spent concocting these designations we shall never know! Previously 'clutch type' levers had operated the exhaust valve lifter and the front brake but for 1924 the more usual inverted levers came into use.

A Binks carburettor could now be specified in place of an Amac for either model. Tyre sizes were 26 x 3 inch for the 624 and 26 x 2½ inch for the 490 but confusion exists concerning a couple of more important specification details. *The Motorcycle's* 1923 Olympia report says that both machines had pump lubrication and that the 490 had a Burman gearbox, whilst the 624 is clearly illustrated with a Sturmey Archer. The *Buyers Guide* March, 1924 lists mechanical lubrication and Burman gears in either case. However a press advertisement appearing in June, 1924 illustrates with microscopic line drawings both models - with Sturmey Archer boxes and obviously without mechanical lubrication!

The 'A' sold at £55 and the 'B' at £50; both prices were exceedingly low since they included bulb horn and gas lighting set. Electric lighting as an extra only appears to have been offered for the 'B'.

The 1925 624cc remained basically unchanged but the exhaust tail pipe had been moved from the left to the right hand side and mechanical lubrication and Burman gearbox now definitely figured in the specification. Mechanical lubrication was by a tiny Showell pump which delivered oil through the sight feed of the Best and Lloyd semi-automatic hand pump on the tank and thence to the crankcase.

The 490cc model had taken on a completely new look. It now had a flat tank with an exposed top tube. A long plated exhaust pipe was followed by a small silencer with a long tail pipe. Previous Quadrants had tool boxes on their rear carriers but the tool box was now on the seat tube.

A 490cc OHV was listed for 1925 but little was heard of it and it was not continued for the following year.

During 1925 a comprehensive range of sidecars was produced, built in a separate factory at Greet. Service Depots were at the time operating at Essex Works, Lavender Hill, Clapham Junction; 157 Lower Briggate, Leeds; 99 Manchester Road, Bradford; and 50 Hardman Street, Deansgate, Manchester. At some time during 1925 the London Depot closed down and its function was continued, for a time at least by Clifford Wilson at 177 Westminster Bridge Road, London SE1. Industrial archaeologists may possibly decide that the Northern addresses were those of existing Quadrant dealers.

It was also in 1925 that word appeared in the press that The Quadrant had closed down. As in the case of Mark Twains alleged death, 'the report was grossly exaggerated' and apologetic disclaimers hastily ensued.

1926 –30

At the same time (October, 1925) the 1926 range was announced showing the marque to be one of the most competitive in the industry. Increased discounts were offered to dealers and those considered substantial could buy on credit terms.

The 624cc model, usually referred to as the 4½hp remained unchanged but there was the choice of 27 x 3¼ tyres 'on special rims' (presumably well based for wired edges).

On the 3½hp 490cc model there was a return to the old type of exhaust system with forward mounted transverse expansion chamber and the tool box had been moved to the carrier. Only a minimal guard protected the primary chain. Engine specification details included an aluminium piston, Amac 'Sports' (sic) carburettor and 'full size' ie four stud magneto.

The tank had an unexpected refinement in the form of a double partition between the petrol and oil compartments, a welcome feature in an era when partition breakdowns were all too common.

Since 1926 was the end of a period of partial stagnation in design it may be a convenient point to 'recap' by saying that both machines had a dummy belt rim rear brake, pan type saddle (choice of Brooks or Lycetts on the 3½) and the tyre pump carried in a pair of awkward looking clips on the seat tube. An insignia on the tank sides still quaintly proclaimed the machine to be '*THE* QUADRANT'. In the matter of tanks it has been said that the flat type were of Norton manufacture which may possibly be correct but may just have been assumed on account of the serrated edges to the seams.

The 1926 Quadrants may have been a little outdated but at £42 10s 0d the 3½ was the cheapest (including the 'P' Triumph) 500cc on the market and the 4½ cost only £48.

In December, 1925 what was intended to be a publicity stunt became, due to bad weather, bad luck and haphazard preparation, a non-event. The object of the exercise was to make fifty ascents of Bwelch-y-Groes with a sidecar outfit. With this aim in view one of the new 1926 490cc Quadrants was ridden by Clifford Wilson, described as 'the well known Quadrant exponent' with an ACU observer in the sidecar. Such an outfit would have cost £53 at the time and, had the bid succeeded sales should have received a welcome boost.

With banks of mist and rain being driven by a half gale of wind, a preliminary ascent was attempted just after dawn. The machine ran out of power on the steepest part and returned to 'base' for a change of sprocket to lower the bottom gear to 20 to 1. By now the expansion box had shed its end plate. On the next climb overheating set in and the plug was suspected. Eventually a racing plug from the kit of one of the accompanying cars was fitted, having been spaced out with six extra washers on account of its longer reach. The opportunity was taken to secure the carburettor with rag which was working loose and observed ascents began accompanied by drenching showers of rain. Overheating seemed to have been overcome and steady ascents and descents were being made in ten minutes for the three mile 'round trip'. On the eleventh trip the machine ran out of petrol and after the sixteenth there was a halt for refreshments. The rain was by now blinding and after the twenty-fifth circuit activities ceased for the day, by which time the speedometer had to be removed and the generator had jolted loose. On the second day the weather was a little better but not ideal and after one successful ascent the engine blew out its exhaust valve cap thus bringing the attempt to an untimely and unspectacular end.

The year 1926 was described in the motorcycle press as a period during which the Quadrant had been 'lying low' although one cannot help but gain the impression that ever since 1920 the manufacturers had done little else. However for 1927 the range consisted of three models of completely different design from their predecessors. It is curious that at a time when other manufacturers were turning their attention to saddle tanks all examples of 'Britain's Oldest Motorcycle' had flat tanks. The possibility that such components were Norton items becomes more credible since they held petrol only, oil in each instance being contained in a six pint separate tank. Common to all models were interconnected seven inch internal expanding brakes, ML magnetos, Amac carburettors, grease gun lubricators for the cycle parts, knee grips, friction dampers on the front forks and steering dampers. The steering damper was a neat and ingenious conical device incorporated in the steering head. Timing gears were now ground to ensure silence and to the same end, a new design of cylindrical silencer had spring steel buffers which were supposed to 'give' to the gas impulses.

All machines had 3.24 inch tyres with wired edges, a refinement which at that time usually signified a more enlightened manufacturer. Various detail improvements had resulted in a much less dated image such as the substitution of a spring top Terry saddle for the old pan seat, a less cumbersome rear carrier, and flat strip instead of wire stays for the front mudguard. The control for the gearbox which was still a Burman, was alongside the tank. Appearance-wise abandoning the saddle tank was a good move for it was not really a saddle tank in the usually accepted sense of the term, and 'Quadrant' without the preceding 'The' now appeared in large block capitals.

The1927 models featured a new OHV with a capacity of 499cc. The bottom-end of the engine was of typical Quadrant design but modified to give a shorter stroke of 88mm with a bore increased to 85mm. Duralumin was used for the push-rods and the rockers ran on roller bearings. The cylinder head had two exhaust ports and, as if to prove that there was a valid reason other than that of appearance for adopting such a design, both exhaust pipes were brought back along the left hand side of the machine, each with its own silencer. Twist grip control was provided for the throttle and likewise the clutch.

The side-valve models employed the same engines, with internal detail improvements as before, but a long exhaust pipe now crossed over the front down tube and led along the near side. The 490 now had more complete enclosure for the front chain and in common with the OHV adjustable handlebars and footrests.

The 624 had footboards. Contemporary reports state that it had fully adjustable handlebars but illustrations suggest that they were still of the stem mounting type. At Olympia in October, 1926 a 624 was shown as a 'tandem' with a second Terry seat and footrests for the passenger, but this model probably did not go into production.

Quadrants were not at the 1927 Olympia show and if a single advertisement for the make appeared in *The Motorcycle* during 1928 I must have overlooked it. 490 and 624 side-valve models and the 499cc OHV are however, listed in the 1928 *Buyers Guide* with a return to 700 x 80mm tyres. Only the OHV is illustrated and with only one exhaust pipe on the left hand side, and that at high level.

It is possible that the make was not markete for 1929 since it does not appear in the *Buyers Guide* for that year, but occasional classified advertisements appeared in the motorcycle press wherein Quadrant Motors of 97 Woodcock Street, Birmingham offered 'spares for all models'.

1927 has been given by one eminent authority as the last year of manufacture, but two side-valve models, still with 499cc and 624cc engines of Quadrant manufacture and with Burman gearboxes are listed in the invaluable *Buyers Guide* for 1930. Only a 490cc OHV Model rates a picture. The engine is a JAP and judging by the price of the complete machine (£56) it must have been one of the Standard as distinct from the Sports or Racing units. It appears to have been a purposeful looking affair with an up-to-date high fronted saddle tank and separate oil tank. The Woodcock Street address is still given. If serious manufacture in commercial quantities was in fact undertaken during 1930, Quadrant Motors went about the job in a very quiet manner and do not seem to have overspent a nil budget for advertising.

RADCO

Very few motorcycle manaufacturers can trace their beginnings as far back as EA Radnall and Co Ltd, manufactures of 'The King of Lightweights' – Radco.

Like at least one other well known motorcycle personality, 'Ernie' Humphries (the part founder of Humphries and Dawes who originally made bicycles, and who went on to make OK Supreme Motorcycles in Birmingham), Mr EA Radnall spent the early days of his engineering career with Smiths of Saltley. In 1895 he set up in business with a man called Harrop as Harrop and Radnall, manufacturers of cycle fittings. The address at that time was usually given at 82 Holt Street, Birmingham. After a few years the partnership was dissolved and the concern traded as EA Radnall and Co which title was registered as a business name in April, 1917. (Circa 1924 the firm became a limited company.)

Early in the century the address became Vauxhall Works, Dartmouth Street, Birmingham. The premises which in publicity line-drawing looked most impressive, continued to house the Radnall concern for many years but were demolished during the early seventies. In February, 1918 permission was granted to erect a timber and corrugated iron structure in Holt Street near Ashted Row but since the building was permitted 'for the duration of war' there can be little hope for local industrial archaeologists who might try to locate it.

Mr Radnall was of a particularly inventive disposition and as early as 1902 he took out a Patent (14825) relating to 'Improvements in brakes for cycles and other vehicles'. By 1911 he had at least nine Patents to his credit and more were granted during the ensuing years. One of his most interesting inventions had no connection with cycles or motors. He proposed a bomb which could be lowered from an aircraft by a winch to the proximity of its target, for example a hostile Zeppelin and then remotely detonated. I have no record of the scheme going beyond the Provisional Patent stage. However, on reading the Provisional Specification (17234, December, 1915) one is left with the impression that in some respects the inventor was many years ahead of his time.

As a postscript to this proposition, it is quite probable that this was the invention that was presented to Sir Arthur 'Bomber' Harris during the First World War when he was a Wing Commander in the RFC. It is well documented in Paul Brickhill's book *The Dam Busters*, although names are not mentioned, and may

1921 $2^1/_2$hp with Radco sidecar

have been why another struggling inventor, Barnes Wallis, had difficulties in persuading Harris to adopt the Bouncing Bomb.

The company lost no opportunity in publicising its wares and in 1911 it even took space at the Turin International Exposition: an ambitious project staged to commemorate the fiftieth anniversary of the unification of Italy. Here an award in the form of a medal and a diploma of merit was gained, thus providing useful publicity for more than a couple of decades – the firm's cycle and motorcycle components catalogue for 1933 was still carrying reproductions of the medal on its cover.

Having for some years concentrated on the manufacture of cycle specialities, the production of complete motorcycles was started in about 1913. The simple little two-stroke Radco was for the most part built within the firm's own factory and at the time in question the air-cooled two-stroke engine as a means of motorcycle propulsion was a comparatively new departure. However, the Radco must from its inception have been a staunch little bike, for during 1915 a correspondent to *Motor Cycling* claimed that his 2¼hp single speeder would take a sidecar and passenger 'anywhere'.

1920-22

As listed for 1920 the Radco was one of the cheapest machines on the market and it had the edge on most of its competitors with a six-inch ground clearance and ample tank capacity – petrol 1⅜ gallons and oil 2¾ pints. The firm's own two-stroke engine had a capacity of 211cc (62 x 70mm). It carried a Lion or a CAV magneto behind the cylinder, driven from the right-hand side by an enclosed chain. Transmission on the £55 model was by chain and belt through a plain two-speed Albion gearbox. A kick-start model or a direct belt drive single-speeder, were alternatives at £60 and £48 respectively. Front forks were of Druid type with two side springs, although a particularly neat fork with a single central spring had been patented by Mr Radnall (no. 23673) in 1914 and was in use on the 1919 models. A peculiarity of Radco engines of the twenties was that the exhaust pipe was attached to the cylinder by a flanged elbow and the pipe dropped vertically into a transverse, cylindrical expansion box. On some models the only outlet from the expansion box was via perforations in the end plates.

By increasing the cylinder bore of the standard machine (also referred to here as the No. 1) from 62mm to 67mm a 2½hp (247cc) was available for 1921: an added refinement was a provision for the decompressor to discharge into the exhaust system. Typical of the 1921 range was the 2½hp Sports. The specification included knee-grips and polished wheel discs. The engine could be dropped from the frame by the removal of three bolts.

Two-speed, chain cum-belt models using Albion gearboxes were listed and there was also a direct belt drive single-speed 2¼hp (211cc). Machines continued to be listed with the same transmission options as for the previous year. Maglita electric lighting could now be specified on any model.

The 2¼hp was discontinued for 1922 leaving just the 2½hp which was offered in a bewildering number of guises. 24 x 2 inch tyres and, where applicable, Burman gearboxes were universal.

There was now more emphasis on the cheaper No. 2 series. These machines had 'No. 2' incorporated in the tank lettering. Features which distinguished the No. 2 from the standard range initially included petroil lubrication, as distinct from 'drip', and a Mills carburettor instead of the usual Amac. More noticeable was that the magneto was directly coupled to the right-hand side of the crankshaft. This feature has in more recent times led some people to believe that the engines were Unions although in other respects there was little or no similarity. The No. 2 came in single-speed, plain two-speed, and two-speed, kick-start versions. The first mentioned weighed only 118lbs. and sold at £34 14s 0d.

Turning to the standard range, which for convenience I shall refer to, although the manufacturers possibly did not always do so, as the No. 1 models, there was a newcomer in 1921 - an open-frame ladies model. The engine was inclined in the

Top, 1921 Ladies Model and bottom, a 1922 Radco No. 2

frame which had a short horizontal top tube and a conventional but shorter than usual tank. A dress-guard of Radnall registered design which acted as a sort of bulkhead behind the engine combined with a one-piece cover over the primary drive and the top run of the belt effectively separated the rider from the 'works'. Footboards were included in the specifications and the belt-rim rear brake was operated by the left heel. A Burman gearbox with its control alongside the tank provided two speeds, a clutch and kick-starter. Inverted control leavers were not used and the ends of the handlebars terminated in miniature 'horns' facing downwards. As to lubrication, *Fletcher*'s states, and *Buyers Guide* implies that this was 'forced' or 'drip' which would have been in accordance with No. 1 practice, but a contemporary illustration suggests that it may have been by petroil. I have described the Lady's as a newcomer but there is reason to believe that it was a re-introduction of a model which had appeared some years previously.

The company must have known what could be expected of a lusty two-stroke engine in a light frame and now introduced an attractive combination. The sidecar, which was of their own manufacture was of rakish appearance, unexpectedly roomy and the pointed tail incorporated a capacious locker. The machine itself could have a two or three-speed gearbox, in either case with clutch and kick-starter, a Maglita lighting system was normally fitted and all wheels on the outfit had aluminium discs.

Three-speed gear was not a normal option on solo models which came in single speed, plain two-speed, and two-speed and kick-start versions. *The Motorcycle's* advance description stated that all No. 1 models would have purple tanks with black and gold lining, CAV or Rumbaken magnetos and Best and Lloyd sight-feed lubrication. It also said that tyres would be of 2¼ inch section, which does not seem to have been the case and that foot boards would be standardised, although it is questionable that they in fact were.

1923-24

The only development of any importance for 1923 was the availability of chain final drive. All-chain models had an external contracting or 'band' brake on the drive-side of the rear hub. Tyres remained of 2 inch section which, bearing in mind the lightness of the machines, 123lbs. for the most simple model, was probably adequate.

Petroil lubricated, belt driven No. 2 models were listed in single speed, plain two-speed and two or three-speed, kick-start versions.

The Lady's model retained its belt final drive and was offered in two or three-speed forms with in either instance a kick-starter. Lubrication was now given as being by petroil.

There were, for this year, no single-speed No.1 models and all had kick-starters. Sports solos were listed only in all-chain form but with two or three-speeds and touring solos likewise.

Three-speed gearboxes were used on all combinations but there was again the choice of belt or chain drive. A box carrier model was added with chain-cum-belt drive and petroil lubrication. Few manufacturers can ever have used a 2½hp engines for eight models in one year!

An otherwise unspectacular 1924 range was enlivened by the introduction of a de luxe sidecar outfit. The sidecar consisted of a pretty Hughes aluminium body mounted on a Radco chassis. Electric lighting was by Maglita and an instrument panel in the chair was equipped with an ammeter, a volt meter and a clock.

Common to all No. 2 models were 2 inch tyres, the side mounted magneto, Mills carburettor, petroil lubrication and belt final drive. The four different versions differed from one another only in the transmission details – single-speed, plain two-speed and two or three-speed with kick-starter. They were unexciting machines, but competitively priced at from £23 10s 0d to £31 10s 0d.

All No 1 Machines now had 2¼ inch tyres and with the exception of the Lady's drip feel lubrication. The Lady's was still offered with two or three-speeds but retained belt drive. Possibly it was thought that it was easier for a lady to slip on a spare belt than to deal with a broken chain?

Solos were offered with the choice of two- or three-speeds. Standard models now had long plated tail pipes and with either footrests or footboards. Sports versions were fitted with long plated exhaust pipes terminating in the maker's own 'Si-le-o' silencer. One contemporary stated that Standards retained chain-cum-belt drive but other indications are that, as in the case of the Sports it was all-chain. Fairly general use was now being made of the curious 'XL All' saddle, notable for its horizontal suspension springs.

During 1924 a design was evolved to provide the engine with a detachable cylinder head but I can find no trace that the project ever got beyond the drawing-board stays. It was also during this year that Messrs Radnall participated in the British Empire Exhibition at Wembley.

1925-27

1925 brought a vast permutation of models but few departures from existing practice, 2¼ inch section tyres were standardised throughout the range. The single speed No. 2, with direct belt drive sold at a modest £23 10s 0d.

If Radco policy to date had appeared to be conservative it must be remembered that the concern had activities other than the manufacture of motorcycles. For instance, during 1926 no less than 10,000 juvenile cycles were supplied to one buyer alone. However, for this year they made their entry into the four-stroke market. The new model had a 300cc (70 x 78mm) side-valve JAP engine with mechanical lubrication and the magneto behind the cylinder. Transmission was all-chain through a Burman box with direct mounted gear leavers. The frame was of the conventional diamond pattern with a long flat tank having a scalloped bottom seam. The front wheel had a little internal expanding brake whilst the rear brake was of the contracting-band type. There were two versions differing from each other only inasmuch as one had two speeds and the slightly more expensive alternative had three.

1926 Radco No 1

There were some small changes in the two-stroke range. The tyre size of the No. 2 series reverted to 24 x 2 inch. Only the single-speed No. 2 had belt drive, the two and three-speed versions were all-chain.

Belt was abandoned for No. 1 models, all of which now enjoyed the benefit of mechanical lubrication. The Lady's followed suit and was now available with two or three-speeds.

At Olympia in 1926 the single-speed No. 2 was one of the cheapest machines at the Show, selling at £22 1s 0d. A reduction of eighteen pence in the price would have made the figure even more spectacular. This was one of the last direct belt drive machines to remain on the market. The manufacturers in their advertisements at that time mentioned No. 2 models with all-chain drive but the 1927 *Buyers Guide* does not list any. No. 1 two-strokes were offered with the choice of two or three-speeds either of which could be supplied as a Lady's model.

The Radco Tradesman Carrier Combination was offered coupled to the No. 2, and this had a smart coach built body with lift up lid. It was enamelled in black with gold lines. The total weight of the body and chassis was 90lbs.

1928-30

The 1928 programme still offered their 'King of the Lightweights' 2½hp two-stroke model, but with the added refinement of Best and Lloyds Mechanical oil pump. The three-speed model 'B' was priced at £33 10s 0d, whilst the two-speed model 'A' could be bought for £23 10s 0d.

Meanwhile, the company had upped production of the four-stroke range. They offered a 300cc side-valve Model C with three-speed Burman box with kick-starter,

Left, the Radco 1928 Team and below, PG Dallison in the 1928 French TT

a 250cc overhead valve Model D, a 500cc side-valve Model H, a 500cc Model J and finally a 500cc OHV twin port (or double port as they said) port Model K. In all cases the four-strokes engines were provided by JAP. All the 500's were named the 'Radco Ace'.

The twin port Model K was the most expensive in the range and cost £58. Maglita electric lighting was available for £5 5s 0d. Other extras included 26 by 3$^1/_4$ inch tyres for 15/-, and John Bull knee grips for 5/- a pair. Of course this was the first year of the saddle tanks, and Radco's pride of place Model K had a new frame to go with the tank, along with 5 inch diameter brakes fitted to both wheels.

Although Radnalls were never keen on entering their own products in racing, many people were, and there are reports of successes in the French and Hungarian TTs for that year with Radco machines. The Company did however like Stock Trials, then under the supervision of the ACU, and entered their own teams with varying degrees of success.

Above, 1928 Radco Model K Ace and opposite, the Ace frame

1929 saw the introduction of two new Villiers engined two-strokes, and the final phasing out of Radco's own design of engine. The Model L had a 147cc (55 x 62mm) single port motor with flywheel ignition, whilst the Model N was a 196cc (61 x 67mm) sports twin port engine. Both models were designed to accommodate the Villiers engine, and also the new shape of saddle tank. A large Brooklands type expansion chamber was slung low down by the back wheel, but on test by *The Motorcycle*, the exhaust noise was criticised as 'being out of proportion to the engine' and was quickly modified. Also introduced was a patent steel cradle, in effect two pieces of angle iron on which were mounted the engine and gearbox. By releasing three bolts the whole unit could be taken from the frame for repairs, overhaul or cleaning to be carried out. On test, the little Model L did 130 miles to the gallon, meaning that oil consumption worked out at 2,400 mpg. (Petrol and oil were bought separately but then mixed together in the tank and hence petrol and oil consumption were directly related.)

For 1930 the range consisted of 147 and 196cc two-strokes, and 250 and 500cc four-strokes. The Radco Ace models were housed in a sturdy loop frame, and perhaps as a sign of the times, these were also available without engine and gearbox if required. Soon the four-strokes were dropped altogether in favour of an all Villiers engined range. Around 1932 motorcycle production was suspended, 'Buyers Guides' showing no new models against the Marque.

EA Radnalls from then on made their money mostly from the manufacture of bicycle components, with the occasional foray into motorcycle production, none of which came to fruition and whose products were quietly shelved.

1929 Radco Model N

RALEIGH

During the early years of the bicycle boom a retired lawyer, Mr Frank Bowden (later Sir Frank Bowden), who had been living at Brighton, exchanged houses and went to live in Nottingham. Here he took up cycling and got in touch with Woodhead and Anguis who were producing, in a small way a bicycle called the 'Raleigh'. He was impressed with the little concern and invested capital in it.

1922 Raleigh

In 1886 he inaugurated the Raleigh Cycle Company Ltd who were to become one of Britain's leading producers of high grade bicycles. In 1894 he patented the type of concentric cables used for brakes and gears which came to be known as Bowden Cables. Although Raleigh toyed with motorcycles in the very early days it was not until after the First World War that they returned to this field of activity with any sign of integrating it as a serious part of the business.

Raleighs built during the vintage period were of first class construction and sound, if not always imaginative, design. They were made of the finest possible materials and plating and paintwork left little to be desired. The machines were at least as trouble free as any of their contemporaries and were usually reasonably priced. The side-valve models were not short of speed while the OHV's were very fast indeed. Few other manufacturers can have spent as much on press advertising, and publicity stunts of one sort or another were undertaken on a large scale.

In spite of this the Raleigh, although it was among the two dozen or so makes which sold in serious quantity throughout the twenties, never enjoyed the share of the market that it could and should have done since the make seemed mainly to attract the purely utilitarian type of customer. This situation arose from a number of causes foremost of which, probably, was that the top level management seemed to have no real enthusiasm for the motorcycle side of the concern. Added to this the machine tended to be sold through the existing extensive network of pedal cycle agents rather than by motorcycle specialists. Another factor which did not help sales was that for some years all Raleighs had outside flywheels and an outside flywheel, rightly or wrongly, was never universally accepted as an entirely good thing.

Much of the money spent on press advertising might just as well have been poured down the drain and there was obviously a minimum of liaison between the technical side and the publicity department. I have in mind a three page advertisement in the *The Motorcycle* devoted to a single model and using identical large illustrations twice. A lot of advertising was carried out in the hope of 'selling' pillion riding but the impact was often lost by an obviously hastily posed photograph showing the passenger perched on a make-shift seat - or on the carrier - with nowhere to rest her feet! Most of the road stunts which took place were of a nature which captured the imagination of the public but which could not have resulted in many extra sales.

However, due no doubt to the exploits of Miss Marjorie Cottle, the Raleigh was more popular with lady riders than any other make, and probably because of, rather than in spite of the fact that there was never a 'Ladies Model'. A point that many manufacturers overlooked was that one of the reasons why girls took to motorcycling was to be as one with 'the lads'. Thus to ride a purpose built ladies model was to defeat the object of the exercise.

As is generally known, Sturmey Archer was part of the Raleigh group so naturally all Raleighs were fitted with Sturmey Archer gearboxes. Usually the boxes were standard production items but occasionally units were used which did not appear on any other make. It is rather remarkable however that the best loved Sturmey box as fitted to the Model 'H' Triumph, and for many years to Nortons, the type with a separate kick-start mechanism (and which was evolved by that brilliant designer Israel Cohen) never found its way on to a Raleigh.

During the early years, front forks with both 'up and down' and 'fore and aft' movements were used. These were either of Brampton manufacture or design and referred to here as 'Bi-Flex'.

1920-21

Raleighs were at Olympia in 1919 with a single model, the 5-6 HP twin but it was not until the latter part of 1920 that any appreciable number of these machines were in the hands of the public, by which time various modifications to the original design had been made. Indeed, it was claimed that 'thousands of pounds' had been spent on development.

The horizontally opposed twin engine was 'over square' with a bore and stroke of 77 x 75mm. The short stroke helped to keep down the overall length of the unit thus enabling it to be mounted low in the frame. The capacity was 698cc often quoted as a 700cc. As was usual with this type of engine an outside flywheel was

1921 Raleigh 700cc flat twin at Banbury 2008

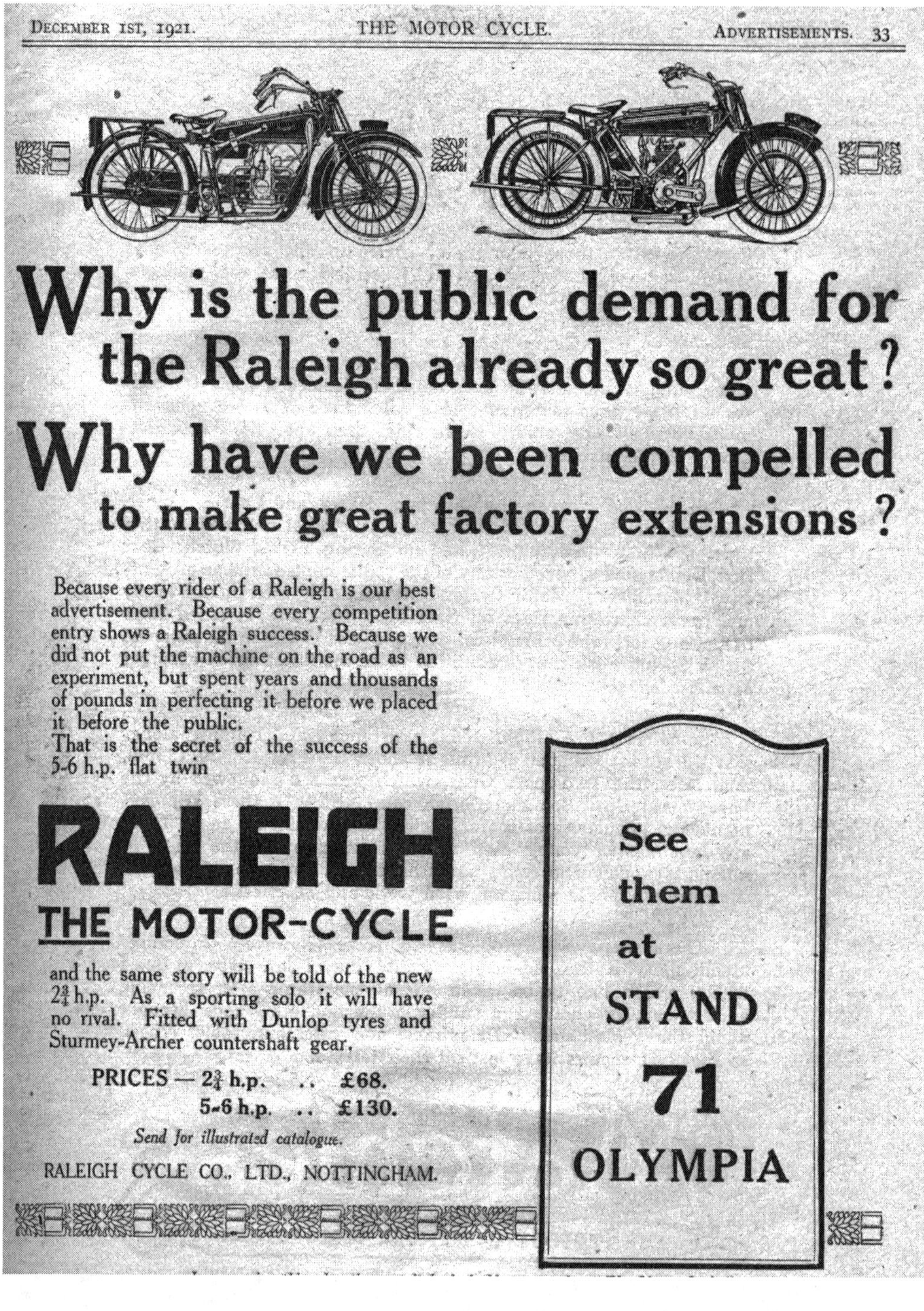
DECEMBER 1ST, 1921. THE MOTOR CYCLE. ADVERTISEMENTS. 33
Why is the public demand for the Raleigh already so great?
Why have we been compelled to make great factory extensions?
Because every rider of a Raleigh is our best advertisement. Because every competition entry shows a Raleigh success. Because we did not put the machine on the road as an experiment, but spent years and thousands of pounds in perfecting it before we placed it before the public.
That is the secret of the success of the 5-6 h.p. flat twin
RALEIGH
THE MOTOR-CYCLE
and the same story will be told of the new 2¾ h.p. As a sporting solo it will have no rival. Fitted with Dunlop tyres and Sturmey-Archer countershaft gear.
PRICES — 2¾ h.p. .. £68.
5-6 h.p. .. £130.
Send for illustrated catalogue.
RALEIGH CYCLE CO., LTD., NOTTINGHAM.
See them at STAND 71 OLYMPIA

employed. The crankshaft ran on roller bearings and roller bearings were also used for the big-ends. Clamp bolts secured the gudgeon pins to the connected rods and conventional small end bearings were replaced by phosphor-bronze bushes in the pistons. This arrangement, which was to become a Raleigh feature, made it almost impossible, it was claimed, for the gudgeon pins to score the cylinder bores. The cylinder-heads were detachable. A yoke across the top of each head made contact at a central point only. Long bolts from the yokes to the crankcase obviated the need for separate fixing for the cylinders and removed any danger of distortion through uneven 'tightening down'. Either head or cylinder could be removed with the engine in-situ, without disturbing the other.

The valves were of a generous 1½ inches in diameter, the exhaust valves being made of tungsten steel. An advanced feature was the fitment of double valve springs. The compression ratio was extremely low at 3.4 to 1 and possibly accounted for the modest power output claimed, 11bhp at 3,500 rpm.

Ingeniously incorporated in the magneto drive wheel, a rotary valve released pressure from the crankcase and created a depression which induced oil through the drip-feed. The usual hand operated pump was also provided.

An Amac carburettor was mounted directly on the timing cover and from it mixture passed through passages in the crankcase casting so that it was pre-heated by the time it reached the inlet ports via short exposed induction pipes.

Apart from the top-tube the frame was of duplex construction throughout. The rear-end was sprung by means of two long quarter elliptical leaf springs attached to a point below the saddle and to the top of a bridge which also formed the front members of the rear luggage carrier. To allow for a total movement of some 4 inches, the rear guard was in two parts.

The three-speed gearbox was of special Sturmey Archer design. Around the cylindrical bronze outer casing pivoted the rear forks or chain-stays enabling the rear suspension to operate without varying the chain tension. Each speed was selected by the engagement of dogs. The kick-start mechanism was fully enclosed and the clutch with cork friction plate had a single spring.

Effective enclosures protected the front and rear chain and each chain case had an inspection point similar to the contact breaker cover on a magneto. Leg shields were 'built in' and looked very much a part of the machine. They combined with foot-boards and efficient mudguards to provide a real 'all weather' mount.

The front forks were Bi-Flex and the front wheel had a dummy belt-rim brake. Incorporated in the rear sprocket was an internal expanding brake which was cable actuated.

This machine continued in production with minimal changes until 1923. It was an interesting model but it must have been expensive to produce and probably had not sufficient power for serious side car work.

1922-4

Single cylinder lightweights were introduced for 1922. They had straight forward side-valve engines with outside flywheel and forward mounted magneto. There was a conventional diamond frame with Bi-Flex forks. Transmission was chain-cum-belt and two-speed and a kick-start gearbox was standard equipment. Both brakes were of the belt-rim type, the rear being heel operated. Models with footboards and touring bars or footrests and sports bars were available.

Basically there was a 2¾hp with a bore and stroke of 71 x 85mm (348cc) and an almost identical 3hp but with the bore increased to 76mm giving a capacity of 399cc. The latter was offered as being suitable for pulling a sidecar. Both types were supposed to come within the 200lbs taxation weight limit and either could be supplied in three-speed form at extra cost.

There were no startling development for 1923 but chain drive was available on the singles. The 2¾ was offered in no less than six forms differing little from each other save in the transmission, chain-cum-belt or all-chain and in the number of speeds, two or three. The 3hp came only with three-speeds and chain drive. The 1923 and all subsequent chain driven models had internal expanding rear brakes.

In the 1924 programme a V-twin replaced the flat twin It was a compact and purposeful looking model. The 7hp outside flywheel engine had cylinders with the same bore and stroke as the 3hp, 76 x 88mm resulting in a capacity of 798cc. The magneto was chain driven from the timing side and mounted in front of the engine. Beneath it was a flat expansion box which discharged into a long straight exhaust pipe cut off obliquely at the end. Lubrication was mechanical via a pump the body of which was integral with the magneto chain cover. A plunger indicator took the place of a sight-feed and there was an auxiliary pump, hand operated.

Transmission was all-chain through a three-speed box. A dummy belt-rim front brake, Bi-Flex forks, aluminium footboards and a seat-tube mounted tool box were typical Raleigh features.

The backbone of the range however was still the 2¾ which was available in various different forms. Readers who have available for reference the 1924 *Buyer's Guide* will notice that the cylinder bore is shown as 76mm and not 71mm as it should be. All models now enjoyed the benefit of three-speeds but the two cheaper versions retained belt final drive. At a pricey £60 the Super Sports Model 5 sported what was a distinct novelty in those days, a plated tank. The 3hp continued almost unchanged and was usually advertised complete with sidecar.

1925-26

1925 was an important year in Raleigh history as it was for this year that mechanical lubrication was first employed on all models. It was also the first year to have a 250cc machine in the programme and the first year for which an OHV was produced.

The OHV designated Model A Sports had a capacity of 348cc and employed the bore and stroke dimensions traditionally associated with the 2¾hp. There was nothing exciting about the design of the engine and the model looked far from sporting, but the performance was quite exceptional.

The engine had the usual outside flywheel and the crankshaft ran on ball and roller bearings, with a roller bearing big-end. A single cam served to operate both valves 'to eliminate wear and to enable timing to be more easily set'. Unlike certain of the firm's earlier engines the gudgeon pin was fully floating. An exhaust pipe of particularly pleasing shape terminated in cast aluminium, the tail pipe of which was slotted.

The frame differed slightly from that of the other 'singles' in that torque stays ran from the rear spindle to a point just below the engine. Even so the engine still rocked gently to and fro when ticking over. In common with the remainder of the models, except the new 250, the front brake was of dummy belt-rim type.

1925 Raleigh 798cc Model 13 at Banbury 2008

Tuning the 348cc OHV was no great problem according to a contributor to *The Motorcycle*. 'Take 1mm off the cylinder base and a ¼mm off the flywheel,' he said, 'polish the inside of the head and the exhaust port, fit a pair of side-valve springs inside the existing ones, give half an inch of ignition advance, ensure a good head joint and 75 mph should be possible'.

Until the advent of the so called 'round tank', BSA were among the few manufacturers of any consequence to market a 250cc side-valve, and its immediate success probably inspired Raleigh to try their luck in the 2¼hp market, thus in the spring of 1925 the 248cc model was announced and at £36 10s 0d was just five shillings cheaper than it BSA counterpart.

Those who, like the writer, are 'bore and stroke students', will have noticed that a stroke of 88mm was common to existing Raleigh models of 348, 399 and 798cc. In conjunction with a bore of 60mm this length of stroke was adhered to for the new little engine. This was an exceptionally long stroke for a 250, appreciably longer than some 350s but not unique since Blackburne were using identical dimensions for their 249cc production. (The exact capacity works out at about 248.8cc). The use of a common stroke for four different engine sizes may possibly have had certain production advantages.

The new small engine closely followed existing Raleigh practice including single-cam operation for the valves (which were of the same diameter as on the corresponding 2¾ model), magneto in front of the engine and the not unnaturally outside flywheel. In common with the remainder of the range for 1925 a mechanical oil pump, the 'works' of which were of 'Pilgrim' manufacture, was built into the magneto chain cover. A hand pump, in addition to its normal function acted as an oil tell-tale – if on being pulled up it was drawn back it indicated that the mechanical pump was working.

Transmission was via a three-speed box with direct-mounted gear lever. A pair of plates secured the gearbox to the rear of the crankcase, giving a 'semi-unit' form of construction.

The frame, although conventional, was not typically Raleigh, lugs being replaced by pin-joints at various points. The lower tank rail was duplicated and chain stays were replaced by a pair of torque stays running from the rear hub to a point just below the gearbox.

Familiar Raleigh features included an expansion box below the timing chest, three point saddle mounting and seat-tube tool box. A new departure was the adoption of normal single-action front forks. Unusual was the brake layout. A drum on the rear wheel housed two internal expanding shoes one of which was hand-controlled by Bowden Cable and the other, heel operated. The tank held 1¾ gallons of petrol and 2½ pints of oil, the wheels had 24 x 2¼ inch tyres, the saddle height was 27 inches and the weight was 172lbs. There was even a front stand.

This was a prettier looking machine than the 2¼ BSA, marginally faster and technically, possibly slightly superior but it did not enjoy the same measure of popularity, although it did sell in fair quantities.

For 1925 the V-twin was virtually unchanged as was the hp. That the latter was primarily intended as a sidecar machine was indicated by the 18 to 1 bottom gear.

The 2¾ at from £45 to £49 10s 0d came wearing four different hats – the belt drive Popular, the belt drive Semi-Sports the all-chain Touring and the all-chain Semi-Sports version which had long exhaust pipes with cylindrical silencers.

Constantly breaking fresh ground for 1926, Raleigh entered the ultra lightweight market but resisted any temptation to dabble with two-strokes, choosing instead to produce a 174cc side-valve machine; a complete break away from tradition in that it employed unit-construction. This was the first example of any engine fitted to a Raleigh being described as of Sturmey Archer manufacture, which seems to suggest that there were hopes of selling the engine-gear unit to other manufacturers.

Two speeds were obtained by sliding one or other of the gears on a countershaft with its opposite number on the left or right hand crankpin. Lubrication was by hand pump. The engine, which ran 'backwards', did not have an outside flywheel and did have the magneto behind the cylinder. The carburettor was to have been of Villiers manufacture but most illustrations suggest that an Amac was the usual equipment.

The engine-gear unit was housed in a neat loop frame with the wedge tank suspended by clips from the top tube. Hand and foot brakes were internal expanding operating within a common drum, integral with the rear sprocket. Tyres were 24 x 2 inch.

That it would 'go anywhere and climb anything' can have been no idle claim for Archie Cocks, a well known accessories representative fitted a sidecar to one of these models and used the outfit on the Isle of Man during the TT period. Whilst he told a representative of *The Motorcycle* that the combinations provided satisfactory transport for two persons, he was not aware at the time that already four of his friends had 'borrowed' it for a joy-riding escapade!

The other models in the 1926 range were practically identical to their 1925 forebears but the 2¾ was no longer offered with belt drive. By way of recapitulation, except where otherwise stated, all Raleighs now had, as in all previous years from 1921, dummy belt-rim front brakes, a magneto in front of the crankcase and a tool box on the seat-tube.

1927

The 1927 programme showed Raleigh to be offering models covering as wide a range of capacity classes as almost any other British producer. To give some idea of the size of the concern in those days, the Nottingham works had a frontage of over a thousand feet, occupied sixteen acres of floor space and employed 5,000 skilled workers. There was a gas plant which supplied a 3,000hp gas engine and a 350hp diesel engine had recently been commissioned. The complex had its own wells for water and its own railway siding. Raleigh, already renowned for fine finish, had just installed new stove enamelling and nickel planting plant, which were probably without equal in the industry. Incidentally, an advertisement which appeared in *The Trade*' during January 1927 hopefully offered the redundant gas-fired stoving ovens for sale.

Although it was capable of producing some pretty fast machines the firm was not as yet taking a very active part in racing. It has been said of Diogenes of old that while his contemporaries were busily preparing to go to war he chose to roll a barrel up and down a hill, arguing that he was doing as much good as they were. In the same manner when other manufacturers were proudly announcing their TT successes in *The Motorcycle* (23 June, 1927) Raleigh were announcing their sweeping victories in the Selanger Hill Climbing Competitions at Kuala Lumpur. Little or no publicity was given by Raleigh to the fact that, under ACU observation, one of their 248cc side-valves taken from stock by Shell-Mex Ltd had, in July of that year, after 2,000 miles on road and tracks, put up a speed of 56.25mph over the half mile at Brooklands. Incidentally, during the course of these tests, three 350 OHVs, a Coventry Eagle JAP, an OEC Blackburne and a Royal Enfield returned figures of 63.85, 63.83 (identical!) and 61.22mph respectively.

The big breakthrough for 1927 was the entry into the 500cc class with a functional side-valve single. The engine, which for a change had inside flywheels and a bore and stroke of 79 x 101mm gave a swept volume of, for all practical purposes, 495cc, but some junior in the drawing office did not get his sums right and the capacity was given as 498cc: the error was not corrected for some years. Lubrication was mechanical but by means of a pump (of the firm's own design) housed within the timing case. Before long it became evident that this pump was not one of the engine's star features.

Oil was carried in a separate tank which housed a hand pump and by the expedient of using this device to force extra oil through the mechanical pump, external oil 'plumbing' was cut down to a minimum. The oil tank was formed into a compact unit with a leather fronted tool box and was mounted on the seat tube. This arrangement was subsequently to become almost standard practice on other Raleigh models.

1927 4.98hp side valve

Once again a Villiers carburettor was originally specified only to be replaced on most production models by an Amac. When the model was first announced the exhaust system consisted of an expansion box and tail-pipe but during 1927 a long pipe with a cylindrical silencer was adopted.

The gearbox was a new Sturmey Archer model which 'lay on its side', that is to say the layshaft was behind the mainshaft and not below it. The box had its main fixing to the rear engine plates thus eliminating the usual gearbox platform. This semi-unit short down-tube form of construction gradually became a typical Raleigh feature. As with all production hitherto and in common with the other 1927 models the 'flat' tank was finished in black, lined in red and gold and with the name 'Raleigh' in the distinctive cursive style.

The front forks were single action Brampton type with centre spring and at last there was an internal expanding front brake

During the 1927 season this Model 21 won the award for the most silent machine in the London – Edinburgh Trial. At £45 it was not the cheapest 500cc motorcycle on the market but it certainly represented outstanding value.

With the exception of the 348cc Light Tourist and the 174cc Model 17 (which, it will be recalled, had both brakes on the rear wheel) internal expanding front brakes were standard and there was a general swing towards wired edge tyres. Otherwise differences from the 1926 range were mostly a matter of detail.

Only the previously described Model 17 relied solely on hand pump lubrication. The remainder were lubricated by mechanical pump with auxiliary hand pump. This, the smallest model in the range, now had an exhaust valve lifter working on a neat quick-thread principle – and a rear carrier. Beaded edge tyres were retained.

248cc examples were listed in no less than four different types. Common to all of them were parallel action twin central spring front forks and front rear stands. They differed little from one another either in specification or price and can briefly be summarised thus:

Model 15
Pan seat, 26 x 2.75 inch wired edge tyres, saddle height 29.5 inches, valanced front guard, weight 182lbs.
Model 15 De-Luxe
Terry spring top seat, 27 x 2.75 inch wired edge tyres, saddle height 27 inches, valanced front guard, weight 187lbs.
Model 14
Pan seat, 24 inch beaded edge tyres, saddle height 27 inches, weight175 lbs.
Model 14 de-Luxe
Terry spring top saddle, 25 x 2.75 inch wired edge tyres, saddle height 27 inches, weight 180lbs.

A steering damper was standard on the 348cc OHV Model 6 at a time when such an inclusion was construed by some people as an admission of defeat. The silencer was now of Ghost manufacture with plated finish. Each machine was supplied with a guarantee which indemnified the customer against any legal costs.

O'Donovan having joined the firm, Raleigh decided to support the TT and took to the Island for the 1928 races with some interesting and competently designed machines, but of the men who were eventually to ride them, probably CT Ashby who had finished third in the previous years Lightweight and TG Bullus (fourth in the 1924 Senior) were of the calibre remotely likely to secure a win. Other workers have said that the power units of those machines were based on current production practice but in fact any similarity to the 'bread and butter' Raleigh engines of the period was purely coincidental.

The Junior entry was ridden by CT Ashby who came in seventh in the wake of three Velocettes and three JAP engined machines, a most creditable performance in a race the tempo of which was such that no Nortons, Sunbeams, AJS's, HRDs or Rex-Acmes completed the course and in which the best New Imperial and Douglas could do was to finish eleventh and eighteenth respectively.

In the Senior, Ashby retired with tyre trouble and Bullus had his carburettor fall to pieces leaving J Duncan to come in eighth and R McGregor to finish sixteenth. Those in the habit of checking statements concerning performances against the Shell-BP guide to the Tourist Trophy Races compiled by L R Higgins circa 1953, will note that an error occurs. McGregor is correctly credited with 16th in one place, but Raleigh are incorrectly stated to have had three retirements in another. Incidentally this was the first TT for both Duncan and McGregor.

One would have thought that these results could have, with advantage, been exploited by Raleigh, but not a bit of it. A three page advertisement in *The Motorcycle* TT Report Number made a passing reference to a Replica in the Junior and devoted a page to a testimonial from a Channel Islands customer who had fitted a sidecar to his 250cc side-valve and was in the habit of going around five-up!

But to return to the production range, in the Autumn of 1927 it was announced that the twin would cease to be listed but would continue to be built to special order. It had probably not been a particularly brisk seller but its withdrawal left the programme short of a machine suitable for heavy side car work. The recently introduced 500cc side-valve barely qualified in this respect in view of its limited power output.

It was thus to fill this gap and at the same time hopefully to attract the more sporting rider, that for 1928 a 500cc OHV model was introduced, designated the Model 23.

Around this time the first ever West of England Trial was held and it was in this event that the machine made its first public appearance in the hands of Harry Viles, gaining the award for the best performance of the day. That Mr Viles happened to be an important personage at Raleigh was quite casually taken for granted. It was accepted in those days that a manufacturer, designer, director or executive should ride his firm's machines in competitive events and it was in this environment that Britain was to lead the World in motorcycle production for so many years.

This new model had a bore and stroke identical to that of the big side-valve i.e. 79 x 101mm but was still usually incorrectly described as having a capacity of 498cc. The bottom half was practically the same as that of the corresponding side-valve model introduced for the previous year. The two-port cylinder-head had stubs for the push fit exhaust pipes. This was not a very clever feature since it was difficult to maintain an effective seal at this point. The rockers which were fitted with return springs were partially enclosed and the push rods totally enclosed. In untuned form but with compression plate removed, 18 bhp was available at 5,000 rpm. What is usually described as a TT Amac carburettor i.e. the type with a small air slide external to the mixing chamber was originally fitted.

When first introduced, tubular silencers were used but at an early stage these were replaced with less sporting looking three sided ones, the top edges of which ran parallel to the sloping chain stays and the bottom edges parallel to the ground.

The rear end of the machine including gearbox mounting and oil tank-cum-tool box assembly was on the previous year's 498cc side-valve, but a soft top saddle was mounted on a bicycle type pillar and there was no rear carrier, although one

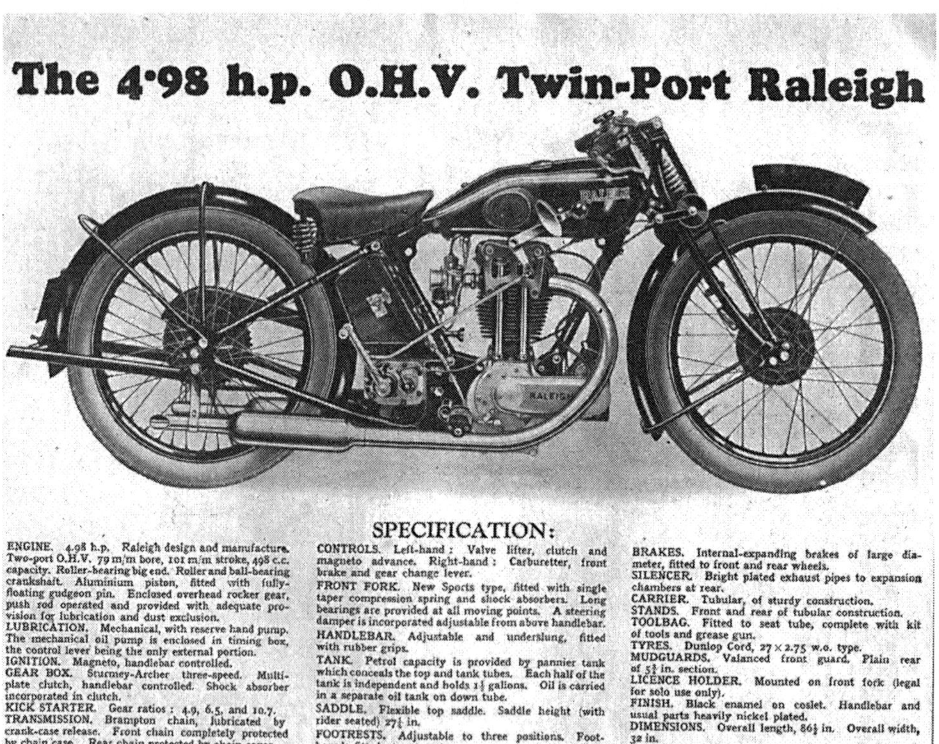

could be supplied as an extra. Typical of Raleigh conservatism was the offer of foot-boards as another extra. The remainder of the frame was re-designed to accommodate a saddle tank which consisted of two panniers each with its own filler cap and petrol tap. The top panels could be finished in 'buff orange' if specified.

Front forks of Brampton type had a single central compression spring and integral friction dampers. Provision was made for special head lamp brackets to be fitted to the spring part of the forks, thus subjecting the lamp to less vibration and at the same time reducing unsprung weight, although the manufacturer's illustrations of the period often showed conventional clip-on brackets fitted. An interesting feature which was rarely publicised was that the friction member of the steering damper (mounted below the head) had fabric inserts similar to those in a clutch. Braking was adequate and well thought out. The front brake had a wide range of adjustment provided by a slotted mounting for the outer cable stop. There was wing-nut adjustment for the 7 inch rear brake and an adjustable stop to vary the pedal height.

Originally the price was set at £5 10s 0d and Raleigh saw fit to invest in a page of *The Motorcycle* advertising space to offer '£100 Reward for information leading to a judgement being obtained against individuals alleged to have stated that the Company had had no intention of marketing the machine at the price'. Despite this astute piece of publicity the price soon found its way up to £55 5s 0d although I can find no record of anyone claiming the reward. Another publicity stunt was the publication around the 1927 Show Time of a questionnaire inviting the motorcycling public to evolve their 'Ideal Specification'. There were forty-two questions but the answers to most of them were obvious i.e. (14) 'Which controls to be right hand' and (35) 'What type of tank do you prefer?' but of this exercise more later.

Production of the Model 23 had scarcely got into its stride before several modifications were made to the design. The threaded filler cups were replaced by quick-release ones and later the rim size was altered from 21 to 19 inches with an increase in tyre section from the somewhat niggardly 2.75 to 3.25 inches. The bottom- end was drastically re-designed to give a positive oil supply to the big-end bearing. Further to this object, the timing case oil pump was scrapped giving place to a sight feed Pilgrim, the body of which was integral with the magneto chain cover casting.

During February 1928 what was claimed to be a model built as the result of the afore mentioned questionnaire, but which was for all practical purposed, a standard 498cc OHV, ridden by High Gibson under ACU observation, covered just over 2,000 miles in ten days returning a fuel consumption of over 99 mpg. Although the route took in most of England and part of Scotland, top gear, apart from of course when starting off, was used throughout.

Road tested by *The Motorcycle*, petrol consumption worked out at about 95mpg and the maximum speed was estimated at 'well over 70mph'. The tester felt obliged to point out that starting was a matter of difficulty since the starter did not mesh until about halfway down the stroke and did not turn the engine over nearly fast enough. This was one of the most serious shortcomings of this model for which there was no excuse, except perhaps the saying that 'blacksmith's horses are always the worst shod'!

For some years Raleigh design and styling had remained basically unchanged and the introduction of the Model 23 would have drawn attention to the fact had 1928 been for the established range, a year of detail improvements only. It was thus obviously expedient to give a face-lift to the more humdrum offerings. At the same time the number of different models, which must in previous years have been a headache to the smaller stockist, was considerably reduced and it was now only the 248cc SV which came in two different forms. The Standard model differed from the 1927 machine in that it had a soft-top saddle, improved front forks incorporating friction dampers and a long exhaust pipe with a cylindrical silencer. This and the 174cc SV were the only models which retained flat tanks with Raleigh in cursive lettering. The De-Luxe had a completely new frame which still carried the engine and gearbox in a semi-unit assembly but incorporated a short seat tube and pannier type saddle tank.

The 350s used diamond frames with conventional top mounting for the gearbox but the SV and the OHV had additional torque stays from the rear spindle forward, and the new pannier tanks. In either case a separate oil tank formed a unit with the tool box in an identical manner to that first employed on the previous year's 498 side-valve. The 350cc OHV was still powered by the out-moded single cam, outside flywheel engine and continued to be offered in 80mph trim for an extra £7 10s 0d.

It will have been gathered that the 498cc side-valve, as far as its bottom half transmission and rear end were concerned, formed the basis for the Model 23, and it now went through another stage of its evolution by having its engine mounted in an identical frame to that of its OHV counterpart.

Finally the 174cc side-valve was completely redesigned. Unit construction was abandoned and an engine closely following standard practice was used in conjunction with a separate three-speed box. The two units were carried in the now familiar semi-unit fashion. Both brakes acted within the rear drum. This was the only Raleigh with hand-pump lubrication and with a three point mounting pan seat. In common with the 248cc machines the gear lever was mounted directly on to the box whereas the remainder of the range had quadrant change levers alongside the tank. It is possible that production of these 174cc models was very limited. I never recall having seen one and it does not figure in the 1925 *Buyer's Guide*.

1929-30

For the 1929 season the Raleigh Group decided to market a comprehensive range of engines with capacities of from 198 to 798cc as proprietary units. Raleigh, or strictly speaking Sturmey Archer Gears Ltd were already supplying about a score of British competitors with gearboxes but the offer of engines did not meet with an overwhelming response. It was however, natural that the engines fitted to Raleigh motorcycles should be designated 'Sturmey Archer' and in consequence distinguished by the letters 'SA', formed into a monogram which usually appeared on the magneto drive cover.

Not all the available types of Sturmey Archer engine were incorporated in Raleigh models; in fact 1929 marked a further pruning of the range. All models now had saddle tanks of pannier construction with ivory side panels, within which Raleigh wass written in block capitals superimposed on a Heron's Head emblem. Common to all machines except the 248cc was the provision of a gearbox driven speedometer let into a recess between the panniers of the tank, and a spring-up rear stand, although the normal mudguard mounted stand-clip was retained. Taper roller wheel bearings were universal and there was a lock nut to prevent adjustment being disturbed during the course of wheel removal.

At last, more accurately described as having a capacity of 496cc, the larger OHV was little changed from the later 1928 version except for the details already mentioned.

For a buyer looking for performance with flexibility and silence it had a distinct appeal but probably many such prospective customers decided that at £55 10s 0d the corresponding BSA Sloper was more than worth the extra 10 shillings. As in the case of all models, the 496cc side-valve now enjoyed the improved lubrication system incorporating a Pilgrim pump which fed oil directly to the big-end bearing. The remainder of the machine closely resembled its OHV counterpart but a rear carrier was standard, the front mudguard was more effective and the gear ratios were more widely spaced.

Still with a bore and stroke of 71 x 88mm the 348cc engine took on a completely new form with inside flywheels and separate inlet and exhaust cams. The unit was almost indistinguishable from the 496cc OHV, as for that matter was the complete machine, although according to published figures it weighed 20lbs less, was lower geared and had slightly more ground clearance. Such a model pulling a rather heavy side car was subsequently used by Audox of *The Motorcycle* for some 2,000 miles which included competing in the MCC London-Edinburgh run. During this period there were no involuntary road stops and no adjustments of any kind were made. Maximum speed was an unwilling 55mph and fuel consumption worked out at about 55mpg. A 348cc side-valve embodied most of the new season's refinements including the horizontal gearbox but at £48 was too expensive to enjoy its traditional popularity.

Although the 248cc side-valve followed the same general lines as its bigger brothers, it differed slightly in some respects, additionally to those already mentioned, particularly in that it had a cylindrical and not a three-sided silencer. Moreover, the gear lever was mounted directly on to the box and there was no separate oil tank. The outside flywheel was retained.

During 1929 there appears to have been available a special 496cc OHV, a Model 25, although I can find no trace of its being advertised. It needed a diet of '50/50' and, for racing, Castrol 'R' or its equivalent. In two-port form a speed of 80mph could be expected, whilst the single port version claimed to be capable of 90mph.

Raleigh was at the Isle of Man in June 1929 but luck was not with the stable. All four Junior riders retired and in the Senior two retired and one finished fifteenth. Nothing daunted, as early as January 1930, DR O'Donovan, already known as 'the wizard of motorcycle tuning' and who was chief of the experimental staff, let it be known in the trade that he had 'some useful items up his sleeve', that he had 'made arrangements with several new and successful riders' and that he 'had his eye on a TT win'. Up to the time of the races Raleighs were taken to be 'dark horses'. The Junior machines were conventional enough, but particularly potent. A single port push-rod engine, bearing little or no similarity to anything which had been or was ever offered to the public, proudly carried the SA emblem. Lubrication was by the total-loss system which meant what it said, for oil from a *one gallon* tank was conveyed to the big-end and to the cylinder wall by means of a duplex Pilgrim pump and the timing case by hand pump never to return again! Riding one of these machines, C J Williams, in what was only his second TT, finished a creditable fifth - a performance he was never to equal on the Island despite a number of subsequent bids on a variety of different makes. Since Williams was only a minute and a half behind the winning Rudge ridden by Tyrell Smith there can be little doubt that in the hands of a more experienced rider, one of these models, even without the advantage of a four-speed box, would have been capable of scoring a win for Raleigh. In the Senior J G Duncan came in tenth. The remainder of Raleigh entrants in the two races retired.

As for the production range of 1930, there were one or two surprises, the 348cc side-valve and the 248cc side-valve had been dropped from the programme to be replaced by models with capacities of 225 and 298cc.

This was a curious move and it is difficult to understand what was behind it since the two new models did not fall into any of the generally accepted capacity classes. The 225cc unit was virtually the 1929 248cc engine but with a slightly smaller cylinder, but the 298cc was of completely new design with the magneto rear mounted. In either case an aluminium shield protected the valve springs

1930 Raleigh MT31 350cc

and tappets, and these engines were housed in frames more or less identical to those used in 1929 for the 248cc model.

The 348cc and 496cc OHVs and the 496cc side-valve model remained almost unchanged in appearance but like the 298cc side-valve all had dry-sump lubrication.

During 1929 the Ivy concern had introduced a three-wheeled van known as the Karryall. This design and name were taken over by Raleigh who themselves put the vehicle into production late in 1930. The Karryall was a 496cc (later 598cc) side-valve motorcycle with the rear end adapted to carry a car-type back axle with its differential gear chain driven by the three-speed gearbox. The driver sat on a normal saddle and steered by means of ordinary handlebars. An enclosed van body suitable for loads of up to 5 cwt was spring mounted.

Raleigh abandoned motorcycle production in approximately 1933 and for 1934 and 1935 concentrated on the Karryall, now considerably refined, and a passenger three-wheeler known as the Safely Seven both with 742cc V-twin engines. It was the Karryall which formed the basis for the first three-wheeled van produced by Reliant, at the time of writing said to be the second largest all-British motor manufacturer.

Racing Raleighs

Raleigh TT history tends to be grossly under-rated since it is usually based on stark statistics without taking the background story into consideration. During Raleigh's four year venture into IOM racing the following finishing places were achieved:

	Junior	Senior
1928	7th	8th
1929		15th
1930	5th	10th
1931	21st	7th

Comparisons, it has been said, are odious and in this case are difficult to make: but for the period in question it is hard to think of any make which did better - apart of course for AJS., Sunbeam, Rudge, Norton and Velocette, all of which were the product of factories committed to a racing policy and which had been at the game for many years. Such legendary Island names as Douglas, Scott, Cotton and Rex-Acme certainly do not qualify. I refer of course to the Senior and Junior events only.

Raleigh's inherent trouble seems to have been that they were racing on a shoe-string and having carried out the design, development and construction of the machines, there was not enough money left to engage experienced riders. With the exception of the 1927 Junior, seventh (Ashby) all the results were achieved by

A racing Raleigh at Stanford Hall

riders who had never ridden in an Isle of Man TT prior to their involvement in the Raleigh racing stable.

Particularly creditable was the fifth place in the 1930 Junior. C J Williams was riding in his second TT and was only about 1½mph slower than the winning Rudge. There can be little doubt in many minds that in the hands of a more experienced rider the machine could have finished in first place, despite its conventional design, 'total loss' lubrication and three-speed box, but of course speculation proves nothing!

It is a great pity that Raleigh did not exploit the experience they must have gained through racing by marketing anything remotely resembling a super sports machine.

RAY

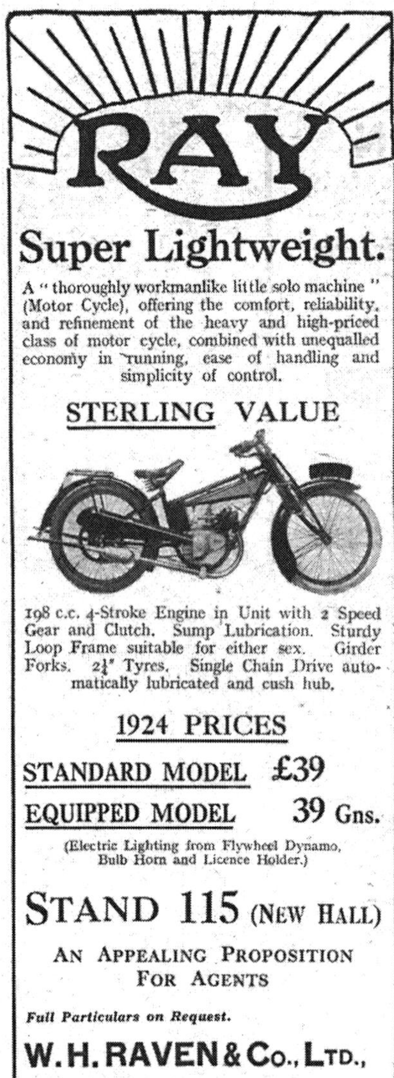

WH Raven and Co Ltd, of Castle Boulevard, Nottingham, were bicycle manufacturers on quite a large scale but around 1923 they turned their attention to the motorcycle field. If this concern's pedal-cycle with lamp bracket in the form of an 'R', dimpled fork crown and distinctive brake linkage bore a resemblance to the product of Raleigh this can scarcely have been coincidental, but the little Ray four-stroke was in a class of its own and showed considerable imagination.

For 1923 only one model was listed. The frame was of the semi-open type suitable for either sex. A single tube formed into a loop became the front down tube, engine cradle, and seat tube. The top tube sloped back at a sharp angle and suspended from it was a wedge tank for petrol only. What would have been an aching void behind the engine was filled in by a neat tool box.

The engine of the Ray design had a capacity of 198cc (60 x 70mm). It had side-valves and was built into a unit with a gearbox.

The cylinder was inclined forward and the crankshaft ran 'backwards', that is to say clockwise. Engine oil was carried in the sump. Unusual for a four-stroke, ignition was by Villiers flywheel magneto which meant an idle spark at the top of every other stroke. There was the choice of Binks or Amac carburettor. The exhaust pipe did not run parallel with the ground but sloped upwards slightly, thus considerably enhancing the appearance.

The gear unit, lubricated from the common supply, provided two speeds and a clutch but no kick-starter. Final drive was by chain on the off-side and a 'cush drive' was incorporated. The chain was well protected and automatically lubricated. Weighing only 140 lbs., and costing about £40 19s 0d, this must have been a most attractive proposition.

At the 1923 show the same machine was offered in Standard (£39) or 'equipped' (£40 19s 0d) versions which differed in detail only. The latter had electric lighting from the Villiers unit. During the 1924 season however, a two-stroke model was brought out.

For 1925 the two stroke became the TS Sports. It employed the 172cc Villiers-Jardine engine-cum-gearbox unit with three-speeds and a kick-starter. This excellent little package was never generally adopted, in this country at least, although Jardines continued hopefully to advertise it for some time. According to its designer, Israel Cohen, the reason was that it put up the price of a complete motorcycle by 'five shillings'. (Literally or metaphorically he did not make clear).

There were two exhaust ports which discharged into a transverse cylindrical box with a tail pipe on the right-hand side. The cylinder in this case was upright of course.

The Super Lightweight, as the four-stroke was called was now available with kick-starter as an extra. Either model could be supplied with 25 x 3 inch tyres instead of 24 x 2¼ inch and hub front brake in place of stirrup type as an extra.

The Ray was not listed after that year. A Lightweight had to be very cheap or very attractive, preferably both, to compete with the 250cc BSA!

REYNOLDS

Inconspicuously sited in a niche beneath the gallery at the 1920 Olympia Show was the Reynolds Runabout. It was being produced by the Jackson Car Manufacturing Co, Pangbourne, Berks, and sold through the sole concessionaires, Ware and de Freville Ltd, car dealers of Walmar House, Regent Street, W1, a concern already well known for its successful legal battle against the Motor Trade Association earlier in 1920.

Whilst the claim 'A car on two wheels' may have been a trifle far-fetched it was an attractive and obviously well designed little vehicle. The machine was really a scooter but with the advantages of reasonably large wheels, provision for carrying a passenger and an engine and transmission system adequate for serious motoring. A horizontal base-frame was swept upwards at its forward end to a steering-head which carried front forks with the fore and aft movement controlled by a horizontal volute spring. The driver sat in a bucket seat mounted on a sprung platform. His feet rested on a floor sixteen inches wide and he had the frontal protection of a full width dash-board. On the inner side of the dash-board were mounted the oil tank and a tool box. There was space behind the driver for a second bucket seat enabling a passenger to be carried in the then legal side-saddle manner, or for a parcel box.

Beneath the driver was an engine compartment its front open, apart from a wire guard for cooling. The sides of the compartment were readily detachable and the petrol tank was between the engine and the seat platform. Wheels were fitted with 550 x 65mm (roughly 21½ x 2½ in tyres). Since the machine weighed little short of 200 lbs the rear stand incorporated a lever in order to operate it more easily.

Initially the engine was 70 x 70mm (269cc Villiers two-stroke) with a Senspray carburettor. Chain-cum-belt transmission was via an Albion two-speed gearbox, its clutch operated by a pedal on the front floor. The starter mechanism was coupled by a rod to a foot-crank which could be operated from the driving seat.

By mid-1921 several alterations had been made, the engine now being a Liberty two-stroke of identical bore and stoke to its Villiers predecessor but equipped with a conventional magneto driven by an extension of the crankshaft. The front fork now incorporated a laminated leaf spring and the clutch was hand operated. £94 10s 0d was the price with £2 10s 0d extra for a second bucket seat. When the

1922 programme was announced manufacture had been taken over by AW Wall Ltd, of Tyseley, Birmingham. Tyre size was now 24 x 2½ inch and the model shown at Olympia had chain final drive. A second long wheel-base version was a full two-seater with rear bucket seat independently mounted so that the passenger faced forwards. The engine was a 70 x 90mm 346cc side-valve JAP driving through a Burman three-speed gearbox. Front forks were by Maplestone, tyres were 26 x 2½ inches and there were internal expanding brakes front and rear.

The two-seater did not appear in the 1922 *Buyers Guide* which indicates a reversion to belt final drive for the original model. The Reynolds did not appear in the 1923 *Buyers Guide* either, but the two-stroke model now being described as a 2¾hp is listed in *Fletchers* for that year with Moss two-speed gearbox, the choice of 22 in or 24 in wheels and all-chain or chain-cum-belt transmission. Ware and de Freville now styled '(1922)Ltd,' are noted in the entry which for 1924 states 'No longer being manufactured'. With more powerful backing the Reynolds might well have succeeded where others had failed.

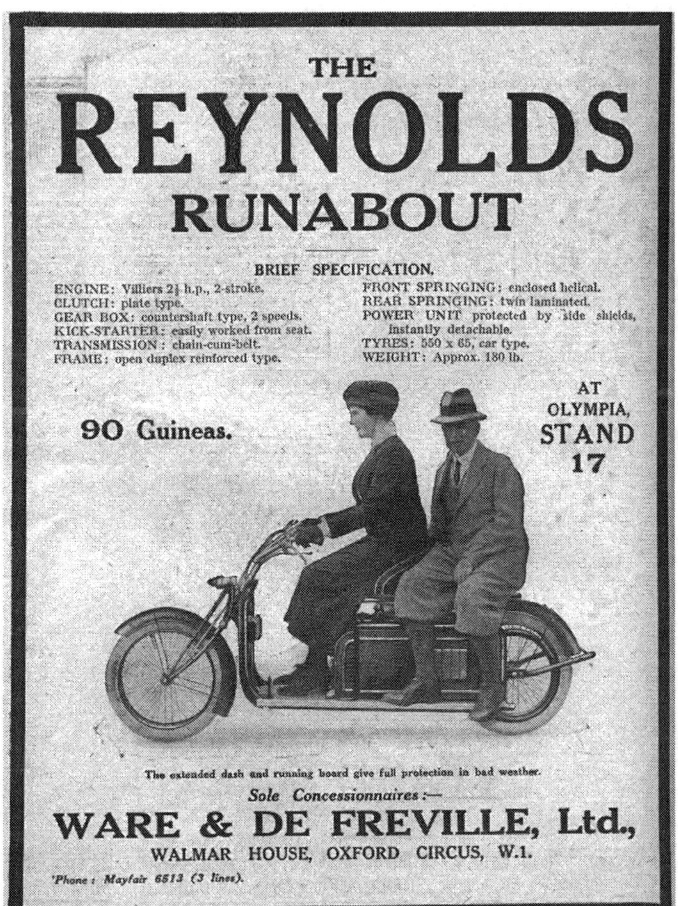

ROVER

In 1920, probably before, and certainly for some years afterwards, Rover motorcycles were produced by The New Rover Cycle Co Ltd, an off shoot of the Rover Co Ltd, Meteor Works, Coventry, an old-established car manufacturing concern of some substance with an issued capital of well over a million pounds. During the early twenties the Rover motorcycle was essentially a connoisseurs machine of straightforward and reasonably up-to-date design, excellent construction and superlative finish. It occupied much the same position in the market as did Rover cars, before their manufacture fell into other hands, and it was priced accordingly.

Single cylinder engines were of Rover manufacture although aluminium castings were produced by the London firm of Fermans Ltd, but twins were by JAP. One wonders why the Company's own highly successful air-cooled flat-twin car engine was never used; certainly it could have been, for many years later one of these units was satisfactorily installed by an enthusiast in a motorcycle frame.

1920-23

The 1920 3½hp had a 499 (85 x 88mm) side-valve engine lubricated by hand pump and with the magneto behind the cylinder. Transmission was optionally all-chain

1918 Rover American Army models

ROVER
The Rover 2½ h.p. Model Price £85.
ROVER
The Rover 4 h.p. Touring Model £95.
ROVER
MOTOR CYCLES
for
1923
provide
AN IDEAL MACHINE FOR EVERY PURPOSE
In particular the new Lightweight Model at £85 complete all on, including Maglita Head and Tail Lamps and Bulb Horn, represents
UNEQUALLED VALUE.
SEE THEM ALL AT STAND 131
and get a Catalogue.
THE NEW ROVER CYCLE CO., LTD.,
COVENTRY, ENGLAND.
DEPOTS:
LONDON: 18, Holborn Viaduct, E.C. Telegrams: "Locomotion." Telephone No. 6459 Central
NEWCASTLE-ON-TYNE: 15, Ridley Place, Northumberland Street. Telegrams: "Rover" Telephone No. 2329.
CROYDON: 9a, George Street. Telegrams: "Rover." Telephone No. 222.
DUBLIN: Lord Edward Street (Wholesale only). Telegrams: "Rover." Telephone No. 1060.
ROVER
The Rover 4 h.p. Sports Model £100.
ROVER
The Rover 5/6 h.p. Twin £115.

1920 Rover TT

or chain-cum-belt via Rovers own three-speed gearbox with foot operated clutch. Primary drive was usually by inverted tooth silent chain.

It was a commendably compact machine with a low riding position of 28 inches. Whilst the front brake was of the stirrup type the rear was internal expanding. Of similar construction the 5-6hp twin had a 654cc (70 x 85mm) JAP engine.

1921 models had dummy belt rim front brakes. The twin could be specified with electric lighting in which case a Lucas dynamo fitted to the seat tube was driven by an enclosed chain from the primary transmission. The 3½hp was now available with 3 speeds and all-chain drive or single speed with direct belt drive. These models were designated logically and optimistically the Standard and the TT respectively. It was also possible to obtain the direct-belt drive model equipped with a Philipson engine pulley. This device allowed the outer flange to move outwards thus lowering the gear ration. The actual movement was brought about automatically by a built-in governor. Some decades later the same principle but with the added refinement of automatic belt tensioning, was employed for the primary drive of Raleigh mopeds. The singles had a large cylindrical transverse expansion chamber in front of the crankcase, 650 x 65mm tyres and B and B carburettors. On the twin the expansion chamber was behind the gearbox the tyres were 28 x 3 inches and the carburettor was an Amac. On chain driven models the primary drive was by inverted silent chains and final drive by special shock absorbing chain. Rovers had competed in the 1913 and 1914 Senior TT events with a conspicuous lack of success, as far as placings were concerned. A further bid was made in the 1921 Senior using orthodox side-valve machines. A team consisting of F Collard, R Elliott (or Elliot) and W Brandish was entered; none of the trio had any previous Island form. Collard does not appear to have started. Elliott retired and Brandish finished thirteenth.

1921 was Rover's last Isle of Man appearance and in 1922, the so called TT model was replaced by a Sports version of the Standard 499cc, but outwardly at least it only differed from that model in having a straight through exhaust pipe and more sporting handlebars. It was catalogued at £110 which placed it amongst the most expensive machines of its class on the market. The Standard 499cc now being referred to as a 4hp was much the same as for the previous year except that, as throughout the range the clutch was hand operated.

A little confusion exists concerning the size of the engine for the 1922 twin. When the model was described on the occasion of the 1921 Olympia show the bore and stroke dimensions were given as 70 x 88mm ie 677cc (usually termed 680cc). Neither *Fletchers* nor the 1922 *Buyers Guide* note any such change.

Late in 1922 a completely new Rover made its appearance. A 2.5hp OHV engine of unit construction was employed with a three-speed gearbox. Primary drive was by a roller chain, the top run of which was taken upwards to drive at engine speed (initially) a four-volt Maglita (ignition and lighting) unit mounted behind the cylinder. This feature was one of the few weak points of an otherwise brilliant design. Chain adjustment was offered by moving the Maglita, which in view of the stresses imposed on it had an extra strong armature shaft running on special Skefko races. The crankshaft ran on ball bearings and the big-end bearing on rollers. There was no small-end bearing, the gudgeon pin being clamped to the connecting rod. Since no great performance was envisaged the piston was of cast iron. A bore and stroke of 63 x 80mm gave a capacity of 249cc.

Lubrication was by an early attempt at a dry-sump system. The one piece aluminium casting which formed the crankcase and gearbox housing had a false bottom with a capacity of a quart of oil. An oscillating plunger pump, devoid of balls or springs and driven from the left hand side of the crankshaft, drew oil through a filter via an adjustable valve and delivered it to the crank chamber where it was distributed by splash. Surplus oil gravitated back into the oil compartment which was in free communication with the primary drive case thus providing the front chain with oil mist lubrication.

The cylinder head was of proper hemispherical shape with inclined semi-tulip valves. Four posts cast integrally with the head provided support for the roller races on which the rockers revolved. The head was secured to the barrel by four long bolts, the barrel in turn being attached to the 'crankcase' by three studs. Separate inlet and exhaust cams were mounted on a common spindle running on ball (inner) and roller (outer) bearings. Having removed the cylinder and piston the crankshaft could be withdrawn by removing a circular plate approximating to a timing cover and on which incidentally was mounted a long gear lever. The gearbox had its final drive sprocket on the right hand side, and it could be withdrawn complete with its own inner housing. Since it had to run in an oily situation the clutch had cork inserts.

The engine-gear unit was mounted in an attractive frame with a 1¼ gallon saddle tank, the effect of which was marred by mounting the tyre pump on top of it. Internal expanding brakes were fitted front and rear. The front forks were of the central spring type, described as 'Rover-Druid'. The bottom links incorporated friction dampers but curiously each side member consisted only of a single tubular member.

Following usual Rover practice a transverse cylindrical expansion box was mounted just forward of the rear wheel but in this case the final tail pipe was on the near side. An interesting feature of the design was the front mudguard continued forward to such an extent that it covered a half of the circumference of the wheel; a good point was the spring-up rear stand. Initially the rear carrier consisted of a flat platform with holes for luggage straps.

The above is a description of the 2.5 hp OHV as it was announced. It went into production as the mainstay of the 1923 programme despite a price tag of £75.

The 499cc single continued to be offered in standard and sports form and the twin now appears to have had the 70 x 88mm, 680cc JAP engine but not the backing of an aggressive sales policy. The days of the bigger Rovers were numbered and the manufacture of sidecars to go with them had already ceased.

1924-30

For 1924 the side-valve single and twin machines were discontinued. Either the New Rover Cycle Co Ltd had ceased to trade or else it was concentrating on pedal cycles, for motorcycle production was now in the hands of the parent Rover Co Ltd.

All activity now centred on the 2.5hp OHV which had undergone several changes since its introduction, some of which had possibly crept in during 1923. Mudguards had lost their valences, front forks were now conventional girder type and the exhaust pipe had been endowed with a miniature fish tail. Modifications to the overhead valve gear resulted in the rockers being encased in an aluminium casting. Most important of all the magneto sprocket was now mounted on separate bearings and one contemporary account states that a 2 to 1 reduction gear was incorporated. What probably happened was that the number of teeth on the sprocket was doubled in cases where a magneto as distinct from a Maglita was specified.

The unit construction Rover became a 350 for 1925 the cylinder bore having been increased from 63 to 74mm giving a capacity of 344cc but which was usually quoted as 345cc.

General construction was much the same as that of the previous year's smaller capacity machine but the valances had been restored to the front mudguard and a longer exhaust pipe had no fish tail. Tyre sections which on previous models had been 2¼ inch were increased to 2½ in and a Binks carburettor replaced the B and B formerly used. In the engine, the rocker-spindles now ran on plain bearings formed by an horizontally split casting the two parts of which were held together with four studs; the lubrication system incorporated a tell-tale.

Tested by *The Motorcycle* (19 March, 1925) the machine handled well but was not considered capable of the 60mph claimed by the manufacturers. Half a gallon of petrol lasted exactly forty-two miles covered in the course of reporting the Victory trial and including much second-gear work whilst oil consumption seemed to be negligible. The tester liked the new oil pump adjustment which though still on the primary drive cover could be operated from the saddle; but he complained that it was to easy to knock the gear lever out of the 'low' notch with the knee and he was of the opinion that the gear ratios were too widely spaced. 1925 has been quoted as the last year of production but an unchanged 345cc OHV model appears in the (February) 1926 *Buyers Guide*. However business can not have been too brisk for the columns of *The Motorcycle and Cycle Trader* dated 26 March, 1926 carried an announcement that in spite of rumours to the contrary they were still able to supply spare parts for any model Rover motorcycle. But things were going badly for the Company and when in December, 1926 the accounts for the year ending the 31st of the previous August were made public they revealed a loss of £123,450 on the year's operations. If motorcycle manufacture was still in progress until this date there is little trace that it continued afterwards.

RW SCOUT

It is an odd coincidence that two widely quoted works of reference both give the home of the RW Scout as The Terrace Works, High Road, Kilburn, but this was the address of the Weatherell factory. The RW Scout was in fact built or assembled at The Motor Works, South Green, Billericay, Essex.

RD Weatherell was in the Army from 1915 to 1918 and during that time he designed his motorcycle. After the War he set up in the motor business with savings of £2,000. In September 1919 manufacture of the RW Scout was commenced: deliveries starting in 1920.

Apparently there was no lack of orders, but for various reasons not the least of which was a lack of working capital, things got out of hand and delivery schedules could not be met. Early in 1921 he was introduced to a person who undertook to form a company to take over the business. Despite the sum of £100 having changed hands in this connection the Company was not formed and before the year was

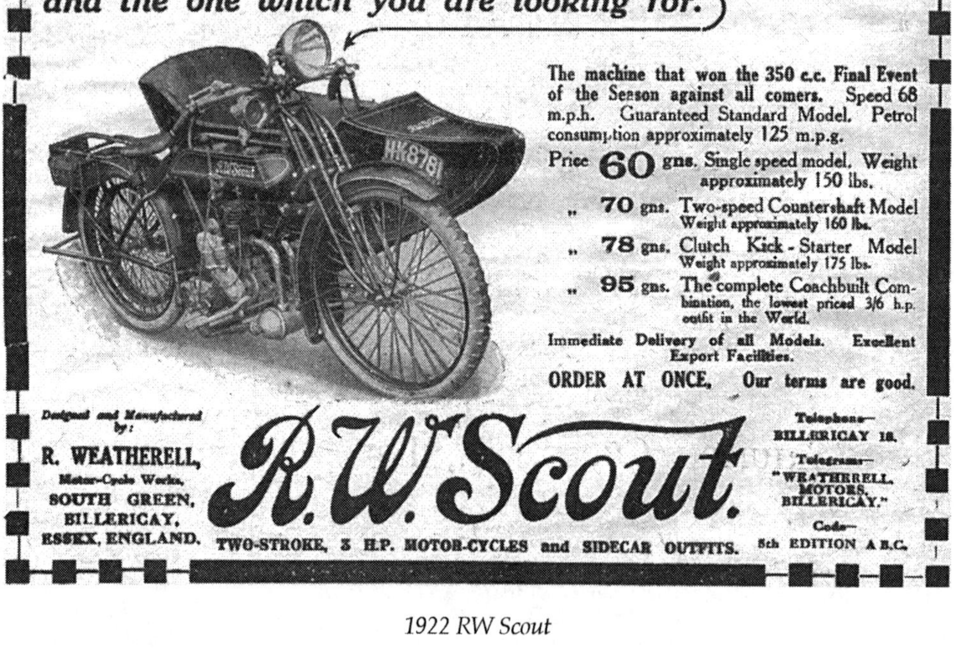

1922 RW Scout

out Weatherell found himself in the unhappy position of having to file a petition for bankruptcy.

At a time when it was difficult to pick out even one feature which distinguished one make of 'assembled' machine from another, the 1921 RW Scout was at least unconventional in one respect - the 318cc (73 x 76mm) Dalm two-stroke engine had twin exhaust ports. This characteristic was not however exploited to its logical conclusion for instead of anticipating future trends and providing two entirely separate exhaust pipes, both ports discharged into a cast aluminium expansion box in front of and below the crankcase.

Transmission was by chain and belt via an Albion two-speed gearbox with kick-starter. The price of this offering was £81 18s 0d although it was available in single-speed form with direct belt drive for the still rather high figure of £63.

It must have been apparent that this was too expensive even for those days - by March, 1921 a 269cc(70 x 70mm) Villiers engined two-speeder (and with Senspray carburettor) was listed for the more realistic sum of £42 2s 0d.

Production presumably ceased during 1921 but apparently the affairs of the business were satisfactorily sorted out and during 1922 Weatherell received his discharge and proceeded to market the Weatherell motorcycle.

RUDGE

Dan Rudge famously kept a Pub in Wolverhampton, but all motorcycles were produced long after his death in 1888. Rudge motorcycle manufacture began in 1910 with 499cc or 749cc singles and twins. One of their more interesting pre-war models, the Multi, used variable gearing by altering the ratios on the engine and rear wheel pulleys, and the machines proved to be extremely successful in Trials. War work ended motorcycle production in 1916, but by 1919 they were back on the market under the name of Rudge Whitworth. All the machines were singles using either the firm's own, or JAP engines. There were three basic variants, Standard, Special and Sports, all with 499cc engine and electric lighting was an optional extra. The success of the 499cc Rudge Whitworth in the 1928 Ulster Grand Prix led to the racing Ulster model, followed by TT Replicas in the following years. Rudge also made a short lived foray into the new world of Speedway, and produced a special that was intended to cash in on the craze that was sweeping the country at the time.

Further Reading;

Don't Trudge it, Rudge it, Brian Reynolds, 1989, Haynes Publishing

SCOTT

The Scott took its name from Alfred Angas Scott who built his first motorcycle at home in Saltaire during 1902. The Scott was way ahead of its rivals in so many ways: by 1912 it had all chain drive, enclosed sprung fork, foot change gear pedal and kick starter. They were of course, water cooled two stroke parallel twins of 322cc. A A Scott developed a shaft driven gun carrier during the war, and in 1919 sold his interest in the company to make the strange Sociable, a sort of permanent sidecar driven from the inside. Under new management during the twenties the firm developed a range of a dozen or so models, using 486cc, 498cc or 596cc engines, each variant being named after a squirrel, (Super Squirrel, Flying Squirrel and the like). From 1929 they also made a few 298cc singles.

Further Reading;

The Scott Motorcycle, the Yowling Two Stroke, Jeff Clew, 1990, Haynes Publishing

The Scott Selection, John Underhill, VMCC

SCOTT SOCIABLE

During the early twenties it was not unusual to produce a motor-cycle, the frame of which had a sidecar chassis integral with it. The logical outcome of this scheme was to use such an assembly as the basis for a three wheeled car as described elsewhere in this work.

Alfred Scott, originator of the Scott motorcycle, evolved his tricar however by using as a basis the three-wheeled gun carrier of his own conception which had been rejected for use in the1914-18 War. The name of the vehicle was the Scott Sociable. According to one dictionary 'sociable' is defined as 'a seat, tricycle, aeroplane etc., for two people side by side'.

Manufacture was undertaken by the Scott Autocar Co, (sometimes quoted as 'Ltd') at Lidgett Green, Bradford, in an ambitious new factory. The venture was (inadequately) financed by Alfred Scott and his brothers. Operations were constantly hampered by lack of working capital and unfortunately Alfred Scott died before the project had a chance to get properly underway.

Except for a cycle-and-sidecar wheel disposition the vehicle owed little to accepted motorcycle practice. The chassis was built up from straight tubes of various diameters pin-jointed together into a space-frame of impressive strength and rigidity. A forward extension, well braced to ensure permanent alignment carried a coil-spring suspended sliding member to which was attached a stub-axle for

The Scott Sociable

the front wheel which incidentally, was devoid of brake. Steering was by a conventional wheel and a rack-and-pinion mechanism.

The water-cooled twin cylinder two-stroke differed in various respects to the Scott motorcycle unit notably in that it incorporated rotary inlet valves and employed petrol lubrication. In the latter respect it is likely that the designer in his wisdom realised that a utilitarian type of owner would not have taken kindly to the idea of having to adjust separate drip feeds to suit the needs of individual cylinders. The engine was well over square - bore 3 inches, stroke 2½ inches. These dimensions were doubtless arrived at by a combination of expertise and expediency. Converted into the more usual metric terms they become 76.2 x 63.5mm, hence the somewhat off standard capacity of 579cc (usually quoted as 578cc).

The carburettor was by Zenith to Scott design. Cooling water circulation was pump assisted. On early examples the radiator was clearly visible giving the unfortunate impression of a car which had lost one of its front wheels. Later versions had a cowl covering the radiator.

The engine was mounted on the right hand side, slightly inclined and with the flywheel facing towards the rear. A metal-to-metal clutch engaged with the flywheel and drove a three-speed constant-mesh gearbox. Bottom gear was sufficiently low to deal with any hill which was likely to be encountered, and a 5 to 1 'top' made for excellent fuel economy - 70 mpg has been reliably quoted. Starting was by hand lever operated from the driving seat from which position it was also possible to 'tickle' the carburettor. An interesting feature was that the clutch control was interconnected with the gear lever.

Independently operated internal expanding brakes were provided to either rear wheel. All wheels, which were of the side type shod with 700 x 80mm tyres were interchangeable. A track of less than four feet, a wheel-base of about five feet and a good steering lock combined to give such a small turning circle that the absence of a reverse gear was no great hardship.

As was the practice with conventional cars of the period, the body was framed with timber but for the body panels however, a form of vulcanised fibre was used. This material seemed to have had the virtue of being cheap, light, durable, easily worked and capable of accepting a fine finish. The front wheel cowling which also housed the fuel tank was however, of metal.

Everything about the Sociable was properly thought out and painstakingly designed. There were no flexible control cables, even the wheels eschewed fixing studs and were secured by a simple, centre-lock device.

Inconspicuously displayed at the 1920 Show, the 1921 model had a single headlamp and two side-lights recessed into the scuttle. No dynamo was provided

with which to charge the accumulator but the rather staggering 260 guineas did include a speedometer.

For 1922 a dynamo was standard, the screen was higher, the radiator was bigger and a solid prop-shaft replaced the hollow one. It was now easier to gain access to the engine compartment. The price had come down to a more realistic £215.

It was not until 1923 that the Sociable found its way into the *Buyers Guide* and at a further reduced price of £176. The car was now being described as having a dickey seat. Lighting had been re-arranged by dispensing with the single headlamp and resorting to two head-cum-side scuttle mounted lights. Vulcanised fibre was replaced by aluminium and the starter lever was geared up to the engine.

1924 was the last year of production and only now, and alas too late, was it a viable proposition as an alternative to a sidecar outfit on the basis of price. In standard form it cost £135 whilst a 'double dickey' model was offered at £140. The front was now fully cowled which greatly improved the appearance and a cast aluminium sill or 'running-board' replaced the former wooden one.

Possibly the undoing of this little tricar was its unconventional appearance although given time the public could probably have got used to it - we take the conventional combination as a matter of course but move the sidecar over to the opposite side and it looks like something out of a bad dream. Technically few three-wheelers could compare with the Sociable but its price must always have been against it. During the twenties tricars appeared and disappeared like ships that pass in the night. The Scott Sociable was no exception but it was one which deserved a better fate.

SUNBEAM

The Sunbeam name was reputedly gained from the description of the black and gold finish that reflected the sun on the early machines. Right until the end of production Sunbeams were well known for the quality of their painted finish. John Marston produced his machines from 'Sunbeamland' in Wolverhampton. Carried over from their earlier bicycle production was the oil bath that became one of the more recognizable features on Sunbeams, and it was sold under the slogan 'The Gentleman's Motor Bicycle'. There were many pre war racing successes, and production continued until 1916. Post war two new models, a 3.5hp single and a 8hp twin were launched, and the company entered and won the 1920 and 1922 Senior TT races. Through the twenties they produced a range of singles, of both a utilitarian and sporting nature. Riders such as Alec Bennett and Graham Walker took the marque to many victories. The late flat tank Sunbeams probably rival the Nortons and AJS's for the title of best looking bikes produced in that period. The senior TT win by Charlie Dodson in 1928 was the last TT victory on a flat-tanker. Despite these successes their fortunes were falling and the firm were taken over in 1928 by ICI who continued production into the thirties, introducing new models, but eventually selling out to AMC and transferring production to Woolwich.

Further Reading;
Sunbeam bicycles and Motorcycles, Robert Gordon Champ, 1989, Haynes Publishing.

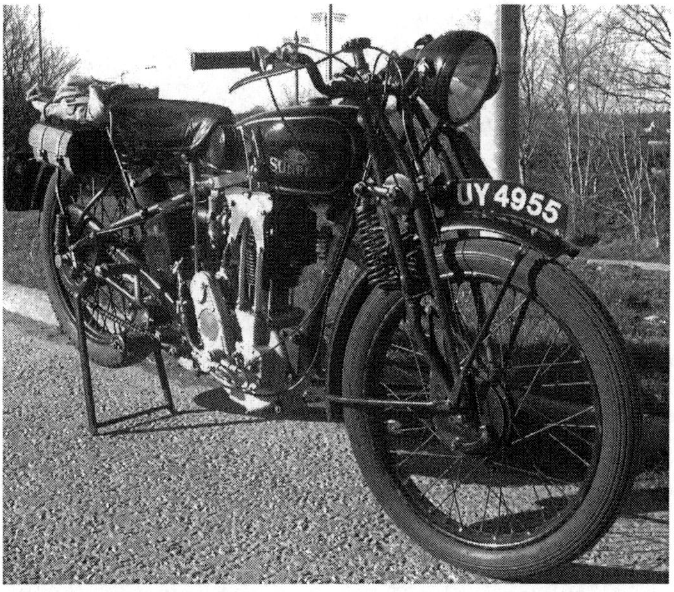

TRIUMPH

It is odd that one of the most British of bikes should have been established by two Germans, Mauritz Schulte and Seigfried Bettman. Their Coventry factory produced Minerva, Fafnir and JAP engined machines before they came up with their own design of a 499cc side-valve in 1907. This model was very successful and was developed over the years, eventually becoming one of the Kaiser Wars favourite despatch riders machines, earning its affectionate nick name of 'Trusty Triumph'. Other models were added, notably the 225cc Baby, and the early twenties saw a 346cc single with unit construction. Perhaps most famous was the 'Riccy', the four valve 499cc single designed by Harry Ricardo, a classic sports machine of its time which lasted until 1926 and was succeeded by a simpler two valve 500. At the same time as UK production was going on, the Triumph factory was supplying engines and components to its German factory in Nurenburg until 1929. By 1930 the company was ailing and it was bought by Jack Sangster who already owned Ariel at the time. Sangster brought in Edward Turner who went on to design some extremely significant bikes for the company and succeeded in reviving their fortunes into the thirties and beyond.

Further Reading;

The Triumph Story, Dave Minton, 2003, Haynes Publishing

Triumph Models Q, P and N at Banbury 2008

TURNER

At least a dozen different makes of OHC motorcycle engines were evolved during the twenties. Only a few of them survived the vintage period. Of the remainder some were never offered to the public and those that were only had a short production life. Typical of the last mentioned category was the Turner which was announced early in 1927 from 87 Rye Hill Park, London, SE15

The man behind the machine was Edward Turner. Later of course he was to find fame with Triumph, but even at the time under review he was not unknown as a designer.

The Turner OHC engine had the bore and stroke dimensions of 74 x 81mm, giving a capacity of 348cc. Identical dimensions were also currently being used by Velocette and AJS.

The lower part of the cylinder barrel was recessed into the crankcase between the two halves of which it was clamped by four bolts. Integral with the right hand half of the crankcase was an approximately square section housing for the vertical shaft which was in effect also the camshaft. The enclosure was completed by a cast aluminium cover secured by sixteen studs. Integral with the casting was the magneto platform which was sited immediately behind the camshaft housing a little above crankshaft height and supported by a stiffening web.

The experimental 348cc OHC Turner Special. Photo: Mortons Media Group Archives

A double-row ball-race supported the driving side main-shaft whilst the timing side main bearing took the form of a self aligning ball race. A bevel wheel on the timing side main-shaft engaged with one having double the number of teeth on the vertical shaft which as a result revolved at the necessary half engine speed.

A short distance up the vertical shaft another bevel engaged with one on the magneto spindle. An exceptionally neat job was thus made of accommodating and driving the magneto, a problem inherent in the design of single cylinder OHC engines. At the top of the vertical shaft were two conventional cams which operated their respective rockers by means of short horizontal plungers. The rockers in turn operated valves set at 80 degrees to each other.

The induction stub was set at an angle to the head bringing the carburettor air intake out to the right hand side of the machine. The carburettor incidentally was a TT Amac with twist grip control. There were two exhaust ports each of which emerged at approximately right angles to the centre line of the machine. The exhaust pipes gave the impression of being straight through but they may have contained internal baffles. An aluminium piston with two rings gave a compression ratio of approximately 5.75 to 1. Its gudgeon pin was fully floating with aluminium end pads. To ensure a gas tight seal between the cylinder head and the barrel, a phosphor-bronze ring was interposed between the two faces of a spigot joint.

One of the most interesting features of this engine was the manner in which the head was held in position. A yoke across the top of the head engaged with lugs on the top of the drive housing and the opposite end was pulled down to a substantial lug on the drive-side half of the crankcase by means of a sleeve nut and two threaded members. On removal of this yoke all that was necessary to take off the head was to disconnect the carburettor, exhaust pipes and plug lead and to slacken back the valve clearance adjusting screws without disturbing the valve timing.

A Best and Lloyd mechanical pump mounted at the base of the vertical camshaft enclosure pumped oil from the tank directly to the top of the camshaft; the oil was thrown outwards through holes in the cam faces by centrifugal force and from there it gravitated to the crankcase. The system strikes one as being somewhat haphazard in comparison with the other features of a brilliantly conceived design.

At the lower end of the Turner frame's front down tube was a forged steel lug from which emerged two separate tubes which swept rearwards to form a duplex cradle. To this lug was also attached the front of the crankcase and towards the bottom of the rear of the crankcase a rod passed through a lug and engaged with brackets on either side of the cradle. There were thus no engine plates and even the top of the rocker box casting was also bolted to a lug on the tank rail.

Transmission was via a Sturmey Archer box giving final ratios of 5.25, 6.98 and 11.45 to 1. There appears to have been no kick-starter. Wheels shod with 650 x 65mm tyres had 7 inch Webb internal expanding brakes and the front forks were by the same manufacturer.

A $1^3/_4$ gallon saddle tank was nickel plated with all but the nose left dull. Oil was carried in a three quarter gallon separate tank which was also dull plated and mounted on the seat tube. Other details of equipment included a 'clean' rear guard, a Lycett soft-top saddle, a steering damper and adjustable handlebars. The quoted weight was only 237lbs, for what was both a handsome and functional motorcycle.

£75 was the price asked, but even at this somewhat high figure it is doubtful if the machine could have been profitably produced and within a short space of time it had sunk into oblivion.

Tyres

It was the Irishman John Boyd Dunlop who patented the first pneumatic tyres in the late Victorian period. They replaced the solid tyres that had been in general use up to that time and proved to be a great boon in terms of comfort and stability, although they were vulnerable to punctures due to the many thorns, horse shoe nails, sharp flints and the like that were strewn across the road surface of the period. Despite this obvious step forward it was not until the end of the vintage period that tyres really came of age.

Initially, practically every tyre that was available was of the beaded edge type, that is to say they were made of rubber and had a ridge moulded into their circumference that fitted into a matching groove on the edge of the wheel rim. Standardisation had not properly commenced at first and neither wheels nor tyres were necessarily of the size they were supposed to be. A new tyre might drop onto a rim and equally drop off after a mile or two. On the other hand it might take three strong men, sweating blood, to lever it on the rim. It was not uncommon practice to fit wheels from a machine of an entirely different manufacturer, after all they were more or less the same, and customers were less bothered about originality than whether the thing would work and get them home on time and in one piece! Belt driven motorcycles also had the added advantage of easy wheel removal. With the two spindle nuts being undone the whole wheel could be taken out very quickly without the need to undo chains, brakes, stays and the like, as was the practice on later more sophisticated models.

Peter Bradley refits the wheel onto the sidecar of his 1928 Sunbeam outfit

Inner tubes were not always of the endless type that is common today. They consisted of long sausage like tubes, and were rolled up and carried in the pocket or round the neck of the rider when not in use. They were designed to be fed into the cover, sometimes without even taking the wheel out, the two ends being placed together and blown up with a pump. The tubes were either completely closed with butt ends, or were designed to fit snugly into each other with either a rubber glue solution or special jelly to provide a good air seal. Valves too were vulnerable and capable of being inadvertently pulled out, so a spare valve and rubbers were carried and could be fitted to a tube if necessary.

Towards the end of the vintage period 'wired on' tyres became common. The main difference between this and the old beaded edge system was that reinforcing wires were built into the carcass of the tyre to provide added strength and rigidity, and rims were provided with a well in the centre to enable the less elastic wired tyres to be fitted. Manufacturers developed standard sizes that really did fit properly, although many let their imaginations have free reign when it came to patterns and treads for all occasions. These, together with circular, sealed inner tubes, formed a much more reliable and safe means of connecting the fast moving machine to the surface of the road.

Above, a Dunlop beaded edge tyre and the BSA wheel it fits. Right a Mosely 'saw-tooth' tyre for competition work.

VELOCETTE

From the beginning to the end, Velocette was a family firm. The Goodman family, who had begun life as German immigrants, produced amongst other things roller skates and rickshaws from their Birmingham factory. In 1913 the 250cc two stroke Velocette gave the company a firm footing in the industry. In the early twenties they introduced a 350cc racer, the first in the 'K' series, which went on to win the Junior TT in 1926. Suddenly Velocette were very popular and orders flowed in. More TT successes followed, and they were the first firm to introduce the combined dual seat, and much more importantly the first production positive stop foot change lever. By 1930 most of Velocette's main production was based around the race and road going 'K' series, so they decided to produce a smaller, cheaper bike and the GTP 250, a single cylinder two stroke was born. This used the engine as a stress bearing member of the chassis, and came with coil ignition.

Further reading:

The Velocette Saga, Titch Allen, 1994, Amulree Publications
Always in the Picture, Burgess and Clew, 1971, Haynes Publishing
Velocette, Ivan Rhodes, 1990, Osprey Automotive

1923 Velocette G3 250cc

W and G

I don't know if market research was practiced in 1928. Had such a service been available one wonders if a demand would have been established for a 500cc twin two-stroke with air cooled cylinders instead of a water heated radiator and selling at about £10 less than a Scott.

However, the sponsors of the W and G, said to have included 'a group of West London enthusiasts', must have felt that such a machine would sell and in July 1927 details of a prototype were released. Design and manufacture were undertaken by Mr A Gough, at what was later described as the W and G Cycle Works, 108 Windmill Road, Brentford. This may or may not have been the same Arthur Gough who was responsible for the earlier Birmingham-built Gough lightweight.

The engine was simple enough in design. The crankcase was in three parts, a main casting with a long plain centre bearing and two castings which housed the side bearings. Four inside flywheels formed the basis of a built-up crankshaft, with provision for roller bearing big-ends. There was also an outside flywheel on the off-side. Oil from a separate oil tank on the saddle tube, fed via an adjustable needle direct to the main bearings. It was claimed that once set the adjustment 'could be forgotten'.

The block was cast in one piece with ample provision for air to pass between the two cylinders. The bore and stroke are variously given as 67 x 70mm, and 67 x 71mm, and the capacity sometimes as 490cc, and sometimes 494cc. Compression ratio was estimated at 6½ to 1.

Chain driven from behind the flywheel, the magneto was situated at the rear of the crankcase, very low down. The B and B carburettor was at the rear of the block. The whole engine was set well down in the frame with the cylinders inclined slightly forward.

An exhaust pipe from each cylinder fed into a flat box beneath the crankcase. These pipes which were flange fitted to their respective ports, had blind ends and were slotted to allow the egress of gas. Long pipes from this expansion chamber were brought out on either side of the machine and these terminated in large, roughly rectangular silencers, the tail pipes of which continued to a point beyond the rear wheel. A Sturmy Archer gearbox was used. This was of the more compact LS type without a separate kick-starter quadrant. Top gear was 4 to 1 and bottom, 10 to 1.

The makers claimed 70mph and 70mpg. *The Motorcycle* seemed favourably impressed by the absence of 'four stroking', the acceleration and the top gear performance. £59 10s 0d was the price at the time.

The prototype looked a trifle 'bitty' but the appearance of the 1928 model left little to be desired. Various modifications had been carried out such as moving the flywheel to the 'drive' side and placing the magneto behind the cylinders in a more conventional manner. A system of oil-ways integral with the crankcase simplified the oil pipework. The petrol tank holding 2¾ gallons was of a much more pleasing design although not of the saddle type, and the half-gallon oil tank looked less like an afterthought. The silencing system, which must have been very efficient was considerably tidied up and blended well into the rest of the design. Top gear was now 3½ to 1.The price had risen to £64 which was a lot of money, even taking into consideration Druid forks with integral dampers, an 8 inch rear brake and 3.25 inch tyres.

Although the W and G appeared at the 1927 Show, I can find no trace of it's ever being advertised. The only subsequent official press reference seems to be the 1928 *Buyers Guide* - possibly it never went into serious production.

The Motorcycle for 20th February, 1930, carried an advertisement wherein a Mr Jeens of 89 Gordon Road, Ealing, was inviting offers for W and G drawings, patterns, castings, frames, tanks and spares, and that is the last trace I can find of the marque.

1927 W and G

WAG

The WAG two-stroke engine was remarkable for two reasons: it was a 50 degree V-twin and it did not employ crankcase compression. The capacity was 494cc, and the two-throw crankshaft was so arranged that firing took place at 180 degree intervals, thus giving the even torque usually associated with a horizontally opposed twin but from a much more compact unit.

The method by which crankcase compression was eliminated was simple and ingenious. In the case of either piston a rod protruded from the centre of the lower side of the crown, roughly corresponding with the piston rod of a steam engine. This rod terminated in a cylindrical plunger which was called the 'stem' and each con-rod was connected to its appropriate stem by means of a gudgeon pin. The stem reciprocated in the bore of a member (the stem guide) which was introduced between cylinder and piston. Gas tightness at this point was achieved by fitting the 'stem' with what was for all practical purposes a piston ring designated a 'junk ring'.

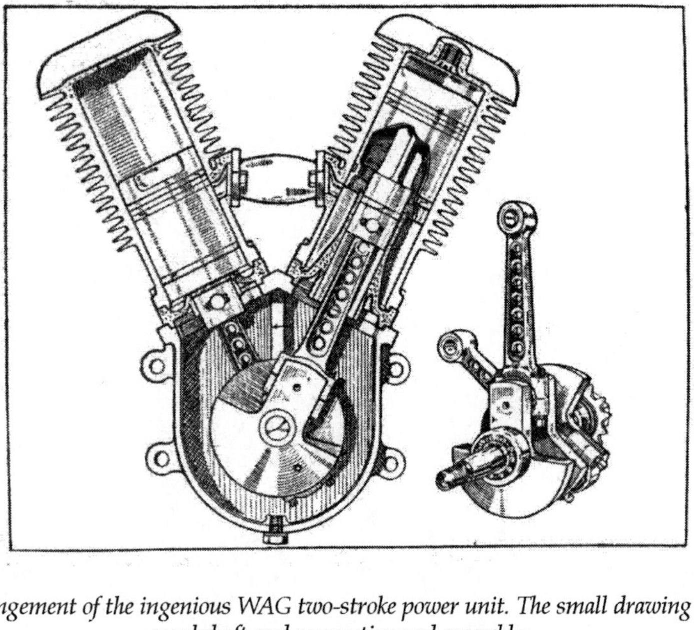

General arrangement of the ingenious WAG two-stroke power unit. The small drawing depicts the crankshaft and connecting rod assembly

Mixture entered the chamber thus formed beneath the piston, where it was subject to a high initial compression and was transferred to the combustion chamber in the usual manner. Lubrication was by splash and one wonders how the cylinder bores fared, since at first view the only oil which could reach them from the crankcase had to pass between the 'stems' and their guides. However, doubtless this point was taken into consideration since a sustained speed of 55mph without overheating was claimed. Petrol consumption was in the order of 75mpg.

The engine, it was stated by *The Trader*, could obviously be produced very cheaply but it is difficult to understand why this should be so. At least three WAG motorcycles were built, and they competed in the 1924 Scottish Six Days Trial, apparently without engine trouble. If any further WAGs were produced there probably weren't many, and in March, 1925 Messrs Wright and Gasking, 114 Rea Street, Birmingham, announced that having carried out the necessary development work, their engine was now suitable to be offered to the public with confidence. They were offering to sell their Patents outright or to grant licences for manufacture on a royalty basis. I have no evidence, however, that any other manufacturer ever adopted the design.

WISEMEN GROUP VERUS, SIRRAH, WEAVER and WISEMAN ENGINES

Few British manufacturers made motorcycles under more than one brand name. One such concern, however, was Alfred Wiseman Ltd, of Glover Street, Birmingham, who produced for some years three distinct makes simultaneously. They were Verus, Sirrah and Weaver, as well as, but with few customers, the Wiseman engines. Wiseman's activities were not limited to the motorcycle field for they were an old-established firm of mechanical and electrical engineers and founders whose products included overhead line material, tramway gearwheels and pinions and castings in iron and non-ferrous metals.

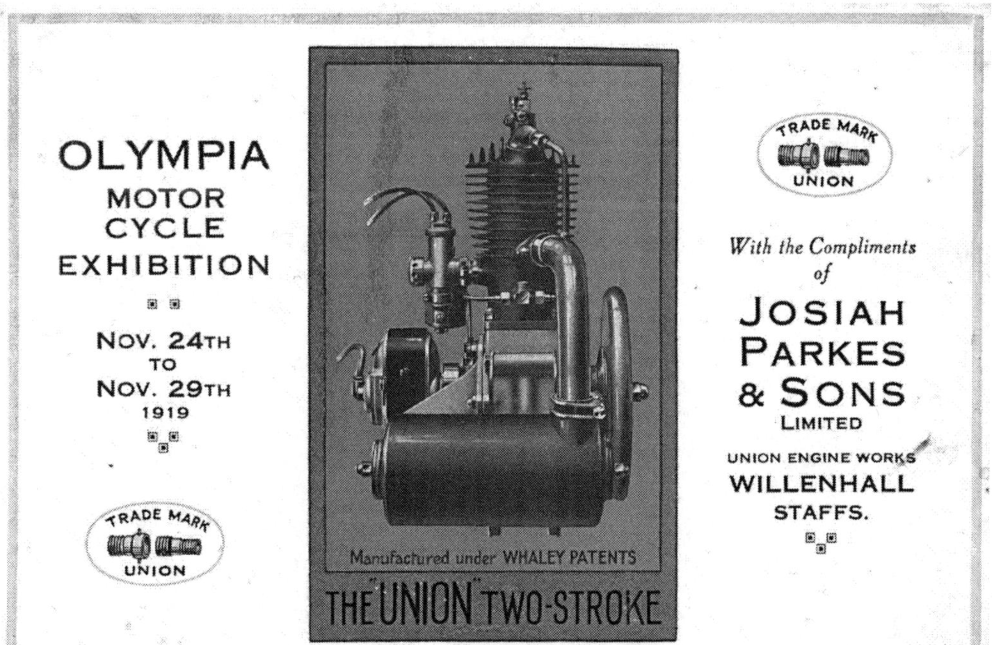

1919 Union engine

During the very early twenties they took up rights to manufacture the Union two-stroke engine both for what these days would be called in-house use and as a proprietary unit. Their rights however were not exclusive. As early as 2nd September 1921 Humphries & Davis Ltd had stated in *The Motorcycle and Cycle Trader* that all genuine OK Union engines had the serial number prefixed by the letter 'D'.

The Jos Parkes produced Union engines had been supplied with the choice of a chain driven magneto or one directly coupled to the off-side of the crankshaft. The 292cc Wiseman version, which they described as the 2¾hp Model 'H', employed the a similar layout, but incorporated a miniature mechanical oil pump mounted on the magneto drive chain cover. The unit came complete with magneto, carburettor, silencing system and engine plates. This attractive package weighed 46lbs, and was listed at £13.

Additionally, the 2¼hp Model 'G' Wiseman two-stroke engine of the firm's own design was also available. It had a bore and stroke of 62 x 70mm giving a capacity of 211cc. At a glance it was similar to the larger unit and employed, where applicable, the characteristic Union dome headed nuts and also the flange fitted induction and exhaust stubs. However, the crankcase was split in two halves in the more conventional manner, the plug was at the rear of the cylinder and there was no detachable cover over the transfer port.

Lubrication was also of a more simple nature. Oil was delivered to the side of the cylinder wall in such a position that it lined up with the hollow gudgeon pin, thus providing a more-or-less direct feed to the small-end bearing. The crankshaft did not incorporate inside flywheels. There was, however, an outside flywheel on the driving side and the magneto drive was the same as the 2¾hp engine. The weight of the complete unit was 38lbs, and the price complete was £12 5s 0d.

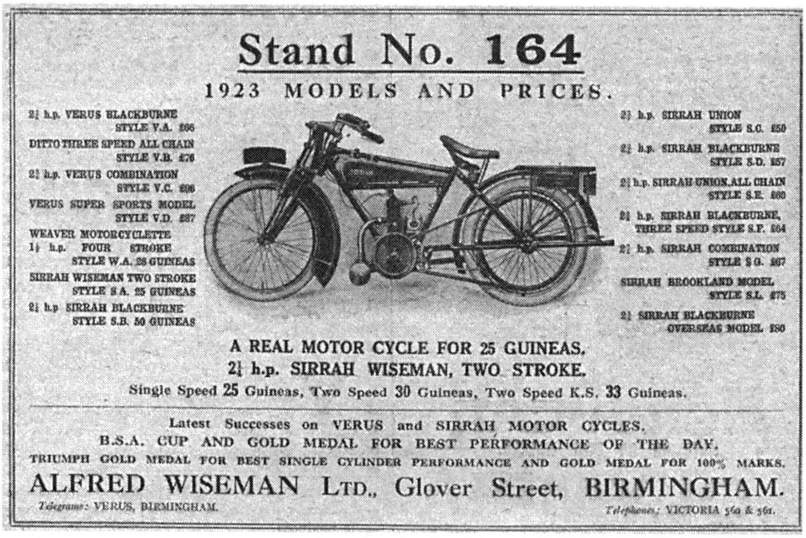

SIRRAH (Wiseman Group)

1922 marks the introduction of the Sirrah. That the word was formed by spelling 'Harris' in reverse has been repeated *ad nauseum*. To begin with it was intended that the Sirrah should be the 'cooking' version of the Verus, or as Wiseman's put it 'the next best thing'. The factory was now facing stiffer competition and prices were reduced to a somewhat more acceptable level.

At the 1921 Olympia Show there appeared a magnificent Verus V-twin with all-chain drive and the choice of 696cc Blackburne or 986cc JAP engine, but it did not appear in the following year's *Buyers Guide*. The same fate befell a projected 248cc side-valve model intended to be sold at £95: the 4hp was discontinued. And so the 1922 Verus programme consisted of only three models which had little in common with what had been exhibited at 'The Show'.

A 2¾hp (348cc Blackburne) had a Burman two-speed gearbox, belt final drive and was identical in appearance to the 1921 example including tank-top tool-box and stirrup front brake. Alternatively there was the choice of a Sturmey Archer three-speed box model with all-chain drive. An attempt to reconcile this machine

A Sirrah at Banbury

with a corresponding one which had appeared at Olympia gives the impression that there was complete enclosure for the chains and an internal expanding front brake.

The sole two-stroke example specified the mysterious 269cc Verus engine (see Verus opposite), two-speed Burman box and belt drive.

By the time the Sirrah went into production the initial programme had been revised and a previously announced single-speeder with 292cc Union two-stroke engine was conspicuous by its absence. There was, however, a two-speed belt-driven two-stroke which could, if required, be supplied as a sidecar outfit. The engine was described as a Verus and since it incorporated the vital statistics 70 x 76mm it would doubtless have been of Union origin.

2¾hp chain and belt four-strokes were to have had Burman three-speed boxes, but they came into production with two-speed boxes by the same manufacturer. The side-valve engine could be a 348cc Blackburne or a 346cc (70 x 90mm) JAP. An example of the latter which appeared at the 1921 Show had 'fir-cone' valve-caps and looked distinctly attractive despite the fact that footboards did not seem to be in keeping with a long plated straight through exhaust pipe.

At the heavy end of the range a common basic cycle could be chosen with either a 5-6hp 550cc single or a 4½hp 796cc twin Blackburne engine, with all-chain drive through a Burman three-speed box. Footboards were standard; the rear brake operated on a dummy belt rim and the front brake was still of the primitive stirrup type.

Left, a 1923 Sirrah Union combination and below, a 1923 Sirrah Overseas. (Photos: mortons Media Group Archives)

VERUS (Wiseman Group)

The first complete motorcycle which Wiseman's produced was the Verus. It was a perfectly orthodox and completely typical 'assembly job' but somehow it seemed to stand out from its competitors and was able to command an appreciably higher price.

Largest and most expensive model for 1920 was a so-called 4hp incorporating an 85 x 88mm, 499cc Blackburne side-valve engine. The top tube sloped backwards to accommodate a wedge-shaped tank and front forks were the ubiquitous Bi-Flex. The exhaust pipe was long and plated and, whilst it might have contained internal baffles, it gave the impression of being straight-through.

Chain-cum-belt transmission was via a Strumey-Archer three-speed box with clutch and kick-starter. The gear lever was mounted high up on the seat tube. No less than £110 5s 0d was the price of this model. How many people bought it would probably have depended on availability at the right time.

Probably more popular was the 2¾hp with a 71 x 88mm 348cc side-valve Blackburne engine for which was claimed mechanical pump, pressure fed lubrication. In this case the gearbox was a two-speed Burman with clutch and kick-starter.

A couple of two-stroke models were also listed for 1920. The 2¼hp had Wiseman's own 211cc two-stroke engine. Transmission was by belt directly from the engine

349cc Verus-Blackburne. (Photo: mortons Media Group Archives)

to the rear wheel. The 2½hp had a two-stroke engine of 269cc (70 x 70mm) which suggests that it was a Villiers. There was, however, the comparative luxury of a two-speed Burman box incorporated in the chain-cum-belt transmission. The prices of these three models were £99 15s 0d, £50 and £75 respectively in 1921. Throughout the range belt final drive was retained. All four-stroke models were equipped with Blackburne side-valve engines of the same bore and stoke and hence the same capacity as those already mentioned. Describing the programme *The Motorcycle* said '.....the Verus range now ranks among the aristocracy of the pastime....' If price was any criterion this was indeed an understatement.

The most ambitious machine listed was the 4hp (499cc) intended for sidecar use. Electric lighting was by Maglita. Carburation was initially to have been by Senspray or Cox-Atmos but, in fact, any make of carburettor could be fitted. Transmission was by Sturmey Archer three-speed box and tyres were of 3 inch section. Features of the design included the ability to remove the engine by withdrawing three bolts.

An inspection cover on the aluminium guard which protected the outside flywheel and the primary drive gave ready access to the clutch. At an initially quoted price of £200 with sidecar, this was one of the most expensive British machines that money could buy, irrespective of capacity.

More realistically priced at £126 was the essentially solo, Light 4hp. From the beginning of 1921 the tax on petrol was discounted (alas temporarily) and in its place came the Road Fund Licence, still quaintly referred to as such by some people. Taxation of solos was now by weight, three pounds a year for one weighing over 200lbs, and thirty shillings if below this weight limit. (The right to attach a sidecar involved an additional one pound a year). The Light 4hp must go down in history as one of the first 500cc machines expressly designed to take advantage of the lower taxation rate. In appearance it was almost identical to the 1920 4hp except that the exhaust system now consisted of a conventional expansion chamber and a tailpipe, and tyres were only 2¼ inch section. 2¾hp models were now available with either two or three-speed Sturmey Archer boxes and chain/belt transmission. If in fact lubrication had ever been otherwise, it was now by drip-feed.

The Buyers Guide for 1921 lists a 70 x 70mm 269cc two-stroke with an engine of Verus manufacture and such a model featured in the 1920 Olympia Show report which appeared in *The Motorcycle*. Whilst the unit may have been a bored out version of the 211cc engine this seems unlikely as specific mention is made of separate oil feeds to the main bearings which were a Union feature. Since reducing the stroke of the Union engine would have necessitated almost completely re-designing it, one can only assume that it was, as in the case of subsequent years a Union type 292cc engine which was used. Transmission was contemporarily quoted as by two-speed gearbox with clutch and kick-starter. The make of box was variously given as Burman and Albion. Despite a price tag of £85, tyres were of a mere 2 inch section. The single speed 211cc continued to be listed.

During the 1921 season, Verus did a fair amount of 'pot hunting' in competitions, some of which were of doubtful status. Exponents of the marque who notched up considerable successes included Bert Kershaw, a factory executive, TH Weaver, CE Stacey and S Dunford. Continental 'firsts', which at least looked impressive on paper, were achieved in Ebnemont Hill Climb, France (K Bartlett), Circuite di Crema, Italy (O Garazini) and Premis Internationale Brecia by the same rider.

WEAVER (Wiseman Group)

For 1923 Wiseman's added to their range the little Weaver. Described as a lightweight, it was in construction more of a motorized bicycle with a saddle height which enabled the pedals actually to be used, if only for starting purposes. It is generally assumed that Weaver took its name from TH Weaver who rode a Verus in competitions. It is unlikely that there was any connection with the Mr Weaver of Coventry Victor fame although statements to this effect have been made in the past.

Various opinions have been expressed as to the pedigree of the engine fitted to the Weaver, but during the short period of the marques currency the unit changed considerably. Originally described as having a bore and stroke of 56 x 61mm, it had a capacity marginally in excess of 150cc. Prior to this no design which had emanated from the house of Wiseman had been anything but conventional, but the Weaver engine represented a drastic break from orthodox practice.

The cylinder and the top half of the crankcase consisted of an aluminium casting with a steel liner. The cylinder-head which housed vertically-disposed overhead valves was secured to what was effectively the top of the crankcase by three long studs, the piston was of aluminium, the gudgeon pin bosses of which replaced the conventional small-end bearing. The gudgeon pin was an interference fit in the 'H' section connecting rod and plain bearings were used throughout. The valve rockers were across the head, operated by push-rods in conjunction with two separate cams which were carried on a common timing shaft. A built-up

crankshaft had an outside flywheel on the left-hand side. Chain driven from the timing side was a magneto of now almost forgotten Fellows manufacture and the carburettor was a tiny Vici (French).

Apart from the single-bladed Brampton spring forks, the cycle resembled an open-frame pedal bicycle. The front tube, however, dropped almost vertically before being formed into a loop which terminated at the bottom bracket. A neat four sided tank was accommodated just behind the steering head between the front tube and the stiffening tubes. The engine was mounted in the cradle at the bottom of the frame, secured by substantial clamps. It could be readily taken out by removing six nuts.

Useful equipment included a carrier, a rear stand and effective mudguards. Tyres were either of $1^3/_4$ or 2 inch section.

Direct drive from the engine to the rear wheel was by V-belt, the top run of which was protected by a guard. The front brake operated on the wheel rim and the other was in the rear hub actuated by moving the pedals backwards. Overall weight was a handy 70lbs, and at £29 8s 0d, the price was not excessive.

WISEMAN (cont. 1923-30)

Turning to the Wiseman range of motorcycles proper for 1923, the factory now eschewed any machine over 350cc. They standardised a common frame with the characteristic sloping top tube and installed therein a confusing variety of engines and transmission systems, with reckless abandon. It is doubtful if any serious quantity of Verus models were sold in this year since they were ridiculously expensive.

The cheapest model in the range retained a stirrup front brake and belt final drive. It had a 349cc Blackburne engine with a transverse expansion box exhaust system and the two-speed gearbox was by Burman. This was priced at £66. At £76 was a similar machine, but with all-chain transmission and in common with all subsequently mentioned all-chain machines, internal expanding brakes front and rear. Such models had cast aluminium chain covers.

Although fitted with a 249cc (60 x 88mm) OHV Blackburne engine, and costing £87, the Wiseman VD used only a two-speed box and belt final drive.

The following, designated as Sports models, were also listed. They had rear guards devoid of carrier, the toolbox being mounted on the right-hand seat stay. Exhaust systems consisted of long pipes with the manufacturer's own cast aluminium silencer incorporating internal baffles. They were as follows:-

Model	Capacity	Engine	Gearbox	Price
VE	349cc (71 x 88mm)	OHV Blackburne	3-speed	£94
VF	248cc (64 x 76mm)	SV JAP	3-speed	£85
VG	346cc (70 x 90mm)	SV JAP	3-speed	£90

A specially designed Sirrah 'Overseas' model was announced for 1923, with a 349cc Blackburne engine, Burman three-speed box and all-chain drive. The standard frame was modified to give, in conjunction with 28 x 3 inch tyres, seven inch ground clearance and the usual wedge tank was replaced by one of the 'saddle' type to provide additional petrol capacity. Both brakes were internal expanding, but the front was so puny that it can have been of little use. Mudguards were deliberately devoid of valances and there was sufficient clearance between them and the tyres to enable accumulations of mud to be cleared out with a stick in the unlikely event of clogging taking place. The model however, does not seem to have gone into production, likewise a projected attractive-looking little Sirrah sidecar outfit. It was to have been powered by a 292cc Union two-stroke engine and to have had all-chain drive. A contemporary illustration of the prototype however clearly shows belt final drive and two exhaust ports.

All Sirrahs for 1923 were, according to information provided by the manufacturers to *Fletchers*, equipped with belt or chain-cum-belt transmission. They were not so specific about gearboxes but two-speed Burmans with clutch and kick-starter would have been the norm. Even if not produced in appreciable quantities the 1923 range included:-

Capacity	**Engine**	**Transmission**
211cc	Wiseman two-stroke	direct belt drive
211cc	Wiseman two-stroke	2-speed, chain/belt
249cc	Blackburne side-valve	
292cc	Union two-stroke	
293cc	JAP side-valve	
349cc	Blackburne side-valve	

It may well be inferred that with the 1923 programme Wiseman's had reached a state of stagnation. Certainly since 1920, the introduction of the Weaver had been the only development of any consequence. 1924 however was obviously intended to be a 'Succeed or bust' year, but one recalls the fate of the settler who chalked on his wagon 'Pike's Peak or bust' - he did not reach Pike's Peak. Nevertheless, at the Olympia Show which preceded the 1924 season, Wiseman's were there with a bewildering display of models.

Any policy whereby a Sirrah was a cheaper example of a corresponding Verus had been abandoned and there was virtually no duplication of models. A new and probably cheaper to produce frame had been evolved. Generally, but not exclusively Verus retained the old diamond frame and Sirrah used the new one. The new frame was of the loop type and had a curious head-stock which, instead of being round, can most easily be described as 'oval' in section but with flat sides. Each side of the rear frame was formed from a single length of tube , instead of consisting of a seat stay and a chain-stay brazed or pin-jointed together. By removing a few nuts the rear frame could be removed, bringing with it the rear wheel and the chain guard.

The frame was made in three sizes and the smallest of these was the basis of the Weaver which had now become a miniature motorcycle in its own right. The pedal assisted model, now the Cyclett was still available. The engine was not totally different and described as a 150cc Vici. The bore and stroke were varyingly quoted as 56 x 60mm and 50 x 66mm This new unit retained overhead valves, but the magneto was now behind the cylinder. All-chain transmission was through a three-speed Burman box with direct-mounted gear lever. The rear brake acted on a dummy belt rim and the front was of the stirrup type, in which Wiseman's seem to have had a vested interest. It was a messy looking little bike but had the advantage of weighting only 100lbs, and costing just £35.

The Verus was listed in four types only. The most spectacular of these used a diamond frame to house a 349cc OHV Blackburne engine. Its exhaust pipe ran back at high level into a cast aluminium silencer which looked as if it needed a rather longer tail pipe. Petrol was carried in a saddle tank finished in mauve and each half had its own filler cap. A separate cast aluminium oil tank was mounted behind the seat tube and had separate adjustable drip feeds to lubricate the chains. There was a Burman three-speed box with the gear lever on the seat tube and, of course, all-chain drive. The sporting appearance was enhanced by the absence of a carrier.

Tyres had a section of 2½ inch and the front forks were the traditional Bi-flex. A reasonably-sized internal expanding brake on the rear wheel was supplemented - one hesitates to say augmented - by a minute one on the front. A little more thought in the matter of mounting the saddle tidily instead of perching it up on top of a bicycle-type pillar would have been the least one would have expected on a machine with a price tag of £86.

Variations on the Verus theme were provided by the incorporation of 349cc Blackburne, 346cc JAP or 248cc JAP side-valve engines. All four Verus models had mechanical lubrication and came well within the 200 lbs weight limit. A completely rakish 'racing' Sirrah was at Olympia but never went into production. What type of racing it was intended for was not made clear, but can hardly have been road-racing since there were no mudguards, only a stirrup front brake and niggardly 2¼ inch tyres. An adaptation of the new loop frame had triplicated top tubes in line with the seat stays which enabled a tiny special racing saddle to be three-point mounted with its top less than two feet from the ground. A long narrow saddle tank held a gallon of fuel. A half-gallon oil tank was supposed to have been mounted just below the saddle, but it does not appear in a contemporary illustration. What does appear, however, is a curious upright tube from just above the gearbox to carry the gear lever. The absence of the oil tank may have been because this particular machine was fitted with 349cc (68 x 96mm) OHV oil-cooled Bradshaw engine which contained its oil within the crankcase. A 349cc OHV Blackburne engine was also available.

The gearbox was a three-speed Burman, but with no kick-starter. Although it never came to anything, this must have been the most interesting motorcycle which Wiseman's ever built.

What should have been another 1924 Sirrah disappeared after Olympia where it was shown with a new Wiseman 60 x 70mm, 247cc two-stroke engine built into the middle size of the new loop frame. Its place was taken, however, by a model with the familiar 292cc two-stroke engine still described as a Union but stated to be made at the Wiseman factory. In its production form it had a Burman two-speed box and all-chain drive. Although they had appeared at Olympia no 211cc two-strokes were included in the 1924 programme.

1923 Sirrah Sports

The 1925 Wiseman range had been ruthlessly pruned, but not so the prices.The Weaver now only came in its 'miniature' form. The OHV engine was described as being of Weaver manufacture and with a capacity of 129cc which figure ties up fairly accurately with a quoted bore and stroke of 50 x 66mm. It now, however, had only a two-speed Burman gearbox.

A typical Verus had a 293cc side-valve JAP engine in loop frame, similar to that introduced for the previous year, but with a conventional rear frame. More powerful engines available were the 349cc Blackburne in side- and overhead-valve form and the newly introduced and extremely potent short stroke 344cc (74 x 80mm) two-port OHV JAP which commanded a price of £95.

There were now only two Sirrah models - a 293cc JAP unchanged from the previous year and an alternative with a 292cc two-stroke engine now described as a 'Wiseman' but obviously of Union extraction.

Using the largest size of frame was a 976cc JAP twin model. Its particular point of interest was that it incorporated a Jardine three-speed gearbox. This excellent unit, designed by Israel Cohen, was never widely adopted. Its Nottingham manufacturers have been said to have been mainly concerned with the production of lace-making machinery and it is known that they took over the once well-known Barlock typewriter business.

Transmission was all-chain (as in the case of all four-stroke models) and tyres were in this case 3 inch section. An alternative machine was listed with a 545cc Blackburne single cylinder engine.

The medium size of frame was also fitted with a 293cc (70 x 76mm) side-valve JAP engine with the magneto behind the cylinder and with fully enclosed drive from the timing side. Neat aluminium guards protected the chains and cast aluminium was used for the transverse expansion box which was positioned in front of the crankcase and outside the frame. Cast aluminium was further employed for the cylindrical tool-box (common to the whole range), positioned below the carrier in the space behind the number plate. Braking relied on a combination of dummy belt rim (rear) and stirrup (front). Alternative power units were 349cc side-valve Blackburne, 349cc (68 x 96mm) OHV oil-cooled Bradshaw and 348cc (70 x 90.5mm) sleeve valve Barr and Stroud engines.

The 1926 season showed the Wiseman group of motorcycles to be on its way out. Such a fate was inevitable since its producers had tended to trade on a good reputation and had made no real effort to keep up-to-date for far too long.

The Weaver was no longer listed and the Verus only in its 344cc OHV JAP form still at £95 and, as an alternative, the 349cc side-valve Blackburne.

Only two Sirrahs were offered, both with Wiseman (basically Union) 292cc two-stroke engines. One was all-chain with three-speed Burman gearbox and the other a single speeder with direct belt drive.

During or after 1926 the factory either closed its doors or concentrated on other activities for the Verus, the Sirrah and the Weaver were not listed for any subsequent years.

THE "WISEMAN" ENGINES

ILLUSTRATION SHOWING SPARE PARTS FOR 2¼ H.P. ENGINE.

When Ordering Spares, it is only necessary to give the Reference Number.

THE "WISEMAN" ENGINES

PARTS FOR 2¼ H.P. ENGINE.

No.	Part	Price
1	Cylinder	50/-
2	Exhaust Elbow Socket ...	3/-
3	Inlet Manifold	2/9
4	Exhaust Washer	3d.
5	Inlet Washer	3d.
6	Rear Engine Plate (R.H.) ...	3/6
7	Front " " (R.H.) ...	3/6
8	Sparking Plug K.L.G. extra	5/-
9	Connecting Rod	18/-
10	Big End Bush	6/-
11	Connecting Rod Cap ...	2/-
12	Big End Packing Piece ...	1d.
13	" Pin, 3% Nickel ...	9d.
14	Small End Bush	3/6
15	Exhaust Pipe, Plated ...	6/-
16	" " Nut, Plated	2/-
17	Piston only	18/-
18	" Rings	1/6
19	" " Grub Screw...	1d.
20	Gudgeon Pin...	3/-
21	Cylinder Base Washer ...	3d.
22	Release Valve Body ...	4/-
23	Release Valve	2/6
24	" " Washer ...	1d.
25	" " Spring ...	2d. (25 and 26)
26	" " 1/16in. Cotter Pin	
27	" " Trigger ...	2d.
28	" " Trigger Body	1/-
29	⅛in. Cotter for Valve Trigger	1d.
30	Cable Adjuster	3d.
31	Release Valve Nut, ⅜in. ...	2d.
32	Cylinder Stud, ¼in. ...	2d.
33	" " Nut	2d.
34	Cylinder Holding-down Stud, 5/16in.	2d.
35	Spring Washer, 5/16in. ...	1d.
36	Holding-down Stud Nut ...	2d.
37	Crankshaft	50/-
38	" Balance Weight	1/6
39	Balance Weight Screw ...	2d.
40	Crank Case, Flywheel side	37/-
41	" " Magneto drive side	37/-
42	Main Bearing, Flywheel side	6/-
43	" " Magneto side	5/-
44	Oil Union Nut and Nipple	9d.
45	Oil Union, ⅜in.	6d.
46	⅜in. Fibre Washer	1d.
47	¼in. Crank Case Stud ...	1d.
48	" " " Nut ...	2d.
49	Drain Plug for Crank Case	2d.
50	Mechanical Pump	12/-
51	" " Screw ...	1d.
52	Crankshaft Sprocket ...	6/-
53	" " Nut ...	9d.
54	Mechanical Pump Connection Nut	3d.
55	Magneto Chain Cover, inside half	3/-
56	Magneto Chain Cover, outside half	3/-
57	Magneto Chain	2/6
58	" Sprocket	3/-
59	Magneto—*See Maker's List.*	
60	" Sprocket Pin ...	3d.
61	" Chain Cover Pin	2d.
62	" Holding-down Plate	1/-
63	" Distance Piece ...	2d.
64	" Holding-down Stud	1d.
65	" Holding-down Stud Nut...	1d.
66	Flywheel	40/-
67	" Sprocket	7/6
68	" Nut...	1/6
69	Silencer, Aluminium ...	20/-
70	" End, R.H.	2/6
71	" Stud, 5/16in.	2d.
72	" Pin, 5/16in.	2d.
73	" Holding-down Stud, ⅜in.	6d.
74	Silencer, Holding-down Stud Nut	2d.
75	Extension Pipe, Plated ...	6/-

We only supply Half Crank Case when customer sends the other half

Wiseman parts list

XTRA CAR

In appearance the Xtra-Car was not unlike a single seater sidecar body to which wheels had been fitted to make it into a tricar. When shown at Olympia in 1921 by Xtra Cars Ltd, London Road, Chertsey, it was equipped with a 269cc Villiers two stroke engine with flywheel magneto and Senspray carburettor, but for 1923 a 342cc Villiers engine was specified with the option of a 247cc unit of the same make. The prices complete with lighting and hood were £99 15s 0d, and £94 10s 0d.

The engine was positioned in the tail behind the seat, mounted in a frame which coil sprung at the front end and which also carried the rear wheel. There were two rear sprockets, one above the other, connected to the engine sprocket by a three-sided chain drive. Each rear sprocket carried a friction disc, either of which could be brought into engagement with a friction drum on the rear wheel, thus giving a clutch action and two speeds. A contemporary description states that the variation in speeds was achieved by the use of two friction discs of different diameters, although an illustration gives the impression that possibly the discs were of identical size but were attached to sprockets of different diameter: either way, the principle is the same. A hand starting mechanism was arranged.

The spoked wheels were fitted with 26 x 2¼ inch tyres. The outer ends of two pairs of flat transverse springs carried the front wheels thus providing independent front suspension. Cycle type wings were used at the front and the rear wheel was partially enclosed in the tail. On the Olympia model the front guards extended down past the body but illustrations of subsequent productions show slightly shorter ones, and a step to assist entry - there were no doors.

For 1924 the specification was much the same, but prices had come down to £75 and £65 which was obviously still too much money for what was offered.

The Xtra Car. Engine and transmission on the left and the body on the right. Advertised as a weather proof three-wheeler of special appeal to the business man. (Photo: Mortons Media Group Archive)

Literature

If you had needed to repair your motorcycle in 1920, the first thing to do was to have a go at it yourself. Much of the knowledge required for this task was available from friends, colleagues, people you vaguely knew, or the fellow up the road who did a bit of work in his shed. And of course there were your own experiences gained as a result of unforeseen breakdowns linked to a basic lack of money and resources to pay someone else to do it for you. Nowadays we have manuals that take the would-be repairer carefully through each step of the way, often with accompanying photographs or diagrams. Although there was some written help at hand, in general terms there was little specific assistance with a particular model unless it came from one of the major manufacturers, and information had to be garnered from a variety of sources.

The starting point might well be one of the books that went through the mechanical theories and practices that were common to all motorcycles and included such titles as *Motorcycles and how to Manage Them*, *Motorcycle Efficiency and How to Obtain It*, or *The Art of Driving a Motor Cycle*. Knowledgeable contributors, often from the motorcycling press of the time, were responsible for writing these and various chapters dealt with for example the carburettor, transmission and gearing, high-tension magneto ignition and so on. They were very detailed and sometimes listed repairs on the more common items of equipment for the more popular makes of bike. If you couldn't work out what was wrong by following the hints and tips contained within those pages then you might have to look elsewhere.

The magazines of the day often printed articles on how to repair, or improve current models. It would pay to go through the back copies of *The Motor Cycle*, or *Motorcycling* to see if there were relevant articles, letters or adverts that might assist. The small ads in the back might just reveal a crucial piece of equipment that would improve performance beyond all expectations. There may be a new design of exhaust system, a different carburettor or super efficient new spark plug that would make your humble old bus go like a TT winner.

Most makes had their own literature, usually in the form of a brochure and a spares list. Depending on how the maker saw the value of publicity, a lot of information could be gleaned from the brochures. Detailed advertising specifications, pictures of the whole machine and close ups could provide all kinds of additional information. In the same way the listing of every single part that went into the makeup of a particular bike, and its designation, were a very valuable resource. Generally speaking however there were no full details on maintenance and repair. From these lists exact measurements, or interchangability of similar looking items could not be easily ascertained. Towards the end of the twenties publishing companies such as Pearson and Pitmans started to publish handbooks aimed at the home mechanic who needed very specific details about his model and the 'Book of the ....' was born. The accessory suppliers usually put out a good supply of detailed information and it was possible to find out, for example, from the Lucas material how your dynamo and the circuit worked, AMAC might show you how to improve your fuel flow, or John Bull would give suggestions about care of your tyres.

THIRD EDITION.
THE ART OF DRIVING A MOTORCYCLE
Published by
TEMPLE PRESS LTD.,
7-15, Rosebery Avenue,
London, E.C.1.
2/6 NET

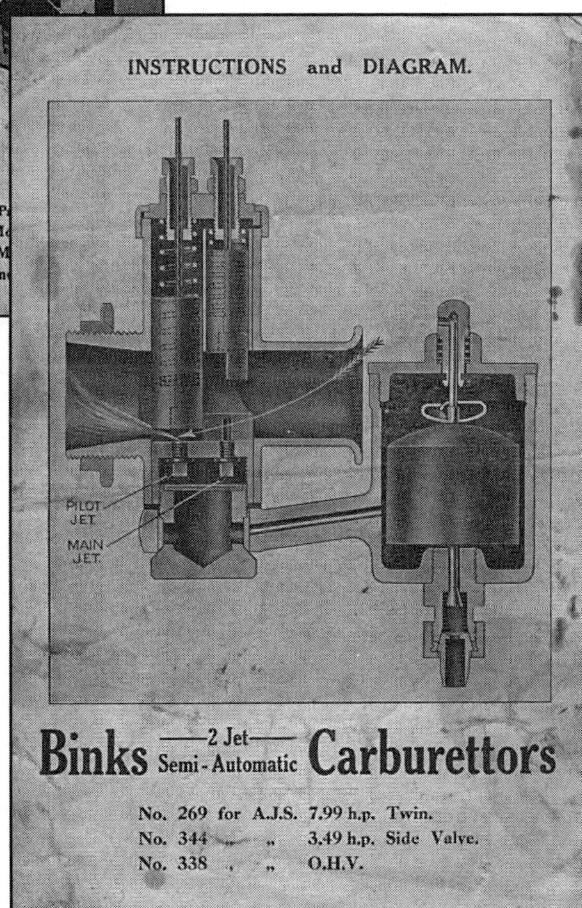
INSTRUCTIONS and DIAGRAM.
PILOT JET
MAIN JET
Binks 2 Jet Semi-Automatic Carburettors
No. 269 for A.J.S. 7.99 h.p. Twin.
No. 344 „ „ 3.49 h.p. Side Valve.
No. 338 „ „ O.H.V.

Bibliography

The following is a list of books that give the reader a flavour of the nineteen twenties. Some of the books are out of print, but most can be found in specialist book shops or on the internet. It is by no means an exhaustive or definitive list, simply suggested reading for those who wish to discover more about old motor cycles.

A History of the World's Motorcycles, R.Hough and L.J.K.Setright, 1966, George Allen and Unwin

Reminiscences of Motor Cycling, Ixion, 1973, E.P. Publishing

Motor Cycle Cavalcade, Ixion, republished 1971, S.R.Publishers

The Land Beyond the Ridge, Roy K. Batson, 1974, Goose and Son

The Roadmender, Michael Fairless, 1926, Duckworth

A Motor Scout in Flanders, Capt. Chas. Gilson, 1920, Blackie and Sons

Early Motor Cycles, Victor W Page, 1971, Post Motor Books

Brooklands Behind the Scenes, Charles Mortimer, 1980, Haynes

Across Europe with Satanella, Clare Sheridan, 1925, Duckworth

Veteran and Vintage Motor Cycles, James Sheldon, 1961, Batsford

Motor Cycles, History and Development, C.F.Caunter, 1955, H.M.S.O.

The Illustrated Encyclopedia of Motor Cycles, Erwin Tragatsch, 1977, Hamlyn

The Encyclopedia of the Motor Cycle, Peter Henshaw, 1999, Regency House

Titch-The Founders Tale, Titch Allen, 2007, Live Wire

Vintage Road Tests, Titch Allen, 1975, Reprinted by V.M.C.C.

British Motor Cycle Directory, Roy Bacon and Ken Hallworth, 2004, Crowood Press

Riding Old Motor Cycles, Reg Eyre, 2007, Blue Hills Publishing

Fletchers Motor Cycle Index 1913-1924, Kenneth Ball, Autopress Ltd, 1964

The Vintage Motor Cycle Club

The Vintage Motor Cycle Club has an online shop where you can buy some of the above books. They are also the principal source of information for those people who enjoy riding vintage motor cycles and they can be contacted at their Burton on Trent Headquarters below.

VMCC, Allen House, Wetmore Road, Burton Upon Trent, Staffordshire DE14 1TR, UK

Telephone: +44 (0)1283 540557, *Fax:* +44 (0)1283 510547, *Email:* HQ@vmcc.net
Internet: http://www.vmcc.net

Panther Publishing

Books on Motorcycles and Motorcycling

Biography

Granville Bradshaw: A Flawed Genius? *by Barry M Jones*

Fay Taylour: Queen of Speedway *by Brian Belton*

Hold ON! *by Stan Dibben*

Makes and manuals

Classic Motorcycling: A Guide for the 21st Century *by Rex Bunn*

The Panther Story *by Barry M Jones*

Panther since 1950 *by Steve Wilson*

Velocette since 1950 *by Steve Wilson*

Rupert Ratio Unit Single Engine Manual for BSA C15, B40, B25, B44, B50

Lost Motorcycles of the 1920s *by Jack Bacon*

Motorcycle adventure and travel

The Rugged Road *by Theresa Wallach*

The Last Hurrah *by Des Molloy*

Daisy's Diaries: Challenging Life on a 1948 Triumph *by Graham Ham*

Road Riders Guide to England and Wales *by Dick Henneman*

Road Riders Guide to Scotland and Ireland *by Dick Henneman*

Motorcycle Trackdays for Virgins *by Simon Bradley*

Children's and cartoons

When Rosie met Anneka *by Steve Wilson*

We've All Been There *by Spider*

Panther Publishing Ltd

10 Lime Avenue, High Wycombe, Bucks HP11 1DP, UK.

Tel: 01494 534778. Email: info@panther-publishing.com

www.panther-publishing.com